SCOTLAND

EIGHT VIEWS ON THE STATE OF THE NATION

Edited by Kenneth Cargill

BBC SCOTLAND

- Cover Photograph Jay Myrdal/Radio Times
- Cover Design by Jim Jackson
- Print Management and Production
  Allister Gourlay, Network Scotland Limited
  74 Victoria Cres. Road, Glasgow G12 9JQ
- Typesetting and Origination
  Scottish Studios & Engravers Ltd,
  170 High Street, Glasgow G1 1QF
- Printed by Strathkelvin Printing Ltd,
  Springfield Works, Bishopbriggs
- © BBC Scotland 1987
- ISBN 0563 205 989

CONTENTS

Preface

Someone else came up with the title *Scotland 2000,* but I take the responsibility for the idea. It was born out of a growing realisation that by the millennium I'd be retired and living on a pension. A pension whose quality and worth depend upon what my children's generation are able to achieve in the world and especially within Scotland.

My parents, now both in their eighties, have seen in their turn the horse and cart grow into the motor car, men stride on the moon and the microchip do in seconds what men and women took years to learn and call — with pride — a trade. They have seen a century full of change: two world wars, famine and starvation, in which a third of the world's population still has a daily struggle for the basic means of survival — and for the Scots, a quality of life undreamt of eighty years ago.

I took the view that as broadcasters we should peer over the horizon and look at what the twenty-first century holds in store.

That was the brief I gave to Ken Cargill, the executive producer of *Scotland 2000.* This book is part of that result.

Patrick Chalmers
Controller, BBC Scotland

INTRODUCTION

I had just returned from a briefing with the British Army in Berlin and West Germany when I was summoned to the third floor of Broadcasting House to see Jim Hunter, the Head of Television. The Controller wanted a major series examining the State of the Nation. In my absence I had been volunteered. Was I interested in editing the series? (Yes.) The Controller had noted down a few headings such as industry, the arts, education and so on. (Sounds interesting.) I would set up a new production unit and I could draw whatever staff I wanted from whichever area seemed appropriate. Would I go away and think about whom I wanted? (Right away.) There were to be film and studio programmes, and we should involve radio as well. (Great.) And filming would start within four months for transmission in February(!)

This book is based on the eight films in that series, *Scotland 2000*, which was broadcast by BBC Scotland during February, March and April 1987. They covered eight broad themes: politics, industry, education, health, land use, the arts, the media and religion. Not completely comprehensive, maybe, but touching as many bases as possible. Each film was scrutinised later the same evening by an expert panel in a studio debate, with the public getting a chance to join in the next morning during a radio phone-in.

Accompanying the series was a specially commissioned opinion poll covering all eight areas. According to the polling organisation, System 3 Scotland, this was the most comprehensive survey of public opinion, across a wider range of issues, of any they had conducted. (See appendix.)

Given that we wanted to stimulate a debate, we had to give a sharp cutting edge to the film programmes — which thanks to BBC Scotland's hard-fought battles to retain the right to opt out of network programmes on BBC1 would be broadcast at the peak time of 8 p.m. Since we could meet our obligations on 'balance' across the range of programmes, we could abandon the usual report by a BBC journalist for committed films by people with strong views.

Having decided the format the next task was to find the presenters – and quick. The logistics imposed their own deadlines: each producer and director would be responsible for two films. Three weeks' filming and six weeks' editing per film meant a commitment per team of eighteen weeks, plus research time, and of course all had annual leave to take and some had current projects to complete. If we were to meet our transmission target, we had to get our presenters picked and start working on the treatments PDQ. After all we would not necessarily be working with experienced presenters, or indeed journalists.

Reaching agreement on the programmes' treatments would be a rather more complex business than usual. Whilst the films would be personal reports, and the presenters would have to defend their editorial lines, we weren't giving them carte blanche to fill fifty minutes of prime time television. As producers we had to ensure that their arguments were factually accurate (without interfering with their right to interpret those facts as they wished); that the programmes were fair (without having to observe the normal rules of balance); and that they reached as far as possible our normal standards of presentation (without ironing out the idiosyncracies that are part of the attraction of personal views).

One other factor had to be taken into account. I wanted to avoid as far as possible party political arguments, not because of a contempt for the political process, but because as an election draws near — and there was at the time much speculation about a spring election — everything a politician does or says is motivated by one consideration alone: whether it will help or hinder victory at the polls. As a result interviews with politicians would produce an even higher than usual element of sterile party political bickering. Politicians would have plenty of opportunities to argue their cases elsewhere on television and radio; I wanted to focus as much as possible on the views of people with first-hand experience, whose opinions had the authority and commitment that come from doing rather than talking.

The next stage was to meet with our shortlist of presenters to test the strength of their views and their televisual qualities. Some choices were more obvious than others, but once we had decided who was wanted, we had a further problem. Even if they wanted to do it, would they have the time? We were asking them for a major commitment: at least two weeks' filming, plus a considerable amount of preparation and scriptwriting. Surprisingly, only one of our choices baulked, with great regret, although two had to withdraw later because of other commitments.

I had decided to take a bit of a risk by starting the series with a film on the governance of Scotland. It was risky because for many people politics is a switch-off; but it was necessary to start with an examination of the political and constitutional framework because that is what largely shapes not simply the answers to important questions but the questions themselves. To present the film we chose Chris Harvie, Professor of British Studies at the University of Tübingen in Baden-Württemberg in West Germany. Chris is an energetic, far from stuffy, academic who lives and breathes politics. Since moving to Germany seven years ago he has come to regard himself as Scottish first, European second and British hardly at all. It struck us that as an historian based in the most prosperous West German *Land* he could offer an interesting perspective: he argues that Britain is regarded by other European states as eccentric in persisting with a high degree of centralisation. Deeply committed to devolution, Chris argues that the débâcle of the 1979 referendum will not be repeated. Too much has changed: in party politics; in the further shift from traditional heavy engineering to the service industries; in the burgeoning financial sector; in the accelerated revival of Scottish culture; and not least, in a disenchantment with London, increased by the Scots' perception of the North–South divide.

Never one to hesitate to stick his neck out, Chris predicts that within five years a Scottish Parliament will once again sit in Edinburgh, and that it will succeed because we now know the kind of work we want it to do.

His whole approach seemed to offer our best hope of keeping out of the party political quagmire: as an historian in self-imposed exile he could offer a more detached assessment of the forces at work in Scotland 1987.

However, our choice was to cause raised eyebrows in New St Andrew's

House because of an article Chris had written for *The Guardian* shortly after Malcolm Rifkind had been reshuffled, and promoted, to the Scottish Office. It was a robust piece of journalism, suggesting that Rifkind must be 'watching his world collapse from the unpleasing windows of New St Andrew's House . . . left in charge of a party not simply demoralised, but actually moribund, the only means of reviving it being totally against the rules of the Tory game'. The word was that the SoS's hackles had risen more than a little, and that he was deeply suspicious of our motives in choosing Chris. In the end, although we were refused access to top civil servants for interview — in a pre-election period in particular, questions on public policy must it seems be addressed to politicians alone — Rifkind gave us his full co-operation, including an interview in which he gave Chris a personal demonstration of his well-honed forensic skills.

The choice of presenter on industry was one of the easiest. Despite being in one sense the grand old man of Scottish industry, Sir Monty Finniston has lost little of the enthusiasms of youth. Now seventy-four, and with an impressively wide career in both the private and public sectors behind him, not least as chairman of the British Steel Corporation, he is still actively involved in many companies and organisations.

Describing himself as a company doctor, he seemed the ideal choice to examine the health of the Scottish economy and provide a prognosis on its prospects. Given his heavy commitments, I doubted at first whether he would be willing or able to devote the necessary time to filming his report, but he responded with great enthusiasm, launching into a list of the kind of points he would want to make. But he had as many questions as answers. He didn't want simply to present the conclusions of more than half a century's experience: he wanted to explore other people's experience, to ask why, and why not. His enthusiasm for new ideas gives force to his argument that Scotland has consistently failed to exploit the natural inventiveness of its people. Those with capital to invest, whether institutions or individuals, have, he says, played safe too often and for too long, forcing inventors and inventions abroad in search of the enterprise culture so lacking at home. He argues that we must accept that the creation of wealth no longer corresponds with the creation of work. Whilst recognising the increasing importance of service industries, Sir Monty points out that a thriving manufacturing sector is crucial to our prosperity, not least because the service sector itself depends on manufactured goods, and the more British they are the better. As is appropriate to a man with such an active and open mind, Sir Monty stresses the importance of education and training, but points out the folly of training people for work that no longer exists. The creation of work is too important, he argues, to be left to market forces.

Given the dangers of settling into a doom-and-gloom analysis, it was heartening to find that Sir Monty became more optimistic about Scotland's economic prospects as filming proceeded and he talked and listened to people who provided the justification for his conclusion that 'all the ingredients for success are there; all we have to do is get the mix right, and be prepared to take a few risks along the way'.

If people are a nation's most important resource, its second is the land. How we use that resource is now the subject of fierce debate. Farming has generally been regarded as the highest priority, but the industry is now the victim of its own success. High technology, greater efficiency and increased productivity have led to the loss of 30,000 farming families and 100,000 farmworkers' jobs on top of that. But they have also led to overproduction and the obscenities of the food mountains. There are demands that land be taken out of farming altogether. But if large areas of arable land are to be released for other uses, what should they be?

We turned to James Hunter, director of the Scottish Crofters' Union and an authority on countryside issues, to present a prospectus for change. He argues that we have been presented with an opportunity to reverse the apparently inexorable decline of rural communities by giving people a new opportunity to live on and work off the land. Surplus agricultural land could be sold off in parcels and put to a variety of uses: homes, small-scale farming, forestry, tourism, sport, conservation. Combining woodland management with agriculture would in James's view counter the trend of blanket forestry which is doing so much damage to Scotland's landscape. Locally owned and locally operated forests on the continental model would bring jobs back to the countryside. Not surprisingly, James regards crofting as a model for a more successful rural Scotland.

Scotland's health record is appalling, all the more so because so much illness is self-inflicted: the result of smoking, drinking too much, eating the wrong food, taking too little exercise. That we are aware of the errors of our ways — even if too many of us carry on slowly killing ourselves — is in no small measure due to highly effective campaigns run by organisations like the Scottish Health Education Group. Its former director, Dr David Player, was an obvious choice to present the health programme. He argues that while many of us are changing our lifestyle for the better, many others living in areas of social deprivation cannot afford to do so. As a result they may be more than twice as likely to die for example from heart disease. Furthermore, what he calls 'the enemies of health' — the tobacco and drink industries — are cornerstones of the economy, providing valuable taxation revenue to governments who preach the health message while pocketing the proceeds. However, David points out that the increased availability of healthy foods in supermarkets is the direct result of public demand, further proof of what can be achieved if profits are at stake. As the National Health Service becomes increasingly a 'patch up' service, under more and more pressure because of the rise in the numbers of old people and the high cost of advanced treatments, David argues that it is all the more important to prevent people from being ill in the first place by embarking on a major campaign of preventive medicine. He ends with the sobering thought that if we cut out tobacco and alcohol abuse completely, at least a hundred and twenty-five thousand more of us would live to see the year 2000.

David argued a strong case in his usual forthright manner — a style, however effective, that had not endeared him to government ministers. They had already announced the abolition of his Health Education Council; it was to be replaced by a Health Education Authority, staffed largely by the same people. David was waiting to be interviewed for the top job — the only one left unfilled. Informed opinion wasn't rating his chances highly, but to his credit, neither in the film nor in the subsequent studio debate with the Scottish Health Minister, Lord Glenarthur, did he pull his punches.

Our ability to succeed depends above all on one major resource: people. The young adults of the twenty-first century are now in the early stages of their education and what schooling does for and to them will determine how well they'll cope with an increasingly complex adult life.

As presenter we chose an Edinburgh head teacher, Margaret Macintosh, who is strongly committed to community education and lifelong learning. Her contention is that our secondary schools are failing a complete generation of young people, by force-feeding them to pass examinations which are for the majority irrelevant. Those who don't like the diet, she says, are cast aside as failures, and boredom and disaffection are the result.

Our primary schools are turning out children well educated in the basics, used to working collaboratively and with an enthusiasm for learning. Secondary schools, on the other hand, regiment young people in a way which ignores their individual abilities and needs. As a result, large numbers think of themselves as failures. Margaret makes a strong plea for a system of lifelong learning which is geared to individuals, allowing them to proceed at their own pace, developing the social and educational skills that will equip them to succeed in a rapidly changing society.

Ask people for a list of priorities for public expenditure and the arts will probably come near the bottom. They are seen as at best a luxury, at worst an irrelevance. Such views seem particularly misguided at a time when Scottish artistic and cultural life is vibrant, symbolised not just by the continued success of the great set piece, the Edinburgh International Festival — or rather festivals — but by the designation of Glasgow as European City of Culture 1990. They also reduce people such as playwright Tom McGrath to a state of apoplexy. In his personal view on the arts he argues that they are a form of wealth for the nation. Not just in the sense that the Edinburgh Festival is good for business — creating employment, filling hotels, cramming the restaurants and putting every available space in the city up for rent. It is also a source of spiritual wealth, giving us a clearer sense of who and what we are.

Art, according to Tom, is produced by exceptional people, the only ones in our society who create wealth out of nothing. It is, he says, vital to nurture talent and imagination and he outlines the importance of community arts projects at a time of high unemployment. As a nation, he says, we are rich in artistic talent of all kinds, but complacency and underfunding could lead to cultural impoverishment by the year 2000.

To present his personal view on the media, we chose John Lloyd who was on the point of moving from industrial editor of the *Financial Times* to the editorship of the *New Statesman*. It was to prove a particularly prescient choice. His standpoint is that the media — press, radio and television — are on the threshold of an unprecedented technological revolution, which throws into sharp relief the eternal issues of ownership and control, accountability and freedom of expression. As the programme was being made the latter — freedom of expression — was thrown into even sharper relief than John could have predicted by the Zircon affair, with the BBC's decision not to broadcast and his decision to print information the government regarded as one of the most secret of secrets.

John warns about the dangers to our national culture of the forces building up thanks to satellite broadcasting and facsimile printing by which the media barons can beam their programmes and their papers to us while having to show no respect for or commitment to cultural minorities. He asks whether Scotland, both as a place and as a centre for emotions, is to wither away under the blast of a multinational media intent on world domination, and with the resources to achieve it. If the big get bigger, will the small become less important and more discouraged? And will our culture, which is largely print-based, be swept away on a tide of instant images?

The series concluded in Easter week with a personal view on religion by the Reverend Stewart Lamont, the journalist and broadcaster who had joined the production team as a producer but who took on the task of presenter when our original choice had to withdraw because of other commitments. Stewart's trenchant views have stimulated and infuriated readers of his weekly *Glasgow Herald* column 'In Good Faith'. He argues that the churches are facing a crisis of faith while the people have lost sight of the non-material dimension to life. The result is that only 10 per cent still go to church on a regular basis, and if downward trends among the young continue, the Church of Scotland will be literally a dying institution. He points to three main causes of the decline of institutional religion – Ageism, Sexism and Neuroticism – but describes two examples of church success against the trend: the Buckhaven Project in Fife organised by a Church of Scotland minister, and the Renew Programme centred on the Archdiocesan Pastoral Centre in Glasgow, both of which demonstrate committed Christianity at work. Generally speaking, however, Stewart is pessimistic about the prospects for the Scottish churches.

Of course his pessimism may prove unfounded. *Scotland 2000* was not designed as an exercise in futurology. Predicting the future is easy: any fool can do it and it is the height of folly to try. Getting it right is well-nigh impossible so long as real life produces shocks, horrors and sensations that even a Jeffrey Archer might dismiss as too fanciful for a work of fiction.

There's an old Scots saying that my granny used to console people at times of anxiety or uncertainty: 'Whit's afore ye, winnae gang past ye.'

That could mean we get what we deserve. All the more reason to make sure we deserve better, and, as they say, there's no time like the present to start.

A series like *Scotland 2000* is a team effort, and I was fortunate to work with one of the best. I'd like to thank the presenters who coped admirably with the frustrations of filming and whose broadcasting skills, if anything, exceeded my expectations; and the producers and directors to whom most of the credit is due: John Milne and Mike Alexander for politics and industry; Bill Dunlop and Dick Colthurst for health and land use; Eleanor Aitken and Adrian Herring for education and the arts; Stewart Lamont and David Richardson for the media and religion. I must also thank the production assistants without whom no programmes would reach the screen, Ruth Allan and Shirley Jardine; production managers John Adams and Geraldine Eardley for keeping control of the budget, and my assistant Julie Adair for her invaluable help.

Thanks are also due to the film crews, editors, studio crews, designers, radio producers and other staff who contributed to the television series, and James Gordon who chaired the studio debates; to Mike Shaw, Jimmy Mack, Kirsty Wark and their colleagues on the *Scotland 2000* phone-in on Radio Scotland; to John McLeod for the title music; Yvonne Bostok for her particular help with the health programme; John Boothman and Heather Lamont for research assistance; and Pat Chalmers, Jim Hunter, Stan Taylor and George Sinclair for their support.

In connection with this book I should like to give special thanks to Patricia Taylor Chalmers for her invaluable advice and help in getting the copy into a state fit for publication; Chris Eynon of System 3 Scotland for his interpretation of the opinion polls; Michael Nicholson, Julie Adair, Robert Tweedie of the *Glasgow Herald* and Bill Brady of *The Scotsman* for picture research; Jim Jackson for his help with the cover; Michael Russell, Allister Gourley and their colleagues at Network; and Una Gallacher for her patience.

Kenneth Cargill

BIOGRAPHIES

CHRISTOPHER HARVIE

Professor Christopher Harvie was born in Motherwell in 1944 and educated at the Royal High School and the University of Edinburgh. He was lecturer in history at the Open University from 1969 to 1980 and is now Professor of British Studies at the University of Tübingen in Baden-Württemberg in West Germany. He is the author of *Scotland and Nationalism* (1977) and *No Gods and Precious Few Heroes, Scotland 1914-80* (1981, revised edn 1987).

SIR MONTY FINNISTON FRS, F Eng

Sir Monty Finniston was born in Glasgow in 1912 and educated at Allen Glen's School, Glasgow University and the Royal College of Science and Technology (now the University of Strathclyde). He has had a wide-ranging career in industry, including the chairmanship of British Steel from 1973 to 1976. Since 1980 he has been acting as a business consultant and is chairman of a variety of companies and organisations, including the Council of the Scottish Business School and the Scottish Enterprise Foundation. Since 1979 he has been Chancellor of the University of Stirling.

JAMES HUNTER

James Hunter was born at Duror in Argyll in 1948 and graduated MA (Aberdeen) 1971 and PhD (Edinburgh) 1974 with a thesis on the development of crofting. He spent five years writing features for *The Press and Journal* before joining the *Sunday Standard*. After it closed he freelanced as a writer and broadcaster until his appointment as director of the Scottish Crofters' Union in 1986. Among James Hunter's books are *The Making of the Crofting Community* (1976) and *Skye: the Island* (1986).

DR DAVID PLAYER FRCPE, FRCPsych, FFCM

David Player was born in Glasgow in 1927. After graduating MB ChB from Glasgow University in 1950, he held a variety of posts in Scottish hospitals and in general practice. Between 1970 and 1973 he was Medical Officer (Mental Health Division), Scottish Home and Health Department and Psychiatric Adviser to the Secretary of State on the Scottish Prison and Borstal Service. In 1973 Dr Player became director of the Scottish Health Education Group, leading among others the Dying Scotsman and the Fit for Life campaigns. From 1982 until March 1987 he was Director General of the Health Education Council.

MARGARET MACINTOSH

Margaret Macintosh was born in Peebles in 1936. After graduating MA from Edinburgh University and attending Moray House Teachers' Training College she taught in Peebles, Inverness, Portree and Oban, and at Napier College of Science and Technology. She was appointed assistant head teacher at Wester Hailes Education Centre in

Edinburgh in 1976 and since 1983 has been head teacher at Drummond Community School in the city. Margaret Macintosh is actively involved in a number of educational organisations, including the Scottish Community Education Council and the Board of Governors of Queen Margaret College, Edinburgh.

JOHN LLOYD

John Lloyd was born in Anstruther in 1946. After graduating MA from Edinburgh University in 1967 he worked for the *Scottish Daily Mail* and *Time Out* before joining Independent Radio News in 1972. Two years later he moved to London Weekend Television, first as a reporter then as a producer. In 1977 he returned to print journalism and the *Financial Times*, becoming industrial editor. Since August 1986 he has been editor of the *New Statesman*. John Lloyd has won a number of awards including Specialist Writer of the Year 1985 (British Press Awards) and Granada Journalist of the Year 1985. He is co-author of two books: *Politics of Industrial Change* (1982) and *The Miners' Strike* (1986).

TOM McGRATH

Tom McGrath was born in Rutherglen in 1940. He was features editor of *Peace News* and founder of *International Times* before going to Glasgow University where he graduated MA in 1971. He was musical director of *The Great Northern Welly Boot Show* before founding the Third Eye Centre in 1974. His plays include *Laurel and Hardy* (1976), *The Hard Man* (1978), *Animal* (1979) and most recently *Kora* (1986). He has also written for television and is an accomplished jazz pianist. Tom McGrath is at present associate literary director with the Royal Lyceum Theatre in Edinburgh.

STEWART LAMONT

Stewart Lamont was born in Broughty Ferry in 1947 and graduated BSc BD from St Andrews University where he was president of the union. He has been an ordained minister of the Church of Scotland since 1972 when he joined BBC Scotland's religion department as a radio producer. For two years from 1980 he was part-time minister at Abernyte in Perthshire but resigned to freelance as a radio and television producer and presenter and as religious correspondent for the *Glasgow Herald*. Among his publications are *Religion and the Supernatural* (co-author, 1985) and *Religion Inc.* (1986).

KENNETH CARGILL

Kenneth Cargill was born in Arbroath in 1947. After graduating MA LLB from Edinburgh University in 1972 he joined the BBC as a researcher. After five years as a reporter on *Current Account,* he became a film director. He has produced a number of current affairs series including *Agenda* and has been an editor of the day on *Reporting Scotland.* Since 1984 he has been Deputy Editor of Television News and Current Affairs in Scotland.

GRASPING THE THISTLE

— *Professor Christopher Harvie*

'You're a' Jock Tamson's bairns' is a line encountered often enough on doorsteps in Scottish elections. The prestige of politics is not high. Politicians are seen at best as a necessary evil, at worst (as perhaps shown in our System Three Poll)* as a self-seeking bunch of parasites. The popularity of a programme like *Yes, Prime Minister* in which the pompous, thick, popularity-obsessed Jim Hacker is directed in circles by his clever, selfish and ultimately nihilistic 'servant' Sir Humphrey is predicated on the old belief that politicians will do 'as much harm as they can and as much good as they must'.

No wonder Mrs Thatcher likes the programme. The view that she shares insists that the more we try to plan, discuss and direct our future, the more the Hackers and Applebys will take over. We should cut back the 'public domain', turn more and more decisions over to the 'secret ballot' of the free market. Odd that this anti-politics line tends to be held by people whose confidence in their own political judgement is unclouded by doubt, but still a popular one.

When politics — the capacity to settle issues by argument — die, however, we are in real danger. Germany, where I now live and work, found this appallingly true in the twelve years which followed 1933. Culturally, the country is still deeply traumatised by the consequences, but politically, in the forty-year career of the Federal Republic and its eleven states, it seems to have developed into a mature, efficient and open democracy.

Now the Germans aren't any better than us at the 'life' of politics, the fixing, wheeling and dealing, etc., but they seem to have evolved, in their federal system, a structure which is closer to the problems it deals with than ours: one which operates openly and in accordance with accepted rules. Two examples: last summer, when the Chernobyl fall-out came, the German *Land* governments set out to inform, not to cover up. In Britain, reassurance came before information. And while I was making my *Scotland 2000* television programme, *Grasping the Thistle*, the offices of BBC Scotland and the *New Statesman*, for which I was covering the German election, were repeatedly raided by the Special Branch in pursuit of a film on a top-secret project which, unobserved by Parliament, had escalated in cost to £500 million. This sort of thing happened in 1962 in Germany, in the raid on *Der Spiegel* news-magazine, but even at that early date it cost the powerful Defence Minister, Franz-Josef Strauss, his job. I don't see many such heads rolling here, and I worry about that.

But if the pianist has gone so far out of control, better to change the instrument than shoot him or her? Have we not had enough — after over thirty years of fairly consistent economic failure — of a centralised structure dedicated to two-party politics, which seems to promote

* see appendix

1

Christopher Harvie in the proposed Scottish Assembly Chamber – *Scotsman Publications*

pointless conflicts, wasteful reverses of policy, and obsessive secrecy, while failing to provide enough organised consent for government to become effective? Given that, in Scotland, consent seems to have become massively eroded (the System Three Poll showed support for the Conservative government at 17 per cent, or less than half its British level), and the institutions of British government have by any standards been pretty ineffective in coping with Scottish problems, how strong is the demand for fundamental constitutional change? Would decentralisation and federalism, of the sort practised in West Germany and Baden-Württemberg, work?

A decentralist trend, now general in Europe, is shrewdly and wittily defended by one of Baden-Württemberg's leading politicians, Manfred Rommel, son of the Desert Fox and now Christian Democrat Oberburgermeister of Stuttgart:

'If we had to ask for everything in Bonn it would take much longer, and the possibility of helping industry and creating a good employment rate would be reduced very much. I think modern society is so complicated that it cannot be well organised without decentralisation, and without initiative for it in the administration.

'I can of course not say if German decentralisation is good or not for Great Britain, but for Germany it is very important, and also our neighbours the French are trying now to change the structure of the nation fundamentally in the direction of more decentralisation. This is very new for the French because the French were very centralised. I think it is better, not only because it offers more well-paid jobs for people like me, but for industry, for economy, and also for social welfare.'

Manfred Rommel was gently mocking about the efforts of his rival, Minister-President Lothar Späth, to cut an international dash with frequent state visits abroad, thus emphasising the lack of an obvious cultural and political identity in the German *Länder*. Rommel is in fact a local politician; but he could have come from Berlin or Cologne, as leading politicians are transferred around Germany by their parties like football aces. There is no Baden-Württemberg football team, let alone a national anthem. German decentralisation is carefully organised and effective, but (Bavaria and the old Hanseatic towns of the north, Bremen and Hamburg, excepted) the German *Länder* are politically-legislative units, not actual nations.

By contrast, in Scotland the Secretary of State presides like – as he himself

6th Duke of Richmond – *BBC Hulton Picture Library*

River Neckar, Tübingen – *German National Tourist Office*

said - a governor-general over a country with its own law, its own Church, its own educational system and (at least in terms of nomenclature) its own health service, trains and buses; and its own acute sense of a separate culture. Within the centralised structure of British politics, the present Secretary, Malcolm Rifkind, a contemporary of mine at university, rejoices in, at least nominally, remarkably autonomous powers:

'The advantage of being a Secretary of State for Scotland is that, although the total resources available to one in Scotland are naturally determined by the Cabinet as a whole, how they are used in Scotland is decided by the Scottish Secretary and by his Scottish ministers and Scottish colleagues. There is a tremendous amount of autonomy here, and that is something which is very attractive from Scotland's point of view because, clearly, the balance between housing and education and roads and law and so forth is a matter which quite often will not be the same in Scotland as in England. These are not matters on which my English colleagues tell me what to do. I have complete discretion, as did my predecessors, as to how I allocate these resources.'

This system has lasted for over a century, since 1885 when the Duke of Richmond entered a revived Scottish Office (it had been suppressed after the Forty-five) based — as it still is — at Dover House in Whitehall. But its ethos is not quite the paradise of adminstrative autonomy Rifkind suggests: it has always been posited on the notion that the governing

4

party could either get a Scottish majority for its overall approach *or* create some form of Scottish consensus behind it. For more than twenty years, however, this certainty has been breaking up, something observed by Roy Jenkins – since 1982 the Social Democrat MP for Glasgow Hillhead as well as a prominent political historian and biographer:

'If I treat the Alliance as one party now, the SNP gives a four-party system as opposed to a three-party system, and that affects the whole set-up, with a different balance between the Conservative and Labour parties in Scotland, though that is a fairly recent development . . . Yet there is still a certain feeling of entrenched armies in Scotland, to an even greater extent than there is in England, except that of course the one army has shrunk to such a size it can hardly be called an army now; it's become almost a remnant.'

Malcolm Rifkind, representing the 'remnant', presently under 20 per cent in the opinion polls, hits back:

'I don't believe that in a democracy government can govern without the general consent of the public. If you are implying that if the government of the United Kingdom does not have a majority in Scotland or in England at any given time, then there is not consent, that implies a nationalist view of life. If you are a Scottish nationalist, and you believe that Scotland should be a separate state, then clearly a government that does not reflect the wishes of the Scottish public on a range of issues cannot have legitimacy. Eighty-five per cent of the Scottish public do not vote for the Nationalist Party. They vote for unionist parties and for others including the Labour Party and the Liberals and Social Democrats as well as the Conservatives, who believe in a United Kingdom and a United Kingdom government. Therefore, the only constitutional mandate, whether in Scotland or in England, is that of a democratically elected British Parliament.'

I find this argument odd for two reasons. One is that it seems to convert elections in Scotland into a running plebiscite for the Union. Two, if the Scots agree, through such votes, to let the rest of the UK decide for them, why should there be a separate Scottish Office, with a steadily widening range of powers over all aspects of Scottish society? On what logic is it grounded? If the *raison d'être* of the Office is the welfare of the people of Scotland, why are they not consulted about the policies appropriate to further it?

The further 'unionist' argument can be made that Scotland is, per capita, a substantial beneficiary through government expenditure, and that this has done more than autonomy ever could to equalise Scots incomes with those in the south. Two points here: not only nationalists would argue that this is a highly nominal *quid pro quo* in return for oil revenues. Two, if this is an act of indefensible generosity by Whitehall, there are now plenty of people in Mrs Thatcher's party demanding that it cease.

But the most penetrating argument about the inadequacy of a purely administrative structure of devolution seems to come when we contrast Scotland with my adoptive country. At the beginning of this century Scotland was one of the most complex industrialised regions in Europe. Baden-Württemberg, with the same population, mainly small peasant-farmers, had about half Scotland's gross national product per head. In 1906 its most famous product was the teddy-bear and Stuttgart seemed to have more palaces than factories.

The Scotland I was born into in 1944 was, by contrast, still the one which featured in the last lines of John Grierson's, Harry Watt's and W. H. Auden's film *Night Mail* (1936), an image which even now I find almost choking in the emotions it provokes:

Dawn freshens. Her climb is done.
Down towards Glasgow she descends,
Towards the steam tugs yelping down
   a glade of cranes.
Towards the fields of apparatus,
   the furnaces
Set on a dark plain, like gigantic
   chessmen.
All Scotland waits for her:
In dark glens, beside pale green lochs,
Men long for news.

The 1906 comparisons are now reversed. Scottish GDP per head is only about half that of Baden-Württemberg, although the latter's population is now over nine million. Unemployment in Scotland is almost three times greater at around fifteen per cent. Baden-Württemberg is the headquarters of world giants like Daimler-Benz, Porsche and Robert Bosch, and manufacturing comes to over forty per cent of GDP, while Scotland's has fallen to under twenty-five per cent (as far as more up-to-date industry is concerned) and is increasingly a branch-plant operation. IBM, for example, operates in both countries, but its European headquarters and research institute are based at Böblingen near Stuttgart.

Now what have politics and administration to do with this? A great deal, I think. A parliament is a means of surveying and organising the whole conspectus of social and economic policy; of debating priorities; and of organising consent for particular strategies of reform and adaptation. This is not glamorous or headline-hitting business, but in a modern state it's essential. Scotland has not only completely failed to evolve such a system, but has gradually become enchained in a neo-colonial form of government. I believe that this has, for some time, been taking an increasing toll of our chances of economic recovery. The reasons for this don't just reside in the 'British malaise', although they're a part of it. They're also peculiar to the evolution of Scots politics since the Act of Union 280 years ago.

My argument is that the amalgamation of the Scottish and English parliaments didn't leave a power vacuum but in fact preserved, in a disarticulated way, Sir David Lindsay's 'three estates' — Nobility, Clergy

Schillerplatz, Stuttgart – *German National Tourist Office*

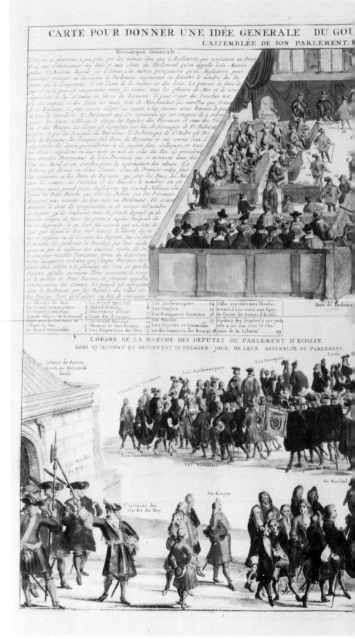

The Three Estates of the Scottish Parliament
(an early eighteenth-century French engraving, artist unknown) – *BBC*

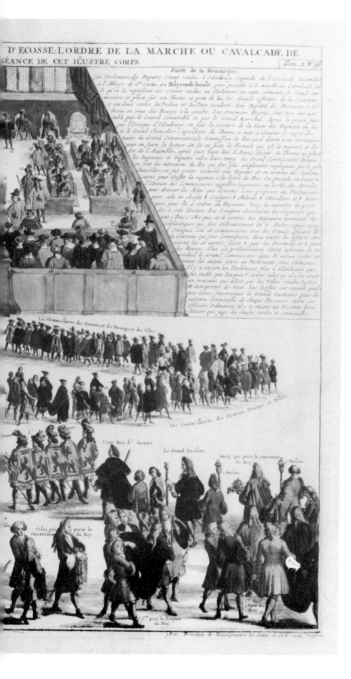

and Burgesses — which had come together in the old Scottish parliament. It preserved their assemblies and their peculiar political consciousness. These changed, of course, over time. Land, well organised by the legal profession, became industrial — and then finance — capital; the clergy became a secular 'clerisy' and then the 'intelligentsia' of writers, artists, academics, and so on; the burgesses both continued in the formal estate of the Convention of Royal Burghs, now the Convention of Scottish Local Authorities, and broadened into the Scottish political parties, MPs, ministers and bureaucrats.

Up to a point this was a reasonably effective form of politics, as it concentrated the mind of the élite on domestic 'improvement' at a time when parliaments were liable to become dangerously involved with foreign intrigues. Its great triumph was Scotland's transformation within fifty years during the eighteenth century from backward province into an industrial economy with a growth rate comparable with that of England; its disaster was its failure to diffuse the benefits of this experience and enable the people of Scotland to control it.

This ambiguous achievement — national in its inception but non-national in its results — added a fourth estate: the working class: organised labour: the Scottish Chartists of the early nineteenth century, the Scottish trade unionists and the Marxist zealots of the Red Clyde.

'We never thought of Scottish politics at all, we treated it with contempt, I think. Scottish nationalism? We just laughed at them. We didn't regard

Police returning from a baton charge in North Frederick Street, Glasgow, 8 February 1919 – *BBC Hulton Picture Library*

10

it as a social issue of any particular importance. My attitudes have changed now, but in those days I think we treated it right, just as a sort of bunch of freaks.'

Thus Harry McShane, the last survivor of the militants who challenged Lloyd George over munitions policy in 1916 and were regarded, both by Lenin and the then Secretary of State as a revolutionary force. To them the future of the Scottish working class was as soldiers of an international revolution:

'The big thing was the class struggle . . . the first thing a Marxist thought about was the class struggle . . . fighting the people in power, overthrowing them. . . that was Marxism. That was treated in the Communist manifesto, it was the classic word put forward by the Marxists at the time and I was a Marxist. I'm still one.'

In many ways it's as well to start with this group, as they had a view of Scotland's place in history: one which appeared consonant with the rationalism of the eighteenth-century Scots Enlightenment, with Adam Ferguson, John Millar and the Marxists' favourite novelist, Walter Scott: from Scotland to Britain to world revolution. But the result of their efforts, Scottish class politics, however powerful, was in Marx's own phrase, 'of a class' rather than 'for a class'. In the words of Christopher Smout of St Andrews University, the leading historian of modern Scottish society:

'The radicalism of the Red Clyde is a myth. It was a movement which involved a very large number of people in the First World War, but not many of them were revolutionaries. A great many were democrats, who believed that they could do something with their own energies for Scotland, and were very concerned about the social problems of Glasgow and of their fellow workers. It was an abiding tradition, but Glasgow wasn't going to be a Leningrad.

'There was always a tension in the Clydesiders between the democratic ideal that you're responsible for your own fate and future and the idea that the State should come in and do something for you. And it was the second that won, partly due to Tom Johnston, one of the great Clydesiders and then an immensely important Secretary of State. The idea of a consensus where you gently prodded England and then the goodies came tumbling out was really the one that eventually the Labour Party, Clydeside and most of Scotland decided was the way to go.'

The dominance of class politics is implicit even today in Labour's position in the opinion polls — hovering for the past year at around forty-five per cent (about ten to fifteen per cent more than in England and Wales) while the Conservatives have dwindled towards extinction. Yet in 1979 this same class-consciousness cut across Labour's commitment to a Scottish Assembly. In the Labour clubs and housing schemes, it appears that, ambiguous as Labour's Commons performance was on devolution, it was — and maybe still is — more than matched by a feebleness of purpose at the grass roots. Donald Dewar, Labour's Shadow Secretary of State, thinks otherwise:

'We were very keen in the late 1970s on forcing devolution through and we did it. I think it was a bravura performance, particularly by John Smith and his colleagues in the House of Commons, with no majority from day to day. We made it somehow, breathless and dishevelled. But we got to the referendum, and then in a sense Scotland took fright. It was partly the kind of parish-pump politics of the Teddy Taylors of this world that persuaded people that it was a swollen bureaucracy, more expenditure, and the vision was lost. I don't think that would happen again.'

Dewar is sanguine, Christopher Smout is pessimistic, seeing Scottish socialism as essentially bureaucratic rather than democratic. By this reckoning Johnston, who really established the ethos of administrative devolution while Secretary of State during the Second World War, formed Labour into a kind of lobby-organisation which could never encourage real involvement and decision-making, even when the pork-barrel at the end of the lobby was found to be empty.

Now this impasse in socialist ideology — the dependence on going through parliamentary conventions rather than creating a democratic movement for autonomy — brings me back to my original thesis. The radical intentions of the political socialists in a deeply class-divided society were dissipated. How?

Were they beaten down by a successful and adaptive capitalism, as has been the case in Baden-Württemberg, where the conservative Christian Democrats have formed the government for most of the *Land's* thirty-six years of existence? (Be it said that Manfred Rommel would qualify only as the wettest of British Conservatives.) It might have seemed so thirty-two years ago. In 1955 the Scottish Conservatives were ahead of Labour both in numbers of MPs and total votes cast. This was in an economy where the Clyde shipyards were still booming and Glasgow still had the second-largest locomotive-building works in the world. The consequence of this success was that the Scottish Unionist Party still reflected the powerful indigenous business interest personified by such as Sir James Lithgow, the Tsar of West Scottish heavy industry, whose word was law in the shipyards of the Clyde, and by implication in the steelworks and coal mines of Lanarkshire.

But their doom had struck. The slump which followed the Suez operation was the beginning of the end of the old industrial order, and the Unionist Party was, anyway, becoming more of a specialist pressure group with a particularly strong emphasis on agriculture. But this too is a thing of the past. Agricultural policy is now decided by the European Commission in Brussels, and the very success of agricultural modernisation has resulted in the Tory electorate of the countryside dwindling away. In one glen in the heart of Tory country the farming population has fallen from twenty-one families in 1966 to eight today.

There was one last attempt to rally. The industrialists evolved Oceanspan, their scheme to run the Clyde again as a major European entrepôt. In 1968 Edward Heath, responding to the sudden challenge of the Scottish Nationalist Party, made the Declaration of Perth, pledging his party to a form of home rule. However, when he came to power in 1970 he ditched this commitment for reasons which the chairman of the subsequent Tory Commission on the Constitution, Lord Home, makes patent by implication:

'As long as the Scottish Office is good, as long as they interpret their

Scottish Office ministerial team, left to right: Lord Glenarthur, Michael Ancram, Malcolm Rifkind, John Mackay and Ian Lang – *Glasgow Herald*

function with a good deal of emphasis towards decentralisation, then I think that we can go on being governed as we are. That may be a bit optimistic but I don't think so. Though there is a lot to be said for decentralisation, modern circumstances are against it. Unemployment being what it is now, if we accepted suggestions of separation from England we could not finance unemployment in Scotland on the same scale as it is done by the UK government. That's one reason why I think people hesitate a good deal before they commit themselves to anything like separation.'

Devolution was a priority political issue to the Conservatives while centralist Labour was in power. When in power themselves, and finding Scotland progressively less inclined to follow them, they postponed it. When Labour opted for devolution, they ditched the commitment altogether. The problem was that this coincided both with the final collapse of Scottish industrial Conservatism and with another, more subtly subversive development, the entry of the party for the first time directly into local government. Albert MacQuarrie, MP for Banff and Buchan, typified this new type of urban councillor:

'The reorganisation of local government overtook the Declaration of Perth because it was found that we had devolved government from central government to the new regional government and district councils. I think that has proved satisfactory. It'd be an absolute disaster if we started talking now about parliaments in Edinburgh when we've got this huge organisation set up throughout the country with the regional and district councils. They proved themselves to be very satisfactory and we still have a control on the legislative people in Edinburgh, in New St Andrew's House.'

The local government Tory was concerned with cutting expenditure and limiting rates, not with expensive strategies for industrial recovery. This was not a view which met with unqualified support from a representative of the more traditional agricultural interest in the party, Sir Hector Monro, MP for Dumfriesshire:

'We thought of devolution in terms of the old county councils and burghs and city councils, virtually non-political, but now the whole thing is so bureaucratic — everything is decided in committee meetings before they actually meet — that I think we have lost the enthusiasm for giving that sort of power to a legislature in Scotland.'

No one could possibly have called most of the Scottish burgh councils 'non-political' in the 1960s, but let it pass. Michael Forsyth, a devoted monetarist of the New Right, took an even more aggressive line:

'We've always been a unionist party and devolution was a diversion from the main challenge facing Scotland, which was to make ourselves competitive in world markets, and create jobs. The experience of regional councils, and particularly of Strathclyde, has convinced all of us that the last thing we want is a kind of greater Strathclyde presiding over Scottish affairs. It would guarantee for the forseeable future a Labour administration in Scotland, and the experience of Labour administrations in Strathclyde and elsewhere is a very unhappy one. It's one of jobs being destroyed and of higher and higher taxation, and as the party which I think is determined to take Scotland into the twenty-first century, we would reject any constitutional barrier which devolution represents.'

For a libertarian, this implies a somewhat draconian curb on the right of voters to make silly mistakes, if that's what a majority of them want to do. Was this the same Michael Forsyth who, in a paper written for the New Right Adam Smith Institute, demanded that Scottish banks be allowed to float the pound Scots against the pound Sterling?

Malcolm Rifkind argues on one hand that devolution is open to constitutional objections but also states emphatically that all Scottish business opinion is against it. Yet Rifkind in fact is the first Secretary of State to be notably distant from Scottish business opinion. For longer than most Cabinet positions, that of Scottish Secretary usually required the holder to 'carry guns' either as a party functionary, like James Stuart, who had been Churchill's Whip, or as a member — like Younger, Noble, Maclay or Collins — of the Scottish landed or industrial establishment. In this context Rifkind, a professional from a middle-class Edinburgh trade background, is something new. He is also the first Jewish Secretary of State (there has never been a Catholic one), something which confirms the WASPish, small-c conservatism of the party he heads.

Rifkind is young, informal and intelligent, but does he 'carry guns'? Can he get on the phone to the leaders of Scottish industry and — like Tom Johnston or Walter Elliot — create the informal structures which lead to innovation? Are there, anyway, any leaders of industry to be reached? He has tried to make the best of a very bad political position by attempting to consolidate the Tory ratepayer vote through the poll-tax scheme he inherited from George Younger (and, I believe, the Adam Smith Institute). But his failures to discipline Guinness in the aftermath of its takeover of Distillers, or to prevent the closure of the Caterpillar plant at Uddingston, suggest that he has little room for manoeuvre, or for the sort of original thinking on planning that someone like Walter Elliot could generate.

Further, elements of his own party may be moving beyond him. According to the opinion polls, a majority of Scots Tory voters now support devolution, and the one remaining major centre of capitalism in Scotland — the financial institutions of Edinburgh — seems to show at least a benevolent neutrality to the idea. The Royal Bank of Scotland group is the biggest operator in what is — in terms of the range of financial services offered — Europe's second-largest financial centre, and its chief executive Charles Winter is guardedly positive:

'The big change which is taking place in the financial sector these days is the increasing use of technology, and that offers opportunities for Scotland which never existed in the past. The need to conduct financial markets now within one tight floor, with the traders standing on the floor, has gone and that means that there must be possibilities in future for these markets spilling out of the City of London. And given the infrastructure which exists already in Scotland, Scotland must have a heaven-sent opportunity to take advantage of that. So far from there being any danger of a drift from Scotland to London, I would have thought that there are opportunities, if properly tapped, for bringing business from London to Scotland. I would not purport to be an expert on the issue of Scottish devolution, but as long as the right climate is created for industrial growth in Scotland and the right environment is provided for the Scottish financial community by politicians of whatever colour, I will be perfectly happy with that.'

The merchant banker Ian Dalziel, who heads Adam and Company in Charlotte Square, and was formerly a Conservative Member of the European Parliament, goes even further and now supports an Assembly:

'I confess I was one of these who were against it in 1978-79, I think because I was living in London and it wasn't, frankly, very well marketed south of the Border. People associated devolution with independence, which is not necessarily the case. But today I feel there is room in Scotland for an elected Assembly.'

This change of heart was prompted by his experience of the European Parliament after 1979:

'I quickly realised that there were people representing regions in France, Germany, Italy, who had a much greater awareness of what the benefits of the community were to their own region. And at the official level civil servants, regional administrators in those areas, seemed to be less inhibited in asking for the impossible, and seemed to be frankly more on the ball than some of us in Scotland. It's almost inconceivable to believe that a development authority in, say, Corsica or in the north of Italy didn't know every single rule and regulation and how to circumvent it to get the maximum amount of money from Brussels for its region. And I got the feeling that because there was a lack of a forum, a place where these views could be aired, sometimes these benefits went by default because there was nobody democratically elected pushing a civil servant or an administrator into answering the question "Why haven't you gone to Brussels and why haven't you got that, and why aren't we getting more?" We are getting a lot in Scotland, one's got to say, but in the last five or six years, with the economy shifting the way it has and so many changes taking place in the financial marketplace, something a little more fundamental than the Scotland–England football game might be a good thing for us Scots to focus on.'

My hunch is that the ructions of autumn 1986; the downright criminality involved in the Guinness takeover of Distillers (in which the Scottish financial establishment was the injured and innocent party) and the questionable future of the City of London after the hype surrounding the Big Bang, has led Edinburgh to distance itself from London. Ian Dalziel suggests, also, a more positive identification with Europe:

'Where I disagreed profoundly with the Devolution Bill of 1977 and again 1979 was that Europe, and Scotland's involvement with the European Community, was of course specifically excluded, along with certain other financial provisions, which were frankly crazy. But a more sensible financial provision and a clear linkage between Scotland and the Community, backed up in a perfect world by proportionality as a form of electing people to that Assembly, supported by all the professional,

The Royal Bank of Scotland Registered Office, Edinburgh – *The Royal Bank of Scotland*

business and economic activities in Scotland, would be an interesting challenge. You would have people responding to it who may not normally respond in purely party political terms to a Westminster situation. Again it's a gamble, but Scotland has to gamble to succeed, on occasion.'

The European dimension is, of course, peculiarly interesting to me, as I teach in Germany and so replicate the inclination of the Scots to seek their fortunes as much on the continent as in London. Tübingen has always had close theological connections with Scotland, and after the Forty-five an oddly pivotal figure, Sir James Stewart, one of the last of the Jacobites and the first great Scottish political economist, was exiled here. In the nineteenth and much of the twentieth centuries, the Empire offered more attractive territory for the Scots to exploit, and did much to complicate the consciousness of the Scots intelligentsia, but the 1960s and 1970s saw what the Germans call a *Heimkehr,* which has helped to create a powerful cultural revival. John McGrath, the Liverpool-born dramatist and founder of the 7:84 Theatre, has been one of its most energetic prophets:

'A cultural revival, if it is really to work, is the sharp end of a political

growth of awareness. There was a huge feeling all over Scotland of a growing sense of national identity during the 1970s, not only because at first there was a Conservative government, which always gives Scotland the sharp edge to its self-awareness, but also because the later Labour government was particularly colourless, and what was going on here was particularly boring in terms of politics. So the grass-roots responses, from people living in Scotland with their own ambitions and their own ideas, led to a qualitative change in their appreciation of what politics was about, and the number of people involved in politics, attending political meetings, going to rallies, going to conferences, was absolutely phenomenal. This was a total change from before.'

McGrath may be overestimating the politicisation of the 1970s. We have evidence that Whitehall administrators thought that the Scots were much more militant than they turned out to be, and many of my friends and colleagues, the political intellectuals (we could call ourselves that at least) thought that, because we had got things right in our minds, the punters would jump into line with us. The Winter of Discontent put paid to this. But as McGrath points out, the impulse of cultural separatism has remained:

'Since 1979 a polarisation has taken place. Many people in Scotland have moved strongly with Thatcher to the right, but the bulk of the population has felt itself totally alienated from Westminster, from the Conservative government, and from the Scottish Office. The Tories have conducted industrial struggles with the kind of ruthlessness, bitterness and personalisation of the struggle which has shocked people in Scotland. This sense of alienation and of shock with the way that a 'Saxon' attitude has come down the line to Scotland has led to a more introverted bitterness than in the 1970s. It's not so self-confident, but it's there and it's coming out in all kinds of interesting ways.'

In the early 1970s, if I had talked about a Scottish film industry or a revival in the Scottish novel or in history writing, no one would have taken me seriously. Even Neal Ascherson, then our leading political commentator, expressed his disappointment at the lack of a cultural dimension to the revival in political nationalism. But all three developments have arrived. Scots are conscious first of being Scots, and the attitude, reiterated so much in the 1960s and 1970s, that an autonomous Scotland would be the cultural equivalent of a Glasgow housing scheme, has vanished. When was the last time that the archetypal English literary gent — Lord Dacre or Paul Johnson — tried to fire off their line about the natural cultural attitude — cringing — of the Jocks? We may have fallen over in 1979; others, McGrath concludes, have fallen farther:

'The main thing about Scottish culture at the moment is that it sings, there's a tremendous amount of music and a lot of words knocking about. Not only the touring companies, but also the Lyceum and the Citizens' Theatre and the novelists, poets and folk singers like Dick Gaughan are doing wonderful work. They are using language with a sense not only of discovery but of origination and invention, compared with the rather arid academic way that the English writers and theatre-makers are trying to force language to obey issues and to obey concepts. This is very, very important and again relates to the same thing: a sense of contact with

Vincent Friel and Alyxis Daly in *The Albannach – Sean Hudson*

humanity in Scotland which I find lacking amongst the intelligentsia and writers in London.'

That said, how do such impulses transfer themselves to politics? Again, the residue of our old institutions lies across the way, particularly in the law, the great instrument whereby Scottish society was modernised in the eighteenth century. As industry has declined, and the trade unions have been politically marginalised, law has become the most important institution represented among Scottish politicians at Westminster: Malcolm Rifkind is an advocate; Donald Dewar and Gordon Wilson are solicitors; David Steel trained as one. Even Jim Sillars, the stormy petrel of the nationalist left, is presently studying law at Edinburgh University. Does this make the Scottish politician a Gandhi sort of lawyer, undertaking a case against the occupying power on behalf of the nation, or does he become a Parliament House clone settling down to a career which conforms to the legalism of the traditional estate? A lot depends on the answer to this question.

Some Parliament House men like Lord Wilson of Langside, sometime Labour Lord Advocate and No-Man in 1979, take a deeply hostile attitude to devolution as the source of an infinitely troublesome series of constitutional conflicts between Edinburgh and London:

'What has happened since 1979 reinforces my view that if the Scotland Act of 1979 had been implemented it would have been disastrous. Compare the tensions that there have been between local government and central government, particularly between local government in Scotland and central government; the absurd tensions which have been allowed to develop. Think what these tensions would have been like if there had been a Labour-Party-dominated Scottish Assembly in Edinburgh and Mrs Thatcher at the head of her government in Westminster. It would have been disastrous for Great Britain.'

The Secretary of State seconds this view:

'I indicated my position the day after the devolution referendum and I haven't changed since then . . . I voted Yes in the referendum and the following day when we saw the result — one-third Yes; one-third No; one-third staying at home and not voting — I said there is no basis for fundamental constitutional change in the United Kingdom if only one-third of the Scottish electorate were actually prepared to vote for it. I haven't changed since.'

But although he is, by implication, still willing to support devolutionary proposals which are backed by a clear majority of Scots, he has strong reservations about current proposals:

'What is ultimately unworkable about the Labour Party's and other parties' proposals for devolution is that they are proposing that Britain should remain a unitary state so far as Scotland is concerned. Now there is, frankly, nowhere else in the world that has such an extraordinary mish-mash of constitutional arrangements and that is why comparisons with Germany or, indeed, the United States or any other country have not yet been made on a valid or convincing basis.'

Up to a point, Mr Rifkind. But for nearly fifty years Northern Ireland's relations with Westminster were governed by exactly this sort of constitutional mish-mash, which has now, since the Anglo–Irish agreement, been replaced by something even more anomalous. Other members of the legal fraternity may feel that the inequities perceived by the Scots — subject, up to now, to pretty severe disciplining by the political parties themselves — are going too far in the other direction.

Enter the third estate, the burgesses, the political professionals represented by the politicians most Scots persist in voting for.

For the Labour Party devolution, something of an optional and not-absolutely-welcome extra in the 1970s, has now become the keystone of Scottish policies aimed at areas with massive unemployment, industrial dereliction and social underprivilege: all too often co-terminous with areas of Labour dominance in Scotland. Yet there's an interesting ambiguity here. John Smith, MP for Monklands — another lawyer — was (rather reluctantly) put in charge of the Scotland Bill in 1978, and then proceeded to win his laurels piloting it through the Commons. For Smith devolution is part of a process of making the British economy again subject to public control:

'We've two things to do with such areas. The first is a real anti-poverty programme; tackling the root causes of poverty means redistributing income in society. Secondly, we have to bring back a different type of industry, and this will not happen against the background of international movements of capital and the like, without determined government intervention, of the type that the SDA has done. It could do a lot more if it were funded and pushed more aggressively. Unless that happens we will become the victims of international forces.'

Donald Dewar, the Shadow Secretary of State, and a man with a record of support for legislative devolution going back to the 1960s, is somewhat more emollient:

'Sometimes it's dangerous to see the problem as standing up against the multi-national corporation or against industrial development across international boundaries. What you've got to do is have the kind of society that can attract industry, which can capitalise on the opportunities it presents, by really having there the educated population, the technical skills and the structure of government that will encourage that sort of enterprise. I am confident that we can do that in Scotland.'

The shift of emphasis here is interesting, given that both Smith and Dewar are on the 'moderate' wing of the Labour Party — indeed were contemporaries at Glasgow University. Dewar is essentially using devolution to reinforce Scotland's traditional strategy of attracting industrial development while Smith, as befits Labour's trade spokesman, sees it from a London perspective as part of a more general restructuring of industrial control and promotion. When challenged about the reaction of 'development areas' elsewhere in Britain to 'privileges' for Scotland, Smith's reply is that Scottish devolution must be set against the greater degree of regionalisation which Labour foresees, including English regional assemblies. Dewar, however, did not commit himself on this, I think wisely, as there's not much evidence to bear out Smith's contention that the English want this sort of reform. Indeed, the sort of protests from the north-east of England with which we were familiar in 1977-79 are already making themselves heard again.

Labour's ambiguity is paralleled by that of the 'traditional' home-rule parties, the Liberal–Social Democrat Alliance and the Scottish Nationalists. The Liberals, or at least their Scottish organisation, have been passing resolutions in favour of home rule for just over a century, but it was the most solidly Liberal areas of Scotland, the Northern Isles and the Borders, which polled the lowest pro-devolution votes in March 1979. However, David Steel, the Liberal leader, rejects this charge of backsliding:

'After the campaign was over John Smith chastised me for not having taken a sufficiently active part in the devolution campaign. I believe that not only was the package of proposals itself flawed, but that the handling of the referendum was quite disastrously mistaken by the government. Unlike the European referendum, they decided to make it a Yes vote, in favour of the government's proposals, with photographs of the then Labour leader on the poster. So they couldn't really expect to have the same all-party enthusiasm.'

Would they react in the same way again? Or what would be their price for co-operation? David Steel is emphatic about the need, while rather unspecific about the means:

'We're going to win some more seats. It's possible the SNP and the Labour Party may pick up one or two each, so that whatever the politics of Westminster, the politics of Scotland are going to be even more anti-Conservative, and rightly so. So the responsibility is heavily on us in politics in Scotland to get our act together. This has been the repeated failure of attempts to get Scottish devolution. The minute the Labour Party has a majority they think, we'll do it our way, and to hell with everybody else. Or if the Nationalists get half a dozen MPs, they think the world is waiting for them to make some dramatic move. Not so. The electorate of Scotland show in opinion poll after opinion poll that they are rooted in common sense. They want to see an agreed measure of internal self-government, which is not excessively nationalist, and not a bit of a facade, as was the last package. It is not beyond the wit of Scottish politicians to agree on what that package should be, but if we go our separate party ways, we won't get it.'

Does this package include changes in the voting system, and introduction of proportional representation, which was something the Liberals tried to press for when they maintained Jim Callaghan in power in 1977-78? According to Roy Jenkins, the Alliance would be prepared to compromise (although not much sign of movement is visible from Labour, who regard any and every move in this direction as an arrow aimed at the heart of socialism). 'I am in favour of proportional representation, but I'm the only member of the Shadow Cabinet who is,' Robin Cook told me in August. And the only thing to have happened since is that Cook is no longer in the Shadow Cabinet.

There remains another option, detailed by the SNP Chairman Gordon Wilson, MP for Dundee East. The SNP isn't the power that it was in the 1970s, but it has been doing respectably in the polls, and somewhat better in local elections. The forecasts are that, unless there's a remarkable Conservative revival, it should have five or six seats in the next Parliament:

'Were we to get a majority of seats at the next election, that would allow Scotland to gain full self-government and allow us to take our part in the world. But if, by some strange chance, we didn't get this then I

SNP Chairman, Gordon Wilson MP launching a new poster campaign, 1980 – *Scotsman Publications*

think the best situation would be, along with our allies in Plaid Cymru, if we were to hold the balance of power. In that situation we would be able to negotiate things of value for Scotland including constitutional changes. We'd then take what we call the Scottish convention route, that is not going for devolution through Westminster, but getting a constitutional convention elected within Scotland that would decide the framework for a Scottish parliament as the Scots want it and not as the English would like it.'

This course has been urged by the non-party Campaign for a Scottish Assembly. But although a precedent for it exists in the Northern Ireland constitutional convention of 1975, most pro-devolution Labour MPs seem deeply hostile to it. The leading left-wing activist of the SNP, Jim Sillars, doesn't seem to place much faith in such possibilities of cross-party action; and doesn't see anything really changing until after the general election:

'Perhaps the most important date is the district-council elections in 1988. We'll know by then either whether we're facing another Thatcher government or whether there's a Labour government probably making a mess of the economy — because I'm unimpressed by Labour's analysis of the English decline. Nineteen eighty-eight is a fixed date; the national movement should be heading for that date and we should be trying to seize administrative power in Scotland at district-council level. We can use that base to fight against whatever government happens to be in Downing Street and Westminster. It can be a leverage for some degree of autonomy, if that's all that people want, or indeed to build up the consensus for independent Scotland within the European Community.'

Sillars sees this crisis coming when falling world supplies force a second North Sea oil boom, coming on stream in the mid 1990s. But this is an awful long way ahead. A twenty-year-old member of the late Scottish Labour Party in 1976 will be forty when that happens. And will there be a Scottish economy by then?

The estate of the politicians contains as many opinions as there are parties, which is only to be expected. That it also shows splits within the parties is likewise inevitable, given the peculiar development of contemporary Scottish affairs. At what stage does the Conservatives' practice of administrative devolution without negotiated consent become a form of colonial government sufficiently irksome for the Scots to take cases about it to international legal bodies? Is Labour prepared to forego its British ambitions to assuage the Scots, and promote representative regional government by taking on proportional representation and reduced numbers at Westminster? As the numbers wanting outright independence rise — from under twenty per cent in 1979 to over thirty-three per cent — when does the SNP gain the impetus to re-launch itself?

Perhaps all these questions will pose themselves emphatically if an MP in one of a couple of dozen marginal constituencies drops dead. The SNP's fortunes in the 1970s owed much to such events. The answer thus still lies in the conventions of Augustus Pugin's masterpiece at Westminster. The West German Bundestag meets for its dull, businesslike sessions in the former Bonn municipal waterworks; while British politicians literally 'play the Palace'. I sometimes feel that our capacity to create a proper democracy in this country would be more than marginally improved if this amazing building with its debating chambers and committee rooms, its thirteen bars, its chapels and libraries and restaurants and portraits, panelling and stained glass were (without injuring anyone) to be burned to ashes — or televised (which amounts to the same thing).

It doesn't do to cross the Whitehall Establishment, which is what the Scots managed to do in the years before 1979, and Whitehall didn't forget it when the reckoning came, as ex civil servant and official Scottish Office historian John Gibson recalls:

'One of our Scottish Office wits did a poem when we were coming up to Referendum Day — St David's Day, 1979 — and the last two lines were: "On David's Day, how shall I choose? Heads you win, tails I lose." Some of us felt that at the time, as I've said in my book, [*The Thistle and the Crown,* 1985] that the package that was on offer was not going to work entirely to the good of Scotland. Others felt the opposite. But both sides did share the belief that if the referendum failed there would be a weakening of our stance in Whitehall. The way in which we'd been able to put fear and trembling into Whitehall colleagues down the years would be a thing of the past. To some extent that's been true. They felt that we had been rumbled.'

The process had, in fact, got under way earlier as, with the foundation of the Welsh Office in 1964, it had already become difficult for Scots bureaucrats to trumpet their successes to their clients without provoking demands for equal treatment from Cardiff (or, indeed, later from Belfast). The result of this was — *inter alia* — to bring to an end a peculiar Scots advantage in Parliament which had lasted, on and off, since 1707: of back-benchers trading their votes for the goodies dispensed through patronage.

For much of this century, as before, Scots MPs competently represented their constituencies but didn't exactly distinguish themselves — although, what with Smith, Rifkind, Steel and Cook, they're certainly doing so now — but they were closely observed by the corps of Scottish political journalists. If we weren't very good at doing it ourselves, we enjoyed watching others doing it. But James Naughtie, Chief Political Correspondent of *The Guardian,* has noticed that things have been changing: the Scottish profile is higher *and* different:

'Westminster in the past few years hasn't seemed to be the be-all and end-all of politics. It's still a place, of course, which is endlessly fascinating and exciting when it works. But I think more and more people see another dimension. A majority of Scots MPs believe that within their political lifetime there will be some kind of institution up there, to which many of them quite openly say they want to return. I don't think twenty, or thirty years ago that was true, largely because there was no prospect of it. Even some of those who are most against it on theoretical grounds still believe it's likely, and many who came to Westminster as young politicians would be quite happy to go back to Scotland. In fact, most of them expect to.

'The idea of a career which bestrides the world stage from Westminster is something which can't be taken as seriously now as it could, even twenty-five years ago. More Scots are looking home to their constituencies and, of course, with the tightening of the party battles, even in Scotland, there are fewer safe seats than there were, and therefore you've got to spend a bit more time on the home patch.'

According to Neal Ascherson, another old Scoto-German hand, formerly Bonn correspondent of *The Observer,* then *Scotsman* political correspondent and now chief columnist of *The Observer,* London's days as metropolis are themselves numbered. The attempt by the City to become an international finance centre to rival New York and Tokyo will, he reckons, push house prices and living costs up to prohibitive levels:

'London, of course, is the highly centralised capital of perhaps the most centralised state in Western Europe, particularly after France has made some move towards devolution. And it is the seat of a gigantic bureaucracy which runs the whole country. This bureaucracy is well paid in its upper reaches. Most of it is not all that well paid and it is going to become impossible for them to live in London. And that means one can imagine that in fifteen or twenty years' time, government will have to face the fact that Whitehall, the centre of British administration, is going to have to move out of London. They're going to have a Canberra solution or an Ottawa solution; they're going to have to create an artificial capital somewhere else. No doubt it will be in England. It will probably be in the south-east of England, maybe somewhere like Milton Keynes. I think that this pull of London is going to die out. London will become inaccessible and, very gradually, the centres of administrative and bureaucratic power will shift away from it.'

This centrifugal tendency may already be visible in the return to Glasgow of Campbell Christie, the new General Secretary of the Scottish Trades Union Congress, after a stint as a white-collar union leader in London:

'It's important that people should look towards Scottish politics and not Westminster as being important. The perception in the South I suppose is that everyone of ability moves south and there isn't much ability left in Scotland, but that's not been my perception since coming back to Scotland. We have people of ability in the Labour movement, in industry and in the academic world; all of whom would be able to make a worthwhile contribution. I think, of course, the situation makes the people. Given that we had an Assembly with new authority where there was real discussion and a real opportunity to take decisions about Scottish problems, we would have the calibre of people to deal with that. Perhaps it would mean that the constant drain of people moving away, both in political and industrial life, would be finished.'

Christie is himself representative of a new breed: a former civil servant to whom the Scottish Labour movement is a specific historical development, and not just something familiar and unquestioned. For him the campaign for an Assembly is part of a restructuring both of Scottish politics and of a Scottish working-class identity whose traditional base and institutions have been eroded.

'There's been a loss of identity in the trade union movement, and the institutions involved with it. The thing that will give the Labour movement a fillip will be the establishment of a Scottish Assembly, not just the present regional structure in local politics. So I set considerable store on seeing an Assembly in Scotland which will be looking particularly at how we take our own decisions about our universities, about education, how we decide about investment in our economy. Having been fourteen years in the South, I see that what's important to Scotland is not necessarily what is seen as being important to the rest of the UK. For instance, Thatcher and Lawson talk about the fall of oil prices being self-balancing in the economy, but for Scotland it has been disastrous.'

It seems odd to think of a Tory banker and a socialist trade union leader making similar cases for Scottish legislative autonomy, but perhaps it's neither historically absurd nor inconsistent with developments in other advanced areas of Europe. I think, in the first instance, of two of the factors which helped accelerate Scottish economic development in the eighteenth century — the sophisticated banking system and the adaptive, educated artisan. I think in the second case not of Baden-Württemberg but of Red Siena in Tuscany, impeccably run by the Communists, fiercely proud of its identity, but also the headquarters of the giant Monte del Paschi bank.

The antics of the City of London — the Guinness, Lloyd's, and Morgan Grenfell scandals — were pretty much what the Scots financial world

Victorian values in the City of London – *Scotsman Publications*

CAMPAIGN FOR
A SCOTTISH
ASSEMBLY

Youth for a Scottish Assembly marchers, March 1986 – *Scotsman Publications*

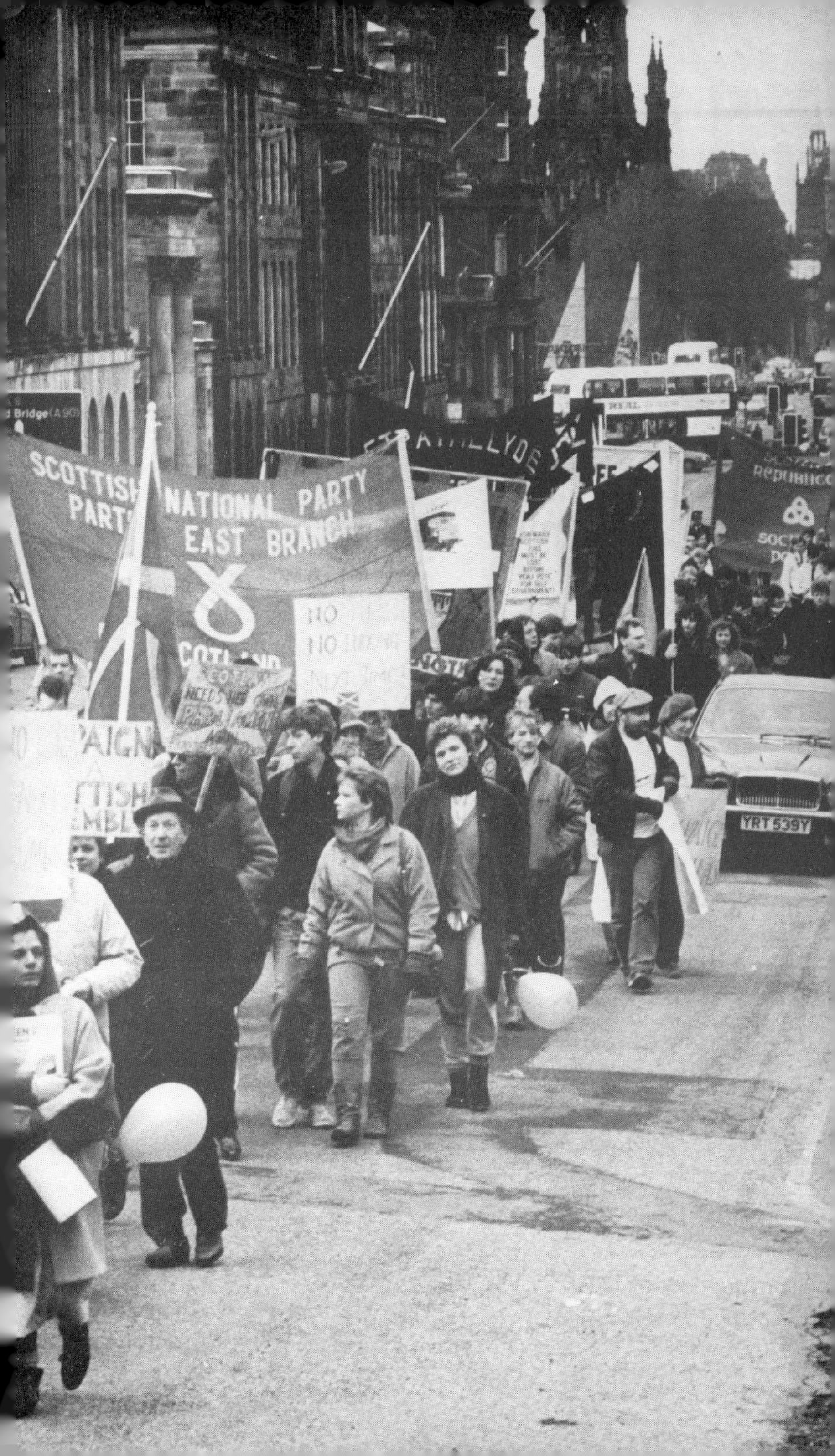
SCOTTISH
NATIONAL PARTY
EAST BRANCH
YRT 539Y

expected to happen. By keeping straight and sober, Scotland may have set itself up not just as a reliable competitor to London but as a potential centre for perhaps the most interesting development in international finance: the economic modernisation of East Europe. Under pressure from the Soviet Union, postwar Finland (the same population as Scotland) emerged as one of Europe's most rapidly developing economies on the strength of supplying high technologies to Eastern Europe. As the Gorbachev regime begins to move the Soviet Union's international trade relations away from a barter basis, might there not be a similar opportunity for Scottish financial services, with their associated manufacturing and service components, to tap this potentially vast market?

'If you look forward just over a dozen years from now, I can give you what I would like to see: that we will have succeeded in setting up a Scottish government. Naturally I hope that the temper of the country will be to have a Liberal-based government. I've always in my political life looked for co-operation with others, for a particular purpose; and I believe that it could be possible to see a Scottish government, in a democratic Assembly, in Edinburgh, with a left-of-centre government based on Liberal ideas. It might have many people in it who wouldn't touch the Liberal Party with a barge-pole at the moment, but Scottish politics has to be allowed to develop its own identity, and not be stuck too rigidly to the English party system.'

Thus David Steel. If I agree with him, it's not because I'm a card-carrying Liberal — which I'm not — but because, as a democrat, I believe that the level of representative government should lie where the public's interest in and information about politics intersects with the place where the political executive can gain consent for its actions, and consequently perform them efficiently. Parliaments are a better forum for getting this than local government or 'workplace democracy', partly because they combine information and participation with theatre and excitement. Westminster is neither participative nor efficient, and, because of this, the theatre it provides is deteriorating: instead of Trollope and Disraeli we have Jeffrey Archer. As my producer, John Milne, put it: 'Westminster is like Dr Who's Tardis in reverse. Once you get inside, it's *smaller*.'

As Scots, never properly fitting in, we've suffered particularly from this, but the survival of our own political conventions — expressed by our 'Estates' — has dulled the blow — in part, as we saw in 1979, by dividing us against one another. This 'multiplicity' in Scotland is recognised, positively, by John Smith:

'We saw some of these tensions displayed in the devolution referendum. I don't think that anything's different today, because while there's a sense of Scottishness, and a feeling that whether you're in Aberdeen or whether you're in Glasgow you're still a Scot, you still know there's a difference between the Glaswegian and an Aberdonian; and the winds of change don't all blow in the same direction at the same time. But my own deep belief is that there is a sense of Scottish identity which ought to be expressed in our political system in a British context and that really is the case for devolution, I suppose, in a nutshell.'

But Christopher Smout sees an irresolution, an acceptance of a client status, which the prospect of constitutional change is more likely to confirm than to overcome:

'I would be very surprised if an Assembly ever came into being, partly because of the fiasco of last time. I would question whether Labour would deliver the goods anyway: there's much more to Labour than the Labour Party in Scotland. If it did, if an Assembly came into being, it seems to me it could go one of two ways. It could either be the beginnings of a genuine national rebirth, in the sense that people would again feel they could do something for themselves and that it was up to themselves to do something. Or it could be just another enormous pressure group to act as a lever on England. I think the second would be very sad, and the first would be very good.'

Smout acknowledges that the experiment could be, against the odds, successful, and I would take up that challenge. To quote the lady, I think there is no alternative. In the last few years several of the fundamental conventions of what Britain means have been destroyed. The divide between North and South has widened and deepened; the possessions of the British State — 'the family silver' in Lord Stockton's words — have been sold off to augment government revenue; the Germans now call British society not a welfare state but a *zwei-drittel Gesellschaft:* one run for the benefit of the two-thirds who are doing well. As the split between Scots and English views of the Falklands campaign showed, the magic power of Westminster to promote a British identity no longer works.

The Scottish Nationalists, in Gordon Wilson's view, see the tide sweeping back to them:

'Every now and again the pressure builds up for change, ebbs a bit and then comes back stronger than ever. In 1979 the Westminster institutions, the Establishment, played for time successfully and the issue lost ground amongst the Scottish electorate. From then on we seemed to go into a "British" phase. Now we're coming out of that, and people are once more looking for Scottish solutions.'

They have, as unionists like Malcolm Rifkind would acknowledge, this much realism on their side: they're not out to solve the problems of both Scotland *and* Britain, and therefore they may have a better chance of success with their limited aim.

Even the complacency of the Conservatives about the British constitution isn't what it was. Lord Home still holds at least a theoretical brief for devolution:

'I generally thought the 1979 Bill was rotten and I said so; but we could have produced a better Bill. If one consulted the Conservative Party now it would be anti-devolution. Let me pass on from that to say if you are going to have decentralisation, a Conservative government could pass a Bill. It would involve an elected Assembly, it would have to do that. It would involve some finance for the elected Assembly under its control and I myself think the Conservative Party could probably agree to the local elections being held on a system of proportional representation of some kind. It could be done, yes; but the climate has changed. So I'm not sure if this Conservative government would take the initiative to do that.'

While the Secretary of State regards himself as keeping an open mind

Polaris submarine base, Holy Loch – *Glasgow Herald*

on the long-term constitutional changes:

'I retain an interest in the principle of devolution and I've always taken the view that devolution is perfectly possible for the United Kingdom which has several countries with different legal frameworks and different national traditions; the federal option is one, but it's only an option.'

But do the 'Little England' tendencies of Mrs Thatcher provide enough will to achieve a difficult and, for the Tories, rather unrewarding solution? In the last analysis, Neal Ascherson argues — as I do — that it's up to us:

'There is no doubt in my mind whatever that if the Scottish people show clearly and firmly that they wish to have a Scottish parliament with wide powers, they will get it. They may get it in the form of devolution but, even if they do, these loaned powers from Westminster will not be taken back because it would create a constitutional crisis of unimaginable dimensions. Westminster wouldn't dare do it. So it is there to be taken. No question about that. If Scottish people want it, they can have it. They may have to struggle a bit for it, but there's the question — how much do they want it?'

An all-Britain solution is a possibility. But we in Scotland haven't the time to wait for it.

We are, perhaps, a strange trio to conclude with. Malcolm Rifkind's family came from the Baltic provinces of the Russian Empire; Neal Ascherson is part German, part Jewish, part Scots. I am totally Lowland Scots, and I work in Germany. None of us is very 'British': all of us testify to a complex Scots involvement with Europe — from the itinerant monks and pedlars to the forefathers of Grieg and Kant — which is now being pieced together again, after both the imperial experience and the appalling events of the Second World War which ended only a few months after I was born.

I am reminded of something Tam Dalyell wrote in his book *Devolution: the End of Britain* (1977). Shortly after he was elected to Parliament — hotly pursued by Billy Wolfe in what was the SNP's first upswing — Dalyell met John Strachey, who told him:

In writing my books I have had to reflect deeply on what happens to countries when they divest themselves of colonies and dominions, and because of that I am most concerned at your result. Now that the Empire is vanishing, we must prevent the 'Balkanisation of Britain' at all costs.

This prospect appalled Strachey and Dalyell; it doesn't appal me. For most of my lifetime Western Europe has lived at peace largely because the sort of nationalism which imperial Britain represented has been in decline; and I myself am more conscious of being 'European' than of being British, more concerned with policies aimed on one hand at preserving and developing the local and specific nature of a community and a culture, and on the other at tackling on a supra-national scale the nuclear threat, the destruction of nature and the exploitation and oppression of the world's poor.

It's impossible to be an historian in Germany and not realise how close we live to the terrible crime of the Hitler regime. Some right-wing politicians try to slide out of responsibility for it, but this is something that the greatest figures of the postwar state — Willy Brandt, Richard von Weizsäcker — have never tried to avoid. Perhaps, under its new administration, Soviet Russia may come to terms with its own, scarcely less terrible, past, and then Western and Eastern Europe can share an historical understanding of the problems they now face.

This isn't something the inhabitants of the British Isles can remain aloof from. There is an island in Loch Broom called Gruinard. Last year it was decontaminated from anthrax germs experimentally released there during the last war by the British government, which was stockpiling anthrax bombs and had contingency plans to drop them on German cities, including Stuttgart. These plans were never carried out; if they had been, millions — chiefly the old, women and children — would have died, and much of Baden-Württemberg would still be uninhabitable. I don't think that Britain has ever come to terms with the other face of her 'finest hour': the destructive madness which overcame all the participants in the war of 1939-45, and the way that this continues to poison our world. This remains our prime example of Orwellian double-think.

Orwell wrote *1984* in Scotland (a country he hadn't previously cared much for) and focused on the destruction of the English language while working in an area — Jura — where a language — Gaelic — was being systematically destroyed. He called Britain Airstrip One, a title we may be particularly aware of because the West finds us valuable as an unsinkable aircraft carrier. Few places, not even Baden-Württemberg, have such concentrations of nuclear weapons. We don't like them and, according to the polls, most of us want rid of them. But these weapons, rather than any views about the rightness and wrongness of small nationalism, or the future of Britain and of Europe, may be the key to whether we get autonomy or not.

Scotland isn't an artificial creation like a German *Land*, but an historic nation. Its relations with the rest of Britain have been political ones, created by an aristocratic élite and maintained by the sort of conventions I have been analysing. The 'union of hearts and minds' has been more limited. When Conservative ministers suggest the inculcation of a 'national' history in schools, the Scottish riposte is to demand greater attention to Scottish studies. This is likely to increase and have long-term political implications. But I think we can only create the institutions of political and industrial recovery if we start now. Ten years ahead may be too late, for Britain as well as Scotland.

As Britain declines and Scottish self-awareness increases, Scotland's powerful tenants must feel increasingly insecure. The information on it will be buried deep in the government archives, but a final question is worth asking: assuming we had got devolution in 1979, did the Foreign Office and Ministry of Defence consider what effect the possible election of an anti-nuclear, left-wing socialist ministry in Edinburgh might have on sensitive defence installations in Scotland? As the tide now seems to be running in devolution's favour, are the same questions being asked again?

Sir Monty Finniston – *BBC*

NECESSITY AND INVENTION

— *Sir Monty Finniston* —

It was Winston Churchill who said 'It is always wise to look ahead, but difficult to look further than you can see.' It might be thought that to predict the state of industry in Scotland thirteen years ahead would not be a task of insuperable difficulty, but in a world of change where a week is a long time in politics, it is just as long in other activities of man; and although Teilhard de Chardin's view that 'the past reveals the structure of the future' may apply to some features of modern society it is a doubtful proposition where industrial form is concerned, as even the most superficial comparison of industry pre- and post-war would evidence.

The Economy

The economy is an umbrella term which covers how people make a living and contribute to the standard of life which their families, their communities and the nation (through taxation) enjoy, (if one can associate taxation with enjoyment). To give some sense of scale to the Scottish economy, its Gross Domestic Product — a financial measure of its economic activity — was £22,809 million in 1984. This is 10 per cent of the GDP of the United Kingdom and almost exactly proportional to the respective populations.

How is the GDP made up? Who does what? The pattern of the Scottish economy — the various sectors of industry which form the totality — is qualitatively identical with that of the rest of the United Kingdom; Scotland has no unique skills or access to natural resources to distinguish it markedly from England and Wales. Manufacturing over the wide spectrum of heavy and light engineering, from shipbuilding to micro-processors, accounts for 25 per cent of the GDP; the remainder covers the service industries, banking and other financial services, local government, transport and the distributive trades, the professions (lawyers, accountants, dentists and doctors) and so on. Quantitatively, of course, there are differences: for example, agriculture represents over 3 per cent of the GDP of Scotland compared with 2½ per cent of the United Kingdom as a whole, and construction 7 per cent compared with 6 per cent. But whatever regional differences there may be between Scotland and the rest of the nation now or in the future, whether in political attitudes, educational system, laws or government, the fact is that the industrial economy of Scotland is, and will continue to be, indissolubly interlinked with the industrial economy of the rest of the UK. To make a success of that economy nationwide will require Scotland to make a favourable contribution to the balance of payments, principally through the exports of its manufacturing industries supported by tourist-attractive leisure services.

SCOTLAND 2000

The Complementarity of Manufacturing and the Service Industries

Britain has in the past, still does, and must in the future depend in the main upon its manufacturing industries to sustain a standard of living which compares favourably with that of other industrialised countries. At present manufacturing industry contributes about 22 per cent to the GDP, (although in the good old days of only a decade ago the figure was as high as 30 per cent), and is still the largest single sector of the economy, whether measured in terms of finance or employment. There are those who claim that the post-industrial society (whatever that may mean) is based on the growth of service industries at the expense of manufacturing. George Matthewson, Chief Executive of the Scottish Development Agency, is one such claimant:

'The major employers will not lie within the manufacturing sector. The major source of employment will lie within the service sector.'

This however is a part truth which does not give sufficient credit to the importance of manufacturing to the economy overall and does not distinguish between the creation of wealth and the generation of employment.

When discussing the growth of service industries there is often an implied conflict in economic, social or political terms between them and manufacturing industries. The fact is that both are essential components of British industry with differing but complementary roles to play in the

Stock Exchange, Glasgow – *Glasgow Herald*

creation of wealth and employment. Service industries for example cater to the needs of society in general and to manufacturing industry in particular through the provision of financial services, transport of people and products, the distributive trades and construction. On the other hand, all service industries depend for their efficient prosecution on the use or sale of manufactured products. I take three examples to which the term 'service' is automatically applied in people's minds — financial, health, domestic.

First, financial services. What bank does not rely for its service to customers upon an electronic computer, a cash dispenser, a word processor or a plastic card? All these are manufactured products. As to the Health Service, what hospital does not depend upon the pharmaceutical industry for its drugs, on the engineering industries for its body scanners, X-ray machines, ultra-sound devices, scalpels, bandages and bed linen? All manufactured products. The reader will have a difficulty in nominating any service industry which does not depend upon manufacturing industry and its products. And on the domestic front, how about the fridge, the dishwasher and the washing machine, the carpet sweeper (and do not forget the carpet) and the telephone, the television set and the radio? One can go on indefinitely. The importance of the success of manufacturing industries should not be underestimated as the principal means of creating sufficient wealth to support our service-based standard of living.

Tourists admiring the view, Edinburgh Castle – *Glasgow Herald*

The Balance of Payments

Not only is manufacturing industry necessary to the service industries it is of even greater importance to the economy as a whole, a fact which may be overlooked when viewing individual factory trees instead of the manufacturing forest. As a country Britain produces only between 60 and 70 per cent of its food, beverage and tobacco requirements and has to import the rest. We have to import the majority of our raw materials and also much of the semi-finished materials and components our industries require. For whatever reason — price, quality, delivery — we prefer to buy the manufactured products of foreign countries rather than our own, or have to, either because we do not make them ourselves or make them less well. And we take advantage of the services which other countries provide rather than home-grown alternatives, e.g. we go on holiday abroad and use foreign airlines to get there.

These imports and equivalents have to be paid for and the major part of the bill, some 70 per cent (and even more in some past years), is paid for by the export of British manufactured goods. In 1985 the UK exported £54.2 billion in finished and semi-finished goods and £23 billion in services, the so-called invisibles — financial services, transport (sea and civil aviation) and travel. The contribution of the service industries to the balance of payments deserves commendation but it remains the junior contributor, every 1 per cent loss in manufactured exports requiring a compensatory 2 per cent increase in active service exports — and in a competitive world that level of increase is difficult to achieve. Two special items of benefit to the balance of payments are the passively (or non-industrially) gained £53 billion in interest, profits and dividends from investments abroad (which count as invisible earnings in the nation's economic statistics, perhaps because they are an indirect contribution) and the visible £16 billion gained in export of oil.

Not all service industries, however, are exportable or attract foreign currency. Internal services like those provided by postmen, policemen, dustmen, butchers, bakers, hairdressers, restaurateurs, bus or train drivers, civil servants and a host of others make little or no direct contribution to the balance of payments; tourism with its infrastructure of attractions — hotels, leisure centres, golf courses, international sports occasions, historical sites and monuments — does gain foreign currency from tourists and foreign industrialists visiting on business. Reo Stakis, and he is not alone, considers 'Scotland one of the most attractive countries in the world' and his hotels are an example of a service industry which caters to this attraction. But those major commercial or industrial services which are directly exportable are subject to increasing competition from other countries offering the same service but with perhaps some special advantages.

As an example of what the increasing thrust of foreign competition can do, take the financial institutions which were once a British sheltered 'near-monopoly'. Today, although London accounts for nearly 24 per cent of all international lending, its share has been falling over the past decade; in the rapidly growing Eurobond market, with turnover last year of $3.2 trillion and new issues of $180 billion, no British merchant bank was in the top ten of dealers; and by allowing outsiders to trade on the

Stock Exchange the 'Big Bang' has subjected what was once a comfortable marketplace for domestic brokers to the full rigour of international competition with ño guaranteed place for specifically British financial services. Today the deutschmark, the yen, the dollar and the Swiss franc are reputable currencies which British companies can borrow more freely than sterling; and the state of the markets in which Britain is concerned is no longer judged simply by the Financial Times index but by the corresponding indices of Wall Street, Tokyo, Hong Kong and many other centres all day long.

So what does the balance of payments look like? Over the past three years the total UK imports of visibles exceeded our exports in value; for example in 1985, exports were £78 billion but imports were £80.2 billion, a deficit of £2.2 billion; in contrast for the same year, credits from invisibles (including interest, profits and dividends from investment overseas) amounted to £80.6 billion, whereas debits from imported services came to £74.9 billion, a positive balance of £5.7 billion, giving an overall balance of payments in 1985 of £3.5 billion. Even if this invisible surplus were to continue into future years, there are ominous difficulties ahead which could reduce the current balance. For example we already live a hand-to-mouth existence in the balance of payments because of the benefit of North Sea oil and gas, which in 1985 yielded an £8.1 billion surplus. It takes no great imagination to work out what will happen if that substantial source of income dries up without any compensating increase in exports from other industrial activities or reduction in imports. The standard of living of the country will fall not just relatively but possibly absolutely. Scotland's contribution to its own economic future and to that of the UK (from which it cannot divorce itself to become industrially autonomous) is best served through increasing its manufacturing sector for which it has the talent, the know-how, the experience and the ability to attract investment, including (for good commercial reasons as it happens) a large foreign element.

Investment in Industry

On the score of investment in industry in the UK, one may ask if we as a nation have become too cautious, even set, in our attitude towards enterprise? Are we too concerned not to lose money and not concerned enough to create wealth because of the attendant risks in a changing world? Peter de Vink engages in industrial investment. When asked whether it was difficult for him to raise money in Scotland from Scottish institutions or the Scottish investor he replied:

'There is a reluctance to commit to ventures that are Scottish. I was asked to raise a modest sum of money for something that would bring great benefits to Scotland — and after four months of pestering Scottish institutional investors, I went to the US and within two weeks had three-quarters of the money.' (As an aside, my personal experience in seeking finance for a cable vision project in Glasgow was not dissimilar excepting that in the end I had to go to Brussels.)

Sir Ian MacGregor, former chairman of British Steel and the National Coal Board, responded to the same question in similar fashion: 'Edinburgh used to be the finest financial capital of the world. There was

Sir Ian MacGregor – *Glasgow Herald*

a time when wealth was being created so fast in Scotland that Edinburgh was looking for places to put their money. We should be looking to our resources to support the venture-capital requirements of today. I wonder whether in Edinburgh people are supporting ventures of that kind today? Are they adventuring as much as they used to? I'm not sure they are.'

Both Raymond Johnstone at the Scottish Stock Exchange in Glasgow and Sir Thomas Risk, Governor of the Bank of Scotland, were defensive on the question of investment in industrial enterprises — which almost by definition carries risk.

First Mr Johnstone: 'Our problem is that we do not get enough of those projects we think justify support.'

Yet the case of John Cruickshank is one which got away. John is a talented engineer who holds many patents in sophisticated measuring devices based on laser technology, which have many applications in all kinds of industries in lucrative world markets. He says, 'I was under pressure from the investors and was forced to sell the basic patents to the Americans for seven thousand pounds, but they assessed them in a value (in sales) somewhere around four billion dollars.'

And Sir Thomas: 'The investors are the people who put up the risk capital. The job of the banks is to lend, and a good banker is a man who has balanced the risk of lending against the reward of getting the interest on what he's lent.' ·

To which John Cruickshank responds from bitter experience: 'When you go to a Scottish bank you go through the fifth degree, the sixth degree and goodness knows how many other degrees, because you have to satisfy one chap, and then another. But abroad, within a very short time they are saying either yes or no.' Colourfully expressed, perhaps — but with some niggling truth?

The need for risk capital in support of Scottish industry is acknowledged and is evidenced by the proliferation of investing institutions — the Scottish Office, the insurance companies, the pension funds, the Scottish Development Agency, the Highlands and Islands Development Board, local enterprise boards, business expansion schemes, etc. etc. etc. All these organisations do their bit but are they doing it on a sufficient scale to create the wealth necessary to achieve an acceptable standard of living or a reduction in unemployment? Or are these well-intentioned organisations inhibited by self-imposed and restrictive criteria of risk?

Jack Shaw, Chief Executive of a new venture-capital organisation, Scottish Financial Enterprise, had this to say: 'Scotland in the UK is a relatively poor region with modest resources. The UK tendency to become introspective, and to look at what is happening in the UK as being the most important feature governing decisions, could lead to the UK becoming as weak in European terms as Scotland has become in UK terms.'

Other nations, however, secure their economic base before invading foreign territories, as witness the industrial history of Japan in recent times and the UK in the more distant past. Some 'introspective industrial planning' for Scotland based on investment from whatever source but including Scottish finance would not come amiss until we could afford to be generous with our money in foreign investments.

While on the subject of investment, Mr Johnstone was challenged on the attractions of non-industrial investment — in Old Masters or cases of wine — which makes a limited contribution to the creation of real wealth and of employment in comparison with industrial ventures. His rejoinder — 'that the money so gained was handed to a third party to invest in industry' — was not supported by any concrete example.

Of merger mania, which although not creating new industry can effect greater efficiency in existing industries, Raymond Johnstone had this to say: 'What is essential for mergers is that there is some system for de-merging, because inevitably there are parts that do not fit together and these are usually fairly badly managed, because top management are not interested in them.' He did however have a well-deserved good word for investment through management buy-outs — a recent and significant phenomenon which revitalises those parts of a business which top management did not reach.

The Broad Vision

Although the economy is enhanced by the growth of a multiplicity of small businesses it is vital to have a broad vision — a strategy for the future. Dundee was a city with a prosperous past but a poor future until the Scottish Development Agency (SDA) came along, not just to start up a company here or there in the city but to plan for the community as a whole. They wanted to bring about a 'change that's big enough for people to feel they've got a platform from which to launch themselves

Ravenscraig – *Glasgow Herald*

into the future'. To achieve it the SDA is creating a new balance between manufacturing and service industries through a multi-directional attack — by promoting links between industry and education in the Dundee Technology Park, by supporting developments emanating from the local university or elsewhere, and by coupling these with environmental improvements to the waterfront area, designed to attract not just tourists but industrialists by providing them, their employees and the community with a new lifestyle. Is this a model for the future or a one-off? Could this broad vision be directed to an even bigger project affecting not just one city but the whole of Scotland?

Steelmaking is a classic example of the problems of bringing Scotland's industries into the twentieth century in preparation for the twenty-first. When the industry was nationalised in 1967 the British Steel Corporation had to control three revolutions at the same time. The first was to organise and administer fourteen public companies, rivals in products and markets, overmanned and in many cases operating with antiquated capital equipment. Secondly there were the technical problems of introducing the latest technologies already being used in Japan and elsewhere to produce lower-cost, higher-quality steel; as an example, the old open-hearth method made 300 tons of steel every twelve hours more or less, whereas the new basic-oxygen system made the same quantity in forty minutes or thereabouts. Thirdly and probably the most difficult to resolve were the industrial-relations problems associated with the multiplicity of trade unions which at the time exercised considerable political power to frustrate change, particularly where this involved redundancies and closures.

Today there are snide comments by industrialists who should know better that the corporation invested on too large a scale and did not cater to market demand. This is knockabout nonsense. Japan, the US and many European countries operating worldwide were investing on a much larger scale to maintain their share of a growing world market. Was the UK to stand still, do nothing and passively watch the decay of an essential industry in which it had a long history and a good reputation? If the UK had been allowed without party political interference to proceed with its ten-year modernisation programme, including closures and rebuilding, this country's position in international steel markets would be much stronger today. (Incidentally most of the 1973 plan as detailed in the White Paper of the time has since been effected by my successors.) The lesson to be learned from the example of steel is the same for all industry in a changing world. It is that the advantage lies with the hare that keeps running and not the lagging tortoise.

Part of that longer-term 1973 plan was the concept of a modern integrated steelworks built on the economically advantageous site of a deep-water port, Hunterston, to replace in due course Ravenscraig when this inland steelworks had exhausted its life expectancy. Steelmaking however is not the only industry that could benefit from a port that, without dredging, could take ships up to 300,000 tons. John Davidson of the CBI in Scotland clearly sees a grand opportunity:

'If we could create a Eurowest port here on the Clyde we could create that vast hinterland of industry which is now the great advantage that Rotterdam — and Bremerhaven and Antwerp — has. It's not just a

Hunterston – *Glasgow Herald*

SCOTLAND 2000

matter of a port, it's a matter of all the industry that that would generate in the West of Scotland as a result.'

So why did it not happen then and is not happening now at Hunterston?

'Because,' says John Davidson, 'too often we are ultra-conservative. I don't think we show enough enterprise, we don't get enough new enterprises started in Scotland and very often now too much of industry and commerce is controlled elsewhere and that's a lack of enterprise on our part.'

So will anything further develop at this barely used natural asset at Hunterston or does the Channel Tunnel, (which itself at the time of writing is not doing too well), exhaust the nation's vision?

The Generation of Employment

Unemployment is a social scourge but society must distinguish between the methods and policies for reducing unemployment and those for the generation of wealth. These two sides of the industrial coin are not as directly related as they were before postwar automation overtook prewar mechanisation, and technological developments made manufacturing industry capital-intensive at the expense of labour. Manufacturing industry today can create wealth without necessarily creating much demand for direct labour. Today it is possible — through robots, computerised machines and flexible manufacturing systems coupled with

Leaving for lunch – shipyard workers disembark from the *Queen Mary* – *BBC Hulton Picture Library*

computer-aided systematics (design, manufacture, integrated engineering, stock warehousing) — to minimise labour while achieving improved productivity and other efficiencies as well as massive increases in reliability and quality. Steelmaking at Ravenscraig and the manufacture of automated devices at NCR are but two examples, but all manufacturing industries — whether of capital, consumer or consumer durable goods — tell the same story. In 1965 there were 8.8 million people engaged in manufacturing industry in the UK; today there are just over 4 million. Since the late 1970s the unemployment statistics have shown a considerable increase in redundancies of manual workers in manufacturing. The general law of industry today is that where machines can economically replace labour, they will.

This restructuring of industry cannot be achieved in transition without painful consequences to some people. Ian MacGregor crystallises this:

'Both you and I [he was kind enough to include me] were looking at the broad landscape and trying to determine what actions should be taken for the survival of the greatest number of people. Unfortunately, as in war, sometimes the general has to sacrifice some troops to achieve an objective. It's a tough decision to make.'

But in my view such decisions can and should be tempered by providing alternative mitigating options. It was to meet such cases as the Cole family, three generations of whom were affected by the closure of Gartcosh, that in 1973 my first act as chairman was to set up BSC (Industry) whose sole function was to provide counselling, retraining, reskilling and redeployment of redundant steelworkers for jobs in other viable industries. This is probably the earliest example of 'caring capitalism', since followed by others. In the thirteen years since its inception, my successors (including Ian MacGregor) have made praiseworthy efforts to implement the scheme and have succeeded in creating several tens of thousands of jobs which otherwise might never have seen the light of day. All markets, even free ones, need planning — and planning well ahead.

It is in the generation of employment however that the service industries have an advantage over manufacturing. Their very nature determines this, since many of them require personal skills applied to individuals and not en masse; for example, no machines have been devised to replace the particular skills of such individual workers as hairdressers, waiters, chambermaids, secretaries, accountants, doctors, nurses and shopkeepers, although many machines are available to them to ease their tasks or improve their efficiency. Even service industries try to minimise their demands for labour. Look at what the automated telephone exchange did to the employment of telephonists. In a recent report from the Institute of Manpower Studies, the authors consider that by 1990 employment in the service industries (mainly incidentally of women) will have increased by 500,000, but that this will be offset by the loss of 650,000 jobs in manufacturing. The redistribution of the wealth created in the manufacturing industries contributes to employment not by direct recruitment but through an increased and affordable demand for services in both the public and private sectors — a further example of the indivisibility of the economy and the complementarity of the manufacturing and service industries.

Apart from the machinery itself there are three essential elements which go to make up industry: manpower, money and markets.

The Importance of Manpower

Manpower is needed in many guises — professionally qualified in some relevant discipline as well as vocationally skilled. I visited the National Engineering Laboratory (NEL) at its main laboratories in East Kilbride and its outstation on the Fenwick Moors. There tests on the latest model of its modern wind turbine (the windmill in new dress) evidenced the creative technological talent which the country possesses and which is

Aerogenerator, Orkney - *Glasgow Herald*

generally acknowledged internationally. This *Scotland 2000* programme was introduced with a fanfare advertisement from the SDA listing all modern inventions for which Scots had been responsible. This impressive catalogue of achievement, if analysed, clearly shows that the inventions and innovations deriving from this technical ingenuity were not exploited on the industrial scale necessary to bring commercial benefit to the economy. On the contrary Scotland exports this inventive talent in the form of patents and licences and even manpower to foreign countries who are not slow to take industrial advantage.

This is not because the scientists, technologists and engineers are opposed to the industrial development of their inventions.

Maurice Daniel of NEL, asked if he would sell his laboratory's patents and know-how to a foreign country, said, 'I'm here to back British industry and if in any way it's going to adversely affect British industry I certainly will not recommend it.'

If however there is no native backing for native invention, what is the alternative if the effort, money and time in sustaining an establishment like NEL is not to be wasted? We hark back to the conservatism of the investing public in exploiting the nation's talents.

I do not agree with our lone inventor John Cruickshank that 'the investment fraternity should never turn away a young man with an invention'. Not all inventive geese are swans and not all inventive geese lay golden eggs. Nevertheless our technical innovators should at least be heard before being rejected sight unseen.

There are areas of concern to the welfare of future generations which deserve special consideration. One of these is the development of renewable energy sources — wind, tide and solar power — to replace in due course the depleting fossil fuels. Development of wind power was undertaken by NEL in conjunction with the Scottish enginering firm of Howden with remarkable technical success. They have a design which generates 330 kilowatts so that 100 wind turbines can provide sufficient power to serve a small town of 20,000 households. Where will this be tried out first? The US of course, and California in particular. Why not here where we could build an international business? Don't ask me.

Not only have we in Scotland the national centre of NEL but we have eight universities and fifteen central institutions engaged in research and development across a range of disciplines and producing the manpower which can continue technological innovation. Universities and industry are co-operating more and more closely, resulting in the growth of science and technological parks as in Edinburgh, Glasgow and Dundee. In the US large firms have special budgets for investment in extra-mural research and development, which gives them first call on new concepts and ideas as well as facilitating the difficult process of transferring the technology from research to manufacture. This concept could well be adopted by Scottish manufacturing industry on a much larger scale than at present.

But industry is not just about technology and engineering, important as these are. Industry is a complex multi-functional activity requiring all kinds of skills — manual and intellectual, professionals, accountants, lawyers, administrators, managers and managed. Is Scotland up to providing these skills? Perhaps the most impressive message I learned while making the programme was the confidence in their workforce expressed by foreign multinational companies with factories in Scotland. When asked why had they come to Scotland in the first place they were frank about the advantages they had gained in grants, rents and rate concessions, and building location. But once here they were reinforced in the correctness of their decision by the response they gained from their workforce. Mr Shiraishi, Managing Director of Nippon Electronic Corporation (NEC) at their Livingston factory, put it like this: 'I am satisfied with our workforce qualities. I have much experience for managing in Japan. Quite at same level as Japanese workforce.'

He was not the only one who spoke highly of the quality of labour and of native management. A wry comment by Mr Shiraishi when I remarked on the youth of his workforce was that he only engaged people between the ages of seventeen and twenty, since they had not by then experienced or adopted the bad habits of other rival firms! He had no doubts about the aptitude of young Scots to learn good industrial habits quickly.

The managment techniques introduced by the multinationals were of interest in the conduct of a modern company and its factories. 'Fundamentally,' says Mr Shiraishi, 'we are harmonising applying the Japanese way and the Western way, so I am usually consulting with the managing staff how to do their best.'

The two major features were hierarchical non-discrimination, i.e. all used the same canteen facilities and toilets were all of a single grade throughout the factory; and the considerable intercommunication between managers and the shop floor on all matters affecting the conduct

Apprentices at the Glasgow Transport School – *Glasgow Herald*

Nicola Brannan (17) with customer in her Bearsden salon, opened with help from Glasgow Opportunities Enterprise Trust – *Glasgow Herald*

of the company's affairs. In some cases this removed the need for trade unions to present the views of the workforce or negotiate for the employees. Gavin Laird, General Secretary of the Amalgamated Engineering Union, ascribed the practice of non-trade unionism to the green-field site and the new opportunities divorced from past history, but although a green-field site may facilitate this non-adversarial environment, it is not in my view an essential pre-condition. Furthermore, the enlightened attitude of the management to up-dating their employees in the latest practices and knowledge of their business was to be seen in their in-house training programmes and in their support of individuals at seminars or extra-mural courses.

Ignorance is not an asset at any time — and certainly not in industry. Education and training are the cures for ignorance. Ian MacGregor drew attention to their importance in two respects. Firstly:

'It is slowly dawning on most of the industrial countries as they are facing increasing competition from the newly developing world and from changes in technology that we have to raise the standards of our training, retraining and education at all levels. People will never finish their education.' Secondly: 'Unless we help people to be prepared to cope with this change and learn skills that aim to take care of the new type of activities that are coming along, we're not doing a good job for them.'

William Emond of the Dundee College of Education when asked if he thought Scotland had come to vocational training too late by comparison with other countries responded: 'Slightly late even although vocational

A welder, Govan Shipbuilders – *Glasgow Herald*

training in Scotland has been going on since the early 1900s. I don't think the push came at the proper time, but we're now catching up with our contemporaries in England and perhaps pushing ahead.'

Training is education in the practise of a skill with specific applications — like learning to machine metals or operate a computer. The government's Youth Training Scheme which was piloted by the Dundee centre I visited supported traditional manual skills for which there should be a continuing demand in industry and in society generally. The kids I saw and spoke to were keen to find work and deserve better from their betters.(I never seem to meet the layabouts whom the press and politicians are always on about.)

But how many will end up with a job after such training? This was left to market forces – another way of saying random luck. One instructor at the centre said, 'There are not the places available for them. And the soul-destroying part of that is we are training them for something that doesn't exist.' So long as it is left to free market forces to decide whether a particular skill will or will not be made use of, any training scheme has limited value. Far better if some planned demand by employers is being catered for.

Govan Shipbuilders also act as agent for the training of what were once apprentices but are now classed as youth trainees. They too teach crafts such as joinery, plumbing, welding, electrical work and so on not just for their own use but for other outside applications. Interesting was the comment of Managing Director Eric Mackie on the new work practices in the yard. Craftsmen no longer confine themselves to their own particular skill but work together as a team with no demarcation. 'They all work together now,' he says. Shades of NEC!

The Importance of Money

All businesses require money to get started, sustain the company through its formative years and then, if successful, support expansion and growth. This money in the main comes from outside sources: from the investing public, ranging from government through banking institutions to private individuals.

Recent government policies designed to create a wider share-owning population may be confused with the investment I believe is essential to the development of industry. I distinguish between investment by the public in the purchase of shares in existing companies and fresh investment in the form of capital for start-ups or for the modernisation or growth of existing companies. The former circulates money in a zero-sum game; the latter can create new wealth. The bustle of talented people doing share deals at their VDUs in the Scottish Stock Exchange is superficially impressive. But Raymond Johnstone, an investment fund manager, did not encourage me on the more creative aspects of the Stock Exchange or of the investing public in general. The Scottish equivalent of the City seemed to show too little understanding of the needs and risks of modern industry and the requirement for investors to match that need and risk with a more relaxed and sympathetic attitude towards investment.

Judging by the massive oversubscription in the privatisation sales of nationalised industries there seems no shortage of money for investment.

Yet in my opinion the country has for the past twenty-five years (some would say longer) suffered and still suffers from economic AIDS — Acquired Industrial Deficiency Syndrome. From whom we acquired this industrial disease is not clear; it may be indigenous, although there are obvious exceptions in the many successful companies we have created in the past. There is great caution among British investors to invest in new enterprises, although that caution appears to be lost when it comes to investing in such developing countries as Mexico, Brazil and Nigeria. Gilts and privatisation attract because there little can go wrong — in the short term at any rate.

Sir Thomas Risk made the distinction that banks are not investors but lenders, and that lending involved taking risks. Maybe, but banks, like other investors, try to contain their risks by seeking collateral in the event that things go wrong. Furthermore while interest rates are at their present level it is expensive to borrow risk capital — one factor which deters individuals from engaging in enterprise. At 2 to 3 per cent over prime rates of 10 or 11 per cent it requires courage to take on this burden as well as all the other risks involved in a new venture. I am sure that the institutional investor does not intend to frighten off the entrepreneur, but the dice are loaded against him. In the industries of today — and even more those of tomorrow — there is no shortage of risk; there is no shortage of capital; but there is a shortage of the combination, which is what Scotland 2000 needs most.

What level of investment would be needed to put Scotland in better competitive condition? The objective is to achieve a neutral balance of payments in the nation's visible exports and to this end Scotland should contribute pro rata to its population and GDP. The present national deficit is roughly £4 billion, of which Scotland would have to cater for 10 per cent, or £400 million. This requires a rise in manufacturing exports of £600 million since one-third of any increase attracts an equivalent increase in imports. Since exports constitute 30 per cent of manufacture-sales overall, an increase in exports of £600 million implies an increase in sales of £2 billion. The ratio of capital to sales in manufacture is roughly 1.25 to 1; thus £2 billion extra sales in manufactured products implies £2.5 billion of extra capital. And £2.5 billion is not an immensely large sum to contemplate investing, particularly if the extra capital expenditure were spread over five to seven years as it would have to be.

The Importance of Markets

The importance of markets should go without saying, but everybody keeps harping on about it as if industrialists ignored the obvious and manufactured outmoded, unwanted products for some peculiar uncommercial reason. Demand for consumer goods is fickle and can be influenced by advertising and other persuasive forces. Consumer durables, and to an even greater extent capital goods, are dependent on performance, reliability, safety standards, ease of maintenance and the provision of spares, cost, delivery and a whole host of variables not all of which can be satisfied at any one time. To retain or regain a market initiative requires changes which take time to effect throughout the manufacturing system. It may well be that we have been too hesitant in the past to change our products and processes, but the reasons have nothing to do with a lack of appreciation of the need to meet customer demands at home or abroad. It does however emphasise that competition in and for markets is a matter for continuing study, particularly of export demands and opportunities.

The Prospects

To determine the prospects for British industry, and hence the Scottish economy, one has to have a view of its strengths and weaknesses and the problems which need to be solved. The major thrust of the economy now and in the future lies in strengthening our manufacturing capability and particularly in increasing our exports and reducing imports whenever possible. The prospects for the immediate future look favourable, although international trade is unstable and can undergo unpredictable stresses (as happened for example in 1973 and 1979 with oil prices), as well as trade cycles, long and short. However in our manufacturing industries there is evidence of improved productivity and lower unit labour costs compared with three years ago,when the hourly-paid manual worker in this country was the lowest paid in the OECD, but because of poor productivity had the highest unit labour cost. Four factors have been in evidence:

First, the reduction in over-manning in manufacturing industries as a whole; second, the concurrent introduction of modern capital equipment in existing industries, which had the double effect of permitting de-manning while allowing increased output per man; third, the change-over of the Scottish economy to the new capital-intensive, high-added-value, high-technology industries of electronics, chemicals and light engineering; and fourth the favourable exchange rate following the depreciation of the pound against the deutschmark (last year amounting to a reduction of 22 per cent) and the wavering dollar. The first three of these factors are the result of industrial decision-making; the fourth is based on an external judgement of the state of our economy.

A further justification for restrained optimism is that world trade is expected to expand in real terms at about 2 to 3 per cent per annum over the next two or three years. Last year the UK had 8 per cent of world trade. What extra share we can gain of the expanded international trade forecast is difficult to quantify, but the greater competitiveness of some of our more important exporting companies should yield some extra, and help to reduce the expected balance of payments deficit for the next year or two. There are however certain adverse conditions — some actual, others potential — which might militate against economic recovery.

Firstly the major markets for our exports are still the EEC and the US. In the EEC restrictive conditions on supply, price and tariffs inhibit trade and particularly expansion. A case in point is steel, but other products covered by the Treaties of Paris and Rome are also affected; the Common Agricultural Policy (CAP), due for change (and not before time), causes considerable dissatisfaction among certain nations. Again the European Monetary System (EMS), although providing some stability to exchange rates between the countries party to it, can also influence the exchange rates of non-member countries and therefore can have a

The *Norsea*, the largest ship to be built on the Clyde since the *QE2,* under construction at Govan Shipbuilders – *Glasgow Herald*

powerful influence on international trade.

As to the US there is a considerable concern about the present direction of its economy and the effects this may have on those countries with which it trades. Consider the anticipated US deficit of nearly $170 billion this year alone and the conventional measures which this country in a comparable plight would have to take. The US with its advanced technological strength might have been expected to exercise its muscle in increasing its export trade; and the deliberate policy of the US Federal Reserve to allow the exchange value of the dollar to fall freely against most international currencies could be interpreted as a complementary measure. These in themselves, given time, would have been expected to succeed. But a policy of protectionism has crept in as well. There were earlier indications of this in the introduction of product quotas (e.g. steel), in bi-lateral agreements and in the earlier multi-fibre agreement on textiles, but the most recent example has the announced intention to impose duties on some EEC products (which would have driven them out of the American market) in retaliation for the loss of US maize sales following the accession of Spain to the Community. There has been compromise on this occasion, but no doubt some other casus belli will present itself and if it were to explode into a full-scale trade war, the effect on the UK and the world at large could only be very damaging.

Conclusion

What then are the prospects for Scottish industry by the year 2000? I tend to take a cautious view because conservatism in risk enterprise has been a notable feature of our industrial investment. For the next two or three years (say to 1990) our manufacturing industries should maintain their trading position in world markets as a result of capital investments, manpower measures and financial controls introduced over the past decade. What is still unsatisfactory is the adverse balance of payments in visibles, a notable feature of the past three years' trading; and the uncertainties in the outcome on invisibles, particularly our financial services following the 'Big Bang'. There are four provisos however even to this reserved optimism.

First, that inflation should not escalate beyond that of our major competitors and better still fall below theirs; second, that exchange rates remain at or about their present levels, hopefully without political intervention; third, that the investing public accepts the priority need for risk capital in innovation, whether in new businesses or existing companies, and that there is a corresponding reduction in the cost of money; and fourth, that the workforce matches up in skills and industrial practices with continuing improvement in productivity and efficiency.

Industry is not static. Invention and innovation create new industries and destroy the technologies of the past. How quickly in the future will Britain, and particularly Scotland, react to the commercial possibilities of technological change which is no longer the sole province of Western industrial society but can emerge from any country large or small or of any political complexion? As a country we have missed out in a number of markets in which we have expertise — computers, robots, space communications and many other hi-tech activities — which if we had grasped our chance would have made welcome additions to our balance of trade. The manufacture of high-added-value products which have a worldwide and continuing demand is the kernel of our industrial future.

I have never doubted the inherent abilities of the Scots to make a success of industry — manufacturing or service — if they grasp the opportunity. Their talents as inventors and designers of engineered products; the asset of an educational system which at all levels compares not unfavourably with that of other countries; a high reputation for research and development; a national pride in achievement and much else — all should have put the Scottish economy in much better shape. I consider it remarkable that foreign multinational companies of unquestioned industrial efficiency (Japanese, American, German) have set up (and are still doing so) important branch factories in the UK; in fact the revolution in manufacturing industry in Scotland from heavy to light hi-tech industry in less than two decades and the high rating these factories have achieved in the efficiency league of their parent companies is a measure of the capability of the Scottish workforce, given leadership. When Mr Shiraishi said in his broken English that his workforce in the Livingston factory was as good as he had had working for him in Japan that unsolicited testimonial boosted my morale.

So what holds up the development of the Scottish economy? Is it the caution of the investing public? That is certainly a major factor. Risk is a four-letter word which Scotland will have to accept as an essential part of the language of modern industry. Scots, with a reputation for thrift consciousness will need to change their attitude and develop a greater willingness to invest in their economic future. We do have the talents, the know-how, the experience, the money, but do we have the industrial and political will to use them? Only the Scotland of the year 2000 will answer that question.

AGAINST THE GRAIN

— *James Hunter* —

One or two are decorated briefly each November with wreaths of plasticised poppies — garish in the otherwise drab autumn landscape. For the most part, however, war memorials in Scotland's country communities stand neglected twelve months out of twelve; and, little by little, the wind and rain erode the long, long lists of names commemorating the men who, in that war with the Kaiser's Germany, are proclaimed by these same memorials to have died that we might live. There is no deliberate ingratitude in our casual attitude to these grey granite monuments. Neither at the going down of the sun nor in the morning can we remember those we did not know. And there are very few of us now who are old enough to recall the faces and personalities of any of these seemingly endless thousands who left Scotland's crofts and farmtowns for the insatiable killing grounds of the Western Front.

But these neatly inscribed stone columns are still capable of evoking a sense of regret: not merely for those young men whose lives were taken from them but also for the society to which they belonged. Much of that society died with them. And, as a result, many of those country places which in 1914 and 1915 provided scores of boys for Kitchener's volunteer armies are today almost bereft of population. In the single human lifetime that separates us from this century's opening decades, the Scottish countryside has been largely emptied of its people, and the small farms that bred so many of the men whose names are still to be seen on our war memorials are now as completely forgotten as the lads who, seventy years or more ago, left these farms behind for ever.

In the early 1930s one of modern Scotland's greatest writers, Lewis Grassic Gibbon, wrote *Sunset Song,* the book that best encapsulates this passing of a way of life. Gibbon, or Leslie Mitchell, was born on an Aberdeenshire croft and grew up, a little to the south in the Mearns, among families who still had access to their own bits of land. Into the mouth of the Reverend Colquohoun, scandalously radical minister of Kinraddie, his quintessential Kincardineshire parish, Gibbon put the words that are an enduring testimony to the worth of his own people, the crofting folk of Scotland's north-east lowlands. The occasion was the unveiling of Kinraddie's war memorial: a plaque fixed to the parish's prehistoric standing stones.

'For I will give you the morning star,' said the minister. 'In the sunset of an age and an epoch we may write that for epitaph of the men who were of it. They went quiet and brave from the lands they loved, though seldom of that love might they speak, it was not in them to tell in words of the earth that moved and lived and abided, their life and enduring love. . . With them we may say there died a thing older than themselves, these were the last of the peasants, the last of the old Scots folk. A new generation comes up that will know them not, except as a memory in a song, they passed with the things that seemed good to them, with loves and desires that grow dim and alien in the days to be. . . And the land changes, their parks and their steadings are a desolation where the sheep are pastured, we are told that great machines come soon to till the land, and the great herds come to feed on it. The crofter has gone, the man with the house and steading of his own and the land closer to his heart than the flesh of his body. . .

These crofters and their predecessors had taken the ground in from the wilderness. They had drained the bogs and levelled the fields; with tools no more sophisticated than spades and picks and crowbars, they had wrenched and levered from the earth the innumerable stones and rocks that had to be removed to make way for their horse-drawn ploughs. These stones they installed in the drystone dykes which are still the dominant feature of the north-east countryside; and so plentiful were the glacial boulders thus extracted from the soil that there were places where the surface of the land itself fell by a foot or more as a result of this immense improving effort. Their reward was to be deprived of the land they had reclaimed. Now their crofts have gone — amalgamated, one with another, to form today's much larger farms. Their houses, though, survive here and there. Some are the refurbished, extended, centrally-heated and double-glazed homes of middle-class commuters from Aberdeen; others, too remote from main roads to be attractive to that type of purchaser, stand derelict, their roofs collapsing, their doors permanently ajar, their rooms serving as shelters for sheep or even crows.

It is difficult to envisage, standing in the grass-grown yard of such a long-abandoned dwelling, that the trends of the last half-century can ever be reversed; that people, in significant numbers, can be brought back to the Scottish countryside. But I believe such repopulation is possible. Change is on the way once more in rural Scotland. Before we reach the year 2000, our countryside districts will experience another transformation. And if we respond imaginatively, we can ensure that, as the next century commences, there will be many more families living on the land.

Since the 1940s agricultural policy applied in Scotland has had a single aim: to increase production. And with the help of techniques and machines that were utterly unknown to Grassic Gibbon's Mearns crofters, that policy has been extraordinarily successful.

At the end of the Second World War Britain and the rest of Western Europe were dangerously short of food. Despite the most stringent rationing, famine was averted only by lavish American aid. And in such circumstances it was both inevitable and proper that successive British governments and indeed the wider EEC should have made self-sufficiency in food a high priority. To this end, farmers were asked, and assisted, to invest in the most up-to-date technology — in heavy machinery, chemical fertilisers, new crops, new breeds of animal. To this end also, we set out to make our farms bigger and, in purely economic terms at least, more efficient — getting rid of as many as thirty thousand smaller Scottish farms inside forty years. In short, we asked our farmers to expand, modernise, increase output. And in contrast to much of the rest of Scottish industry — which failed miserably to re-invest, re-equip, compete and generally adjust to changing conditions — our farmers responded magnificently. But now, paradoxically, they are paying a high price for their own success.

James Hunter – *BBC*

Just outside Catterline, on the seaward edge of the Mearns, is one farmer who did just as he was asked. His name is Angus Jacobsen. He is in his early forties and he is a good, progressive agriculturist. Today, however, he is forced to reap a bitter harvest. Today men like Angus Jacobsen are told by the same politicians who, no more than three or four years ago, were urging them to step up their output still further, that they have produced too much, and indeed the consequences of overproduction are plain to see. Land values, which soared throughout the 1970s, are now falling every bit as fast. The financial institutions, which were once so eager to buy into farming, are now pulling out. Farmers generally face mounting debts and tumbling returns. Nor can they any longer look to government for help. Bit by bit, the stream of public money which has flowed into Scottish agriculture is being turned off.

'My farming experience goes back twenty years,' says Angus, and in that time, he explains, yields have expanded massively. 'I am now growing half as much again on every acre as I was in 1967. That's particularly true of cereals. It's been done by using new varieties of grain; by increasing the inputs of chemicals and fertilisers; by using new technology.'

Now, Angus acknowledges, people like him are being forced to cut back.

'I took the new methods on board,' he recalls. 'I expanded and I borrowed the money I needed to finance that expansion. Then I found

Grain store, Ormiston, West Lothian – *Scotsman Publications*

that, in the new circumstances, the business wasn't generating enough profit to pay back the money I'd borrowed. And, of course, the bank rate moved against me. In the end, I had to sell off most of one farm to get back on to a sensible financial footing.'

Angus Jacobsen does not conceal his anger. He was neither greedy nor reckless. He was simply farming in the way that he had been taught — in the way that government expected. 'I feel really bitter about it; still, I'm wiser now, though I'm also a lot poorer.'

Just how much poorer? 'Perhaps half a million pounds poorer,' he replies.

A major contributor to Angus Jacobsen's problems is to be glimpsed in a former aircraft hangar on the north-eastern outskirts of Dumfries. This wartime building is now a warehouse and for all its immense size, it is piled high with barley. This single building's contents are worth £2 million. And there are several similar buildings, all of them equally full, within a few hundred yards. But even this enormous quantity of grain, some of it already several years old, constitutes only a minuscule proportion of the EEC's steadily growing grain mountain. There are hundreds, even thousands, of such warehouses in other parts of Scotland, other parts of Britain, other parts of the EEC, and quite apart from barley, wheat and other cereals, there are surpluses of beef, butter, milk, wine, olive oil. . . the list seems endless. It is consequently quite apparent that the EEC's publicly financed Common Agricultural Policy (CAP), which has brought these food surpluses into existence, cannot continue indefinitely; not just because the various mountains and lakes are costing all of us so much money but because, to the public at large, there is plainly something seriously wrong with a system which piles up so much food here in Scotland while elsewhere people die of hunger.

The gut response, when confronted with bulging food stores on the one hand, and television pictures of starving Ethiopian children on the other, is to ask: Why not send our unwanted grain to Africa? But the real world, according to James Provan, a Scottish farmer who is also a Conservative Member of the European Parliament, is not that simple.

To store a ton of cereals here in Britain, or in any other part of the EEC, he points out, costs £25 each year. 'To send that same ton of cereals to Ethiopia would cost £265, and that cost is very difficult to meet.'

Nor is it necessarily doing African countries a favour to supply them with limitless quantities of externally produced foodstuffs. Famine relief is obviously essential in the short term. Nobody is quarrelling with that. But in the longer term, James Provan insists, 'We have to encourage African producers to grow more food themselves.' That means enabling African farmers to find a worthwhile local market for their output — something that will not exist as long as subsidised European cereals are freely available.

James Provan is no out-and-out critic of the EEC's much-maligned agricultural policy. The CAP, he points out, was brought into existence to remedy the Common Market's own inability, as recently as the 1960s, to produce the food its people needed. To ensure a basic level of production, European farmers were given an assurance that, even when markets were depressed, a minimum price would be paid for their crops. It is this mechanism which ensures, for example, that barley which does not fetch a certain price on the open market is purchased by a publicly-financed intervention board. This support has certainly produced the intended upsurge in production and it has also ensured that agricultural producers have been protected from the market vagaries which, in the past — most recently in the 1930s — were responsible for many Scottish farmers being reduced to poverty. As long as the intervention board simply stored its grain purchases until the open market could again provide the necessary customers, then no great harm — and quite a lot of good — resulted. But now the customers are just not there. The market is saturated. Grain has to be stored indefinitely. 'The intervention mechanism,' as James Provan comments, 'has ceased to be a safety net and has all of a sudden turned into the main market for the product.'

That means that remedial action will have to be taken, he stresses. 'Something must be done. We cannot go on storing surpluses and producing more than we consume, and it isn't only a Scottish problem, or a British problem or a European problem. There are similar surpluses in America, Canada, Argentina, Australia, New Zealand — wherever you like to look, really.'

Should we be looking, then, at developing alternative uses for the land that is now devoted exclusively to agriculture? Yes, we should, in James Provan's opinion. And we should be making the necessary readjustments as a matter of urgency. 'The EEC,' he warns, 'cannot afford to store any longer the immense amounts of food that we now have in our warehouses.'

Valley of Ae from the Craigshiels viewpoint – *Forestry Commission*

An obvious alternative to farming is forestry. We may be producing too much grain, too much beef, too much milk; but we are certainly not growing too many trees. Britain, one of the least-afforested countries in Europe, still has to import over 90 per cent of its timber and wood-product requirements — at an annual cost of some £4000 million. And the EEC as a whole, while more self-sufficient than the UK, is also a net importer of timber on an enormous scale. Not surprisingly, then, successive British governments have favoured an expansion of forestry. And much of that expansion has been concentrated in Scotland where recently some twenty thousand hectares annually have been going under trees. That trend seems set to accelerate. 'A continuing expansion of forestry is in the national interest,' the Secretary of State for Scotland has told the House of Commons, 'both to reduce our dependence upon imported timber in the long term and to provide employment in forestry and associated industries.'

Providing more jobs in the countryside has always been a stated aim of British forestry policy. But the employment record of the modern forestry industry is rather less than impressive. The overall pattern can be illustrated by the particular example of Glen Duror Forest in that northern part of the former county of Argyll which has now been included in Highland Region. The Forestry Commission began planting here in the early 1920s — Glen Duror, indeed, was one of the commission's first forests. And my reason for focusing attention on the place is simply that I have a long-standing family connection with it — both my grandfathers and my father were for many years members of the Forestry Commission's Glen Duror workforce.

That workforce, however, has diminished sadly in recent years. When my father joined the Forestry Commission at the end of the Second World War, following demobilisation from the army, he was one of more than fifty people picking up their wages each Friday afternoon at the commission's office at the foot of the glen. But things are different now. The office itself has long since been demolished. Lawrence Sinclair — the head forester who when I was a boy in the 1950s and 1960s ran all the commission's local operations from it — is dead. Administration has been centralised. There is no head forester in Glen Duror: the important decisions are taken far away. And though the Forestry Commission now own three or four times more land in and around Glen Duror than in the 1940s, they presently employ less than a fifth of the number who then worked here.

In forestry, as in farming, increasing mechanisation is one part of the explanation for this drastic reduction in employment. One man with a single machine can now tackle a job that would once have required the labour of a dozen individuals. In purely economic terms, that represents a massive increase in productivity.

There is, however, a price to pay for this kind of efficiency. With the thirty thousand Scottish farms we have lost since the 1940s, we have also lost thirty thousand farming families. At least one hundred thousand farmworkers' jobs have gone on top of that; and as we have seen, forestry too has been shedding labour.

As jobs in farming and forestry have become fewer, so more and more young people have had to leave the countryside. So there have been

Felling a Douglas Fir in Dunkeld Forest – *Forestry Commission*

fewer children in the local school, fewer customers in the local shop, fewer passengers on the local bus. Depopulation has inevitably resulted in poorer services; and as schools and shops and churches and hospitals are closed, as public transport is withdrawn, so it has become steadily more difficult for those families who remain. The outcome has been the setting in motion of a downward spiral of decline — a decline that has sometimes seemed unstoppable.

The consequences can be seen in the Central Highland parish of Laggan, some ten miles to the west of Newtonmore on the road to Spean Bridge and Fort William. Towards the end of the eighteenth century, just before the Highland clearances, there were as many as three thousand people living here. By the mid 1970s, however, Laggan's population had slumped to three hundred. Now it is only one hundred and sixty.

But Laggan, encouragingly enough, is neither dead nor dying. A few years ago, when the local shop seemed certain to shut down, the community clubbed together, formed a co-operative and took it over. And when Highland Regional Council, based in distant Inverness, threatened to close Laggan's little primary school, the community again rallied round. A protest campaign was quickly organised. Regional councillors were obliged to change their minds. And the school remained open.

Elsewhere in the Scottish countryside in recent years there have been similar indications of a new assertiveness on the part of rural communities, signs of a new determination on the part of country people to establish the right to a greater say in their own future. For all that, immense difficulties remain. Today there are eight pupils in Laggan Primary School. In the year 2000 those children will be men and women in their twenties. If Laggan then has neither work nor prospects for them, one more of our rural communities will have died.

Once all the jobs that Laggan needed were provided by Ardverikie Estate. Now, for all the apparent grandeur of its turreted mansion house on the shore of Loch Laggan, the estate too is struggling financially. That the struggle still goes on — the latest piece of Ardverikie enterprise being a plan to establish a privately owned and operated hydro-electric power station — is largely due to Patrick Gordon-Duff-Pennington, whose family have owned Ardverikie since Victorian times. He remains determined that Laggan should remain a viable community.

'As a family,' Patrick Gordon-Duff-Pennington insists, 'we're totally committed to this place. We feel that if the people who are here now weren't here, then we wouldn't want to live here either. One of the things that worries me, of course, is that there aren't enough people. And if these places are going to survive, we have to find a way of employing more people — a way of enabling more people to make a living. The prime use of land, I believe, is for the employment of people.'

That is not the sort of sentiment that one automatically associates with Highland landowners. But Patrick Gordon-Duff-Pennington is not at all a typical laird. An unlikely-sounding rebel he may be, but a rebel he most certainly is: a man who has campaigned for a more imaginative

Loch Laggan – *HIDB*

rural and agricultural policy; a man whose underlying love of the land is
reflected in his verse, 'Leaving Loch Laggan'.

Will it be there
That I must find my destiny
Among those crowded city streets
Where men no longer smile
Learning their lust for gold

Or here
Where in my youth I lambed the ewes
Finding the harmony of wind and sky and hills?

Should it be there
Among those cultures of an alien race
Where men forget the poems of the Island seas
And sunset on the silver sand
Should it be there I am condemned to die?
I would fear death
But here among the timeless Highland hills
I learned to love so long ago
My hair brushed by the breeze
My eyes alight with sky
This is the Scotland that my fathers fought to keep
For which I too am quite prepared to die.

If I could have one single wish
It is to lie eventually among the tartan moss
Where first I crawled so long ago
Through herds of autumn deer
Under the shadow of the eagle's wings
Watching the woods below
The yellow banks of tormentil.

There I would wish to stay at rest
Above the diamond waters of the sleeping loch
Nursed by the memories
Of all the people who have taught me how to love this place

As part of me, as part of life
Far and away beyond
All greed for gold.

For this is home and these,
These are the people and the land for which I fight
And here among these hills
For them
I would not be afraid to die.

   What, then, are the obstacles in the way of realising Gordon-Duff-
Pennington's ambition of having more people living in the shelter of the
Laggan hills?

'It's just a matter of money,' he says. 'It's very expensive here. And there is such limited employment. We are at a real disadvantage compared, for instance, with the place in Bavaria where my daughter went to work in a pickle factory. There people had three incomes — one from tourism, one from farming and one from the pickle fctory. We have nothing like that. We have idiotic planners hellbent on creating "growth points" like those we've seen at Fort William or Invergordon. That results in the local community, as well as lots of people who have been brought in, becoming dependent on a single business. Then that business, the pulp mill or the aluminium smelter, goes phut. And the community is left with nothing to support it.'

So how should country people respond? By obtaining more control of their own affairs, in his opinion. 'Whether here in Laggan, or in Cumberland or Devon or Yorkshire, we are seeing more and more decisions being taken by people in London — or in Edinburgh. And we're seeing the Treasury — that most inflexible, stupid, idiotic government department — frustrating anything that's likely to cost a penny. Well, they ought to devolve things, not centralise them. People in the rural areas must have more control of their own destiny.'

Those of us living in the Scottish countryside have little such control today. Administrators in some distant urban centre can close our schools, suspend our bus services, disregard our aspirations. Nor do we have any real rights to our own resources. Here in Scotland fewer people own more of the land than in practically any other country in the world. Much the same is true of enterprises that depend on access to our land. Forestry is the classic example. In most of Western Europe, country people own and manage the bulk of the available woodlands. In Switzerland, for instance, two-thirds of the nation's forests are owned by rural communities. Local ownership is also prevalent in Germany, France and Belgium — while in Sweden and Finland nearly a quarter of all forestry is integrated with agriculture at the level of the family farm. In Scotland, in contrast, there is practically no such integration and, not coincidentally, local ownership of Scottish forests is virtually unknown. Indeed a recent survey in Sutherland has shown that no fewer than 80 per cent of forest owners in that district have home addresses in London and the Home Counties.

That is the inevitable outcome of government policies which seek to channel investment into forestry by making substantial tax concessions to wealthy individuals who choose to deploy part of their financial resources in this way. And though these policies have recently been criticised extensively, Mike Ashmole, the man in charge of the Scottish operations of Fountain Forestry, one of the two or three management groups now dominating private-sector forestry, is convinced that rural communities, as well as urban investors, are benefiting from afforestation of the Sutherland variety.

'It's only the investment that's coming from far away,' he says. 'The trees are here. They're going to grow here. They're going to be harvested here. And it's then that the funds coming into forestry are going to benefit people in the rural community.'

But the benefits to people in the Scottish countryside would be so much greater, to my mind, if they, like their counterparts on the continent, had a direct stake in the forestry which is expanding all around them. Farming could then be closely integrated with forestry to their mutual benefit, bringing Scotland much more into line with the rest of Western Europe where farmers and smallholders traditionally regard their woodlands, which they generally manage very well, as ordinary income-earning assets which contribute to their total revenue in much the same way as their stock or crops.

The farmer who is also a forester has a more intimate knowledge of local conditions than have the employees of a larger, more remote forestry concern. He can modify planting patterns in accord with these conditions. He can apply more intensive and more careful management to his trees. He can make the best possible use of shelter belts and forest grazing systems. The same farmer can provide forest products for farming systems — supplying his own fenceposts, building material and firewood. He can utilise farm machinery for forest operations. He can provide both himself and his family with worthwhile employment at otherwise slack times in the farming year. Above all, he can counter the otherwise prevalent tendency for forestry profits to be appropriated for the benefit of essentially external investors.

Smaller-scale forestry on these lines would have one further advantage. It would considerably reduce the likelihood of future blanket afforestation of the kind that covers entire glens and hillsides with an impenetrable blanket of sitka spruce and lodgepole pine — something that has been condemned, on environmental as well as scenic grounds, in a series of well-publicised reports from organisations such as the Nature Conservancy Council, the Royal Society for the Protection of Birds and the Ramblers' Association. Forestry of the kind with which we are increasingly familiar, these reports conclude, is inflicting irreparable damage on our landscape. And that landscape is important. It includes some of Britain's few remaining tracts of genuine wilderness — places like the Cairngorm plateau and the ancient pinewoods that still survive on Deeside and in Strathspey. The leading expert on these localities, and on their wider significance, is Aberdeenshire scientist and naturalist Adam Watson.

'A wilderness,' he explains, 'is a piece of wild land which is more or less as nature left it. In the world today, of course, there is no wilderness in the strict sense. Human activities now produce measurable effects, in the form of radioactive pollution and acid rain, for example, even in the most remote areas. But the Cairngorm plateau and the pinewoods are as close to wilderness as anything in Europe. The old pine forest, for example, is totally different from a modern plantation. There is tremendous variety. The trees are all different. Some of them are very old. Some are dead. Others are young. There are open spaces in one spot, dense thickets in another. Compared with all that, the modern plantation is completely uniform, completely boring; every hundred yards looks just like every other hundred yards.'

Scotland's wilder localities clearly mean a lot to Adam Watson. 'I've had inspiration from places like these since I was eight or nine years old,' he comments. 'Wilderness is important not just because it's valuable from the standpoint of nature conservation. It's important as a place to be in and to enjoy. It's important to people just to know it's there. It's important

Glen More, Cairngorms – *British Tourist Authority*

Adam Watson – *Chris Lowell*

in a spiritual sense. Wilderness, then, isn't just a geographical area. It's a perception of the human mind.'

But he makes a critical distinction between that type of wilderness and the man-made desolation which is so characteristic of so much of Scotland's countryside. Empty glens and empty houses where people lived not long ago are not at all the same as the high tops of the Cairngorms. Such dereliction is described as 'sad' by Adam Watson. And like Patrick Gordon-Duff-Pennington, he contrasts the Scottish experience with that of places like Bavaria. If our rural communities had owned their own land, and if they had been run on similar lines to those in Norway, Switzerland and the alpine parts of Germany, Adam Watson believes, their fate would have been so much better.

Adam Watson, then, sees nothing appealing in a depopulated countryside. Nor does Roy Dennis, Highland officer of the RSPB and spokesman for an organisation which, with many more members than there are people living in all of northern Scotland, exercises no little influence on government. There are those who do not welcome the growing political clout of the conservation lobby; those who believe that the aims of conservationists and rural residents must invariably conflict; those who consider conservation and development to be incompatible. I do not share such views; nor does Roy Dennis. Like me, he wants to see many more people living and working in the Scottish countryside.

'I live in a most beautiful part of the Black Isle in the eastern Highlands,' says Roy Dennis. 'There we have a fine mix of farming and forestry — the sort of mix we could easily have in other parts of Scotland. And from the RSPB's point of view, from the point of view of conservationists and birdwatchers, that would be good both for wildlife and people.'

But in what way exactly would people benefit? 'There has been too much concentration on making these things super-efficient in manpower terms,' he explains. 'But that leads to a loss of people. A more mixed countryside, in contrast, employs more people. And it assists birds.'

The present crisis in agriculture, Roy Dennis is convinced, will result in a move in the direction he favours. 'People are increasingly horrified by what has been going on,' he insists. 'They are horrified by agricultural surpluses. They are horrified by the decline of rural communities. Conservation can help here. What we need is a greater awareness of the capacity of our natural heritage to increase the number of jobs and to improve both our countryside and its economy.'

The more mixed and diversified rural economy advocated by people like Roy Dennis is by no means impossible. It is commonplace in much of the rest of Western Europe where farmers are not only frequently involved in forestry but, as Patrick Gordon-Duff-Pennington remarked, often combine farming with industrial employment. Even here in Scotland there are indications that a growing number of people are coming to appreciate the benefits of developing a wider range of enterprises on the land.

Jimmy Oswald, head keeper on the Glen Tanar Estate on Deeside, sees sport as one necessary element in the countryside equation. Today's sporting estate, he stresses, is no rich man's playground. It is, and has to be, a commercial enterprise. And there is no lack of customers for the facilities on offer at Glen Tanar. Businessmen and industrialists from all over Europe, the Middle East and North America shoot regularly on Deeside. 'And that's good for the local economy,' Jimmy Oswald says, 'because the folk that come bring their wives and their friends. The hotels are full. The shops are busy.' And on the estate itself, where farming alone would provide comparatively few jobs, there is employment for about twenty-five people.

In the opposite corner of Scotland, at Brighouse on the Solway coast, farmer Tom Gillespie has similarly diversified. He is a first-rate agriculturist, a man who is recognised as one of Scotland's leading cattle breeders. But if he confined himself to farming, he would employ just four people. Tom Gillespie has not so limited his activities, however. His farms cater for 250 caravans. He provides a wide range of countryside pursuits for the 30,000 visitors he receives each year. As a result, his total workforce is now thirty-two.

And not only are Scotland's farmers having to diversify in response to changing circumstances. They are also having to re-examine the way they work the land itself.

Donald Clerk used to be employed as estate manager on 900 acres of top-grade arable land. There he practised the typically intensive type of agriculture which has produced the surplus problem and which, because of its heavy reliance on chemical aids of one kind and another, has arguably inflicted serious damage on the natural environment. Now Donald Clerk is himself a tenant farmer; and he has turned his back on high technology. On his 135-acre holding outside the Perthshire town of Meigle, he is making the slow transition to organic farming. It takes three years to wean each of his fields away from its previous dependence on chemical fertilisers, weedkillers and pesticides. But eventually he will grow grain and potatoes without recourse to chemicals — just as he is already producing organically-grown soft fruit.

'The advantages of organic farming are threefold,' says Donald Clerk. 'First, we're producing better-quality food and that's what the consumer wants. Second, we're working in harmony with nature — unlike the conventional chemical farmer — and so we're creating a more sustainable

Royal Deeside, near Cults, looking west – *Popperfoto*

agricultural system. Third, we are bringing people back into farming. For example, if you look at my soft fruit, you'll see it contains a fair bit of weed. We use no chemical weedkillers, of course. So there's a lot more handwork to be done in getting rid of that weed. On my own small farm, I'm not making a big contribution to employment. But as agriculture overall moves towards less reliance on chemicals, we'll see a lot more work being provided.'

Right at the other end of Scotland's farming spectrum is Maitland Mackie — running 2000 Aberdeenshire acres and a multi-million-pound agricultural enterprise which includes everything from dairying to the development and marketing of farmer-oriented computer software. Maitland Mackie is the epitome of a modern agri-businessman. But he, too, just like Donald Clerk and Roy Dennis, is convinced that farming as we have known it since the 1940s is no longer viable. The taxpayer, he maintains, will not for ever meet the soaring costs of present policy — costs now running at some thirty billion pounds a year across the EEC. The surplus problem, if untackled, will get worse, he warns, as new scientific advances bring even higher output. The only answer, in his opinion, is to get a lot of land right out of high-yield agriculture. Removing such land temporarily from mainstream farming — the so-called 'set-aside' policy which government has been considering — will not be sufficient, he argues. Instead, as much as 20 per cent of Britain's best arable land, some six million acres in all, should be removed from farming on a permanent basis. Some former farms might be used to grow beech, oak, ash and other hardwood trees — 're-creating Sherwood Forest', as Maitland puts it. Other farms should be broken up and sold to people prepared to find new uses for them. Thus the surplus crisis would be solved, the appearance of the countryside would be enhanced and rural areas would be repopulated. It is a radical approach and one which depends on the overturning of the conventional view that most existing farmland should always remain in intensive agriculture.

At Cults, on the western outskirts of Aberdeen, Maitland Mackie looks out across the Dee valley and explains what he has in mind. 'This is a perfect example of what I call conventionally sacrosanct land,' he says. 'In fact, this particular area is sacrosanct twice over. It's part of the Aberdeen green belt — so it can't be used for housing or for industry. It is also reasonable land from an agricultural point of view — something that also puts it out of bounds to other land users. The latter restriction was perfectly reasonable in the past. But now we have to rid our minds of the idea that farmland is there only to produce food. It isn't. It's there for people to use.

'Now if you look over there, across the river,' he continues, 'you'll see a nice eight-acre field where, for some reason or other, someone's managed to get permission to put up a new house. He already has broadleaved, parkland-type trees growing there. If you can imagine how that piece of ground will look in fifty years, you'll see that it will then be every bit as attractive as the little bits of woodland which our forefathers planted in Victorian times. That's what we need to encourage. We need to let ground go out of farming — and into eight- or ten-acre plots where people can develop a home and have their land around them.'

The Maitland Mackie approach, of course, represents a complete

Harvesting winter barley – *Glasgow Herald*

reversal of the long-prevailing tendency for farms to get steadily bigger and for the rural population to diminish year by year. Will we really see such a drastic turn-about as we move into the next century?

'I don't know what we *will* see,' he comments. 'But I know what we *could* see. We could see a lot more people living in the countryside. Instead of having islands of pleasant scenery surrounded by seas of intensive agriculture, we could have islands of intensive agriculture surrounded by much larger areas where people will have taken over the land to do all the other things, apart from intensive farming, that they would want to do it they had the opportunity.'

Already there is one part of Scotland where the land is used primarily

Gathering the peats – *Sam Maynard*

to support a worthwhile rural population. In the crofting areas of the Highlands and Islands there are few big farms and very little in the way of intensive agriculture. Here many farmers already occupy eight- or ten-acre plots of the type advocated by Maitland Mackie. And it is as normal there as it is abnormal in the rest of Scotland to combine a little bit of farming with quite different kinds of work — such as employment in the Gaeltec electronics factory at Dunvegan in the north-western corner of Skye. Donald Maclean is a Gaeltec quality controller. He is also a crofter.

Like many other people who have grown up in the Scottish countryside, he left in search of work. Unlike most of his counterparts, however, he

Ness, Isle of Lewis – *Iain MacLeod*

was able to return — because, at home in Skye, he had access to both land and employment. Now he is successfully running the family croft as well as holding down a skilled job in electronics.

'At Gaeltec,' he says 'we work flexi-hours. If I want off during the day to attend to my sheep, I'm free to leave for a few hours. And I go into the factory in the evening to make up my time. Then when we're shearing the sheep during the summer, we might get a dry day on a Wednesday, say, and you've got to take advantage of that. So I take the Wednesday off and perhaps come in to the factory on the following Saturday when it's possibly wet outside.'

That is a pattern which has long been prevalent, as has been said, in places like Bavaria where it is fairly standard practice for car workers and other industrial employees to be part-time farmers as well. But outside the crofting areas of the north-western seaboard, this particular approach to rural development has not been much tried in Scotland. There is no reason why that should continue to be the case, and every reason to believe that the extension to other parts of Scotland of something approximating to crofting would massively assist the repopulation of the countryside.

To begin to glimpse the possibilities inherent in such a development it is necessary only to visit Ness at the north end of Lewis. Here, at the outermost extremity of the Outer Hebrides, the weather is unusually wild and stormy and the land far from fertile. So unappealing is that land from a purely agricultural standpoint, in fact, that if it were located in practically any other part of Scotland it would be occupied by no more than two or three farms, each of them providing a less than generous income for a single family. In Ness, however, a quite different arrangement has long since been adopted. The land is divided into long, narrow strips — often no more than a few yards wide. Each one of these strips, perhaps half a dozen acres in extent, if that, is a separate croft. And on each croft stands a house. As a result — since there are hundreds, even thousands, of these diminutive holdings in this part of Lewis — Ness, for all its climatic disadvantages, is the most densely populated part of the British countryside.

No crofting family, of course, relies entirely on the very modest financial returns generated by the working of one of these little strips of land. People here invariably combine their crofting activities with other occupations. One such occupation is the weaving, usually in a shed immediately adjacent to the croft house, of Harris tweed that will eventually be sold in fashionable urban outlets around the world. Other crofters are also fishermen, lorry drivers, oilmen, local government administrators, postmen, building contractors, forestry workers, teachers and lecturers. There are crofters who run fish farms; crofters who manage guest houses, pubs and hotels; crofters who are butchers, and bakers, and even candlestick makers.

It has long been the fashion, in the rest of Scotland, to hold crofters and crofting in fairly low esteem. And when national policy for the countryside was almost exclusively concerned with maximising agricultural output, crofting was not, admittedly, a self-evidently sensible way of organising the land. But now — as is being said repeatedly by Patrick Gordon-Duff-Pennington, by Roy Dennis, by Maitland Mackie, by James Provan and many others — national policy for the countryside can no longer be formulated in narrowly agricultural terms. We have to find other uses for the land; uses that will reduce, not increase, agricultural output; uses, ideally, that will make it possible for more people to obtain their livelihoods in our rural areas.

Crofting offers one way forward. 'The important thing about crofting,' says Angus MacLeod, the Lewisman who took the lead in establishing the recently-formed Scottish Crofters' Union and who is now its Honorary President, 'is that crofting has kept people on the land — whereas farming, on the other hand, has emptied the countryside.' Angus MacLeod looks out across Ness with its rows and rows of houses. 'Crofting has kept the people here,' he repeats. 'And people are what is important.' That is an appropriate note on which to come to a conclusion.

'The crofter has gone,' wrote Lewis Grassic Gibbon, 'the man with the house and steading of his own and the land closer to his heart than the flesh of his body.' But in Ness, in Skye and in other long-neglected corners of the Highlands and Islands, the crofter has survived the coming of what Grassic Gibbon called the great herds and the great machines. And so there are still people here; people in large numbers; worthwhile human communities of the kind that have all too often disappeared elsewhere. That is why a seemingly bleak and windy place like Ness has a message for the rest of rural Scotland.

There are major changes coming to the Scottish countryside. But these changes need not be for the worse. I believe we are about to be presented with an opportunity — an opportunity to put more people on the land. Such a transformation, of course, is not inevitable. But if we respond imaginatively to present pressures we can make it come about. So I hope that we can learn something from the crofting townships of the Western Isles. I hope that, in the year 2000, the rest of the Scottish countryside will look a little more like Ness.

A SICKENING WASTE

— *Dr David Player* —

Every year more than three and a half million people fly from Scottish airports. As they wait to board their planes, there's a certain air of apprehension. Despite all the evidence to the contrary, people still believe they're taking a considerable risk by flying. And yet, the very things they indulge in to calm their nerves in airport lounges — smoking cigarettes, drinking excessively, eating junk food — carry much greater risks of premature death than boarding a plane.

Smoking kills nearly ten thousand Scots every year, and Glasgow has the worst record for lung cancer in the world. Not only that, it also has the world's highest heart-attack rate. A large proportion of these deaths are, in a sense, self-inflicted, resulting from our own bad habits: we smoke too much, our leisure activities are based around alcohol, and our diet includes too many fry-ups and sweet desserts.

The situation in Scotland is now so bad that last year more than thirty thousand people died as a result of patently preventable causes. This incredible statistic is the equivalent of 165 fully loaded shuttles crashing every year — and who would fly under conditions like that?

Of course Glasgow's problems are infamous, but the rest of Scotland has nothing to be proud of. If you live on the Clyde estuary, you're more

David Player – *BBC*

likely to die from a stroke, or from cirrhosis of the liver, than anywhere else in Scotland. Aberdeen has a high incidence of death from bowel cancer. In Dumfries and Galloway, death from skin cancer is at its worst. In Fife and the Islands the cervical cancer death rate is higher than anywhere else in Scotland.

The unhealthiest place of all is Motherwell, with Britain's highest rate of premature death. Death is supposed to be the great equaliser, but the Lanarkshire town highlights the inequality of death in Britain. For every one person under sixty-five who dies in, say, Ipswich, three will die in Motherwell. The general pattern is undeniable — southerners live longer.

For a long time we entrusted our health entirely to doctors and nurses. The feeling was that our only contribution was taking the medicine the doctor prescribed, or agreeing to have an operation the doctor recommended. The result of this passive approach to health is a National Illness Service which costs a vast amount to run, yet is unable to cope with the demands put on it by an ever-growing population.

Nowadays, however, there's a new awareness that our health is in our own hands — instead of relying on doctors to cure us, we ought to avoid becoming ill in the first place. Hence the daily ritual in the park, as exercise becomes part of our regular routine. Jogging isn't everyone's cup of tea, but sports centres, and evening classes in yoga, aerobics and dancing, are doing a thriving business.

Eating for health is part of the new lifestyle too. High-fibre cereals, brown wholemeal bread and low-fat milk are now replacing sugar-coated, refined and processed foods with all the goodness taken out. But let's not fool ourselves; a health movement there may be, but health for all there certainly is not.

Scotland in the 1930s was a land of poverty, economic depression and bad housing. The young suffered through poor nutrition; tuberculosis

Children at play in backstreets, 1930s – *BBC Hulton Picture Library*

Young resident of Possilpark, Glasgow, 1986 – *Glasgow Herald*

and infectious diseases were widespread. Chronic overcrowding was common: sometimes whole families shared a single room, so infections spread rapidly.

Fifty years later, the stark reality is that there are still places in Scotland which are not very different. Material deprivation is still with us in the 1980s: throughout Scotland you'll find areas with poor housing, and a lack of decent shops, schools and transport. For many, a shortage of money means that, even if they want to take heed of health education advice, they can't afford to buy the healthy lifestyle. Despite the NHS, manual workers are more than twice as likely to die before retirement than people in professional jobs like lawyers and teachers. A child born to an unskilled manual worker is twice as likely to die before his first birthday as a child born to parents in the professional class. Accidents to children vary just as greatly, according to class. So, just as in the 1930s, people who live in poorer areas suffer far more ill health than their better-off neighbours.

This is no vague theory. Report after report after report has highlighted the relationship between poverty, deprivation and ill health. One of the most famous is the Black Report on 'Inequalities in Health'.* It's quite a rare document: it was published by the government on a bank holiday in 1980, and only a few hundred copies were printed. The Black Report and all the others recommend that if health is to be improved poor living conditions must be tackled. The trouble is that those in power don't seem to be listening.

It's about time they did start listening, because health is a political issue that goes far beyond party political arguments about NHS spending. Doctors, health and social workers and others are only too aware that not everyone is able to adopt a healthy lifestyle and that there are social and political constraints on health. In October 1986 a conference on deprivation was held by the Royal College of Physicians and Surgeons in Glasgow at which doctors and other health professionals highlighted the need for wide-ranging social action.

One of the delegates was Dr John Womersley, a community medicine specialist with the Greater Glasgow Health Board. He described how our chances of succumbing to particular illness can depend on where we happen to live.

'If we compare the fifth of the population living in the most affluent parts of Glasgow with the fifth living in the least affluent or most deprived, we find there are about two-and-a-half-fold differences in death rates between the two areas. This varies from a difference of five-fold in the case of lung cancer to about three-fold in the case of heart disease in women. The most marked differences we find are between the areas of Bridgeton, which has a standardised death rate [a way of measuring the number of deaths in the population compared with the national average] of about one hundred and sixty and that of Whitecraigs which has a standardised death rate of forty. So between these two areas there's a four-fold difference in the death rate. In practical terms, if you live in Bridgeton and you're aged twenty to forty, your chances of dying in the next five to ten years are four times greater than if you are the same age and live in Whitecraigs.'

*DHSS, 1980

Another delegate was Sue Laughlin, a Senior Health Education Officer with the Greater Glasgow Health Board. She believes there is a very strong relationship between poverty, deprivation and health.

'The poorer people are, the greater the risk of ill health, because they don't have access to good housing. They're not likely to be able to get good food. People in areas of deprivation are likely either to be in low-paid jobs, or the risk of unemployment is much higher. And that all affects their health.'

That view was supported by Dr Alex Scott-Samuel, a community physician in Liverpool.

'People's disposable income has a big effect upon their health, and one of the most important aspects is food. Individual diets are important, but so is access to good nutritious food. Obviously if the food is available, but at a supermarket several miles away and you don't have a car, you're less likely to shop there.'

Dr Scott-Samuel believes that there is a connection between poverty and reliance on social props such as tobacco and alcohol.

'It's been clearly demonstrated that smoking and drinking and other unhealthy behaviours are strongly related to social class. In other words, working-class people are more prone to these things. But that leads people into a very simplistic conclusion: "Well then, you — the working classes — have got to do something about it", when in fact a lot could be done by health boards, local authorities and governments.

'People usually smoke for good reasons. They smoke because they're under particular kinds of stress; they smoke because they have monotonous boring jobs; they smoke because there is pressure from people in their peer groups, particularly among adolescents. Appalling social conditions reinforce this and I see it as a fundamental issue, something for social and political action, not just for the health education of individuals.'

If social pressures lead to bad health, unemployment can only make matters worse. Living off Social Security is not easy by any standard, but it's not just poverty that can have an adverse effect on health: the evidence is that the sheer misery and humiliation of being unemployed is damaging. Put simply, I would say that unemployment itself causes bad health.

Mel Bartley, a graduate student at the Department of Social Policy at Edinburgh University, has collected evidence about the effects of unemployment on health, from the 1930s to the present day. She has also carried out a number of original studies in Scotland and the UK:

'You have to divide the relationship between unemployment and health into the effects on mental and physical health.

'I don't think anybody now doubts that someone who's had a spell of unemployment is at a considerably higher risk of serious illness and even of dying in a five-to-ten-year period following their spell of unemployment. Anybody who's ever experienced a spell of unemployment begins to feel less needed, one's role in the world becomes uncertain; applying for benefit and working out all the complexities and red tape can cause a lot of anxiety; when income drops, anxiety increases. The effect on people's physical health is that they can afford a less good diet, and are less able to heat their houses sufficiently, particularly in Scotland.

A scrabble for jobs at an employment office – *BBC Hulton Picture Library*

'The physical effect is also due to the insecurity which results once you've been made unemployed. You may have been working in the same industry for twenty-five years, you may be a middle-aged person, so you're going to find it extremely difficult to get back into the same kind of secure job as you had before. And even if your spell of unemployment isn't particularly long, there's a very high probability of you having to move back into the workforce in a job which is more hazardous, more stressful and at a lower rate of pay — all of which affect the physical health.'

But it's not just people who are actually out of work who are at risk.

'People who manage to remain in the labour force but who have always worked — for example in catering or in building — are now at higher risk of what I call an increasing casualisation of work. This has become possible because high levels of unemployment make people less able to organise themselves and fight for better conditions, but also because employers are now able to hire and fire much more simply than they were before. They don't have to hang on to people, they don't have to pay attention to the sort of rules and regulations which the Health and Safety and the Employment Protection legislation of ten years ago imposed. I believe that the casualisation of work is a greater danger to health than the effects of single spells of unemployment per se.'

When people are under stress they look for what I would call a prop. Sometimes it's a cigarette or a stiff drink. The trouble is these legal drugs cause untold harm to our health, and not only are they readily available, they're a cornerstone of the British economy. Take this excerpt from *Yes Prime Minister,* a conversation between Prime Minister, Jim Hacker and hisCabinet Secretary Sir **Humphrey Appleby**:

Prime Minister: It says here: smoking-related diseases cost the NHS one hundred and sixty-five million pounds a year.

Sir Humphrey: Yes, but we have gone into that. It's been shown that if those extra hundred thousand people a year had lived to a ripe old age, they would have cost us even more in pensions and social security than they did in medical treatment. So, financially it's unquestionably better that they continue to die at about the present rate.

Prime Minister: Humphrey. When cholera killed thirty thousand people in 1833, we got the Public Health Act. A commercial drug kills half a dozen people and it gets withdrawn from sale. Cigarettes kill a hundred thousand people a year and what do we get?

Sir Humphrey: Four billion pounds a year. Around twenty-five thousand jobs in the tobacco industry. A flourishing cigarette export business, helping the balance of trade. Two hundred and fifty thousand jobs indirectly related to tobacco — newsagents, packaging, transport.

Prime Minister: These figures are just guesses.

Sir Humphrey: No, they're government statis . . . facts.*

Of course, I'm not suggesting that the attitude of Whitehall is quite as cynical as that. But in the UK at least £100 million a year is spent promoting tobacco — the single largest avoidable cause of illness, disease and death in Britain today.

Despite that the tobacco companies consistently refuse to accept the relationship between smoking and health.

The government might be expected to take a more considered view; but when they actually give financial assistance to a company which wants to manufacture a new tobacco product, Skoal Bandits, which you suck rather than smoke, you really begin to wonder exactly where health comes in their priorities.

Alison Hillhouse, Director of the Scottish Committee for Action on Smoking and Health — ASH — argues that such decisions are indefensible.

'As far as I can make out there are only thirty to thirty-five jobs at stake there, which does not seem very many for the expenditure of a million pounds. If that factory were manufacturing heroin there would have been no question of allowing it. But because it is tobacco there is no mechanism to prevent it — tobacco comes outside all the legislation that covers safety of drugs, medicines and food standards. Tobacco is exempted from the existing legislation and therefore we find ourselves with a new health hazard on our doorstep.

'The irony is that Skoal Bandits are not actually proving popular. There's been such a public revulsion that most retailers are refusing to stock them and as far as I can understand very few children have actually come across them, although they know quite a lot about them.'

The tobacco industry operate a voluntary agreement restricting the ways in which their products can be promoted, and part of that says that no attempt will be made to attract children to smoking. But is that agreement sticking? Alison Hillhouse thinks not:

'At this moment we have something like forty per cent of the children in Scotland smoking either regularly or occasionally before they reach

*Jonathan Lynn and Antony Jay

sixteen which, of course, is the age when it's legal to sell them tobacco.

'I'm sure that everybody has seen the shops covered with cigarette advertising. These are the places where our children are going and where they're buying their cigarettes. The voluntary system simply doesn't work. It must be replaced by legislation.'

But tobacco companies even now dispute that there is a cast-iron link between smoking and bad health.

'The tobacco industry is the only one saying that these days. The link between smoking and lung cancer, heart disease and chronic obstructive lung disease has been established for over thirty years now and we are still finding more unpleasant things that smoking does to people. For example, in Scotland around four hundred legs are amputated every year, of which ninety-five per cent are from people who smoke.

'Adult smoking is going down, a lot more people give up smoking every year, and so the tobacco industry has to recruit a new young group to smoking or else they'd be out of business within a generation. So they are looking at the younger generation, children still at school — although they would deny that — and also the very vulnerable teenage group. The other group is this country which seems to them a possible means of expanding their market is women, because still fewer women smoke than men.'

The tobacco companies have agreed to all sorts of voluntary restrictions on their promotion. Did Alison Hillhouse not agree that they are being reasonable?

'There is no way that the tobacco industry is going to agree to anything which seriously damages its economic health. What we have is a package of restrictions which have certainly helped, have cut down on what direct

Young boy smoking – *Juliette Radom*

advertising can say, but the industry goes around the agreements. There is a legal ban on advertising tobacco on television, so what do we have? Something over three hundred hours of sponsored sport on the BBC every year. Something like half of the children between eleven and fifteen watched the snooker finals last year. The industry would have us believe that that's got nothing to do with selling cigarettes, but nobody really believes them any more.

'What we need is a complete ban on all forms of tobacco promotion and that means not just advertising, it means sponsorship. It means an end to point-of-sale advertising and an end to sportswear with cigarette logos on it. All the things which attract young people particularly will have to go. That is the most important part of any government package to reduce smoking disease.'

I asked Alison to summarise the changes she would like to see between now and the year 2000.

Glasgow's No Smoking Bus – *Scotsman Publications*

'The most important one is to see that a generation of children do not start to smoke. I'd like to see much more work done on research on how to help people to stop. Two-thirds of smokers would like to stop. Basically we need to create an environment in which children do not grow up to think that smoking is normal, and that will mean cutting down on smoking in public.'

I agree with Alison Hillhouse that what's needed is a complete ban on all forms of tobacco advertising and promotion, including the most cynical of all — sports sponsorship. But while politicians dither, others have taken direct action. In Australia, a group known as BUGA UP, or Billboard Artists Against Unhealthy Promotions, have launched their own offensive against the industry — by defacing billboards. Many of the campaign members are health professionals who are happy to be associated with illegal action.

Here in Britain a similar group has sprung up — the Campaign on Using Graffiti for Health in the Neighbourhood, or COUGHIN. Little is known about them, but already their activities are in evidence in Edinburgh.

Tobacco may be the biggest killer, but the social prop which is most closely woven into the fabric of our society is alcohol. We use it to stimulate and to celebrate, to calm and to console. Every day in Scotland we spend £3.5 million on alcohol — more than 7 per cent of all consumer spending, and worth £5 billion a year to the Exchequer.* But there's a

*Annual Abstract of Statistics, CSO 1982

Edinburgh pub interior – *Scotsman Publications*

price. In the UK, lost production and the cost to the medical and social services of caring for the victims of alcohol abuse are conservatively estimated at £1 billion a year. Since 1976, when the licensing laws were relaxed, cirrhosis of the liver in Scotland has risen considerably in comparison with the rest of the UK — up by a third.

The ad men are good at their job, and the push for ever-increasing profits has produced the glossy advertising images of the good life — cool and sophisticated, young and trendy; special, dry, on the rocks — but never down and out.

If tobacco and alcohol can be major causes of illness, another unhealthy prop can be obtained in a rather surprising place — the doctor's surgery. It's hard to see your GP as a pedlar of bad health, but overcrowded waiting rooms mean that the average consultation with a patient lasts just five minutes. All GPs would like to spend more time exploring and discussing their patients' problems. But in practice many patients who display symptoms of anxiety or tension leave the surgery with another social prop — a bottle of tranquillisers.

Apart from antibiotics, pharmaceutical companies produce more hypnotics and tranquillisers than any other drug. Worldwide, business is worth more than a billion pounds a year.

I talked to a group of women who meet regularly at a support group in Edinburgh. They're all tranquilliser addicts, trying to help each other come off the constant diet of tablets. It's thought that four times as many people are hooked on tranquillisers as on hard drugs such as heroin. Recognition of the dangers has led to a recent drop in their prescription, but tranquilliser addiction remains one of today's least recognised but most disturbing problems.

One woman told me:

'They said to me at first it was post-natal depression. They put me on tranquillisers to calm me down and I was still very depressed; so he said, now we'll have to give you something to pep you up. So I was on tranquillisers to calm me down and anti-depressants to pick me up and sleeping tablets to help me sleep.'

Another's experience:

'I just seem to get the same prescription year after year, month after month. I used to pray to God at night, Please what's wrong with me? and when I started getting really bad the doctor said, We'll have to up your dose. I said, Oh no, you can take the dose. He said, It's your nerves, and I said, I've heard you can come off these tablets, and he said, Don't listen to these neurotic women, don't listen, don't watch these programmes.'

And a third:

'I was back and forward at the dental hospital and they kept saying to me, there's nothing wrong with your teeth, but I was having severe pain and it's only now I've discovered that it's been the withdrawal that's caused it. Some people have had their teeth taken out because they couldn't discover what it was, and I think that's quite sad.'

Coming off tranquillisers can be harrowing, and the trouble according to one of the group is that doctors don't seem to be aware of the symptoms:

'I think doctors should be educated as to what the withdrawal symptoms are, so that when you are on tablets and you go to them with these different symptoms they can turn round and say, now look, that's because you are coming off the tablets.'

If tranquilliser addiction has received little recognition, heroin addiction is quite the opposite. Hardly a week passes without shocking statistics of how many of our youngsters are involved, how quickly the situation is worsening, and how easily this ultimate social prop can be obtained.

Dr Roy Robertson is a GP who works in an area of Edinburgh where heroin use is common. He questions our assumptions about heroin addiction and suggests the whole issue has been blown out of proportion.

'You've got to remember that heroin abuse is not necessarily a continuous and an inevitable process; people stop using heroin at the same rate as they start using. Studies from America and our own country show that a large number of people give up using heroin and apparently remain quite well or unaffected in the long term and, therefore, it may be a temporary phenomenon, at least for some people. They go through a phase of heroin abuse that may last from two to five or ten years, and then they may just stop using it spontaneously. It is usually not connected with any treatment or any particular event; it just seems to happen.

'I don't think heroin abuse is a good thing, I don't think it's something we should encourage at all, but I do think we've got to recognise that it isn't necessarily a disease with a clear cause and a clear treatment. There are all sorts of factors that make people use heroin, and they're not related to any individual personality type or mental instability or anything like that.

'The point is that it's representative, it's a symptom of an underlying multi-dimensional problem: it's related to poor housing, to unemployment, to poor prospects amongst youngsters.'

This notion has been put to the test. Dr Martin Plant of the Department of Psychiatry at Edinburgh University has studied the relationship between drug abuse and unemployment:

'My colleagues and I followed up the progress of a thousand school leavers in the Lothian region and found that, at the ages of nineteen and twenty, people who were unemployed weren't drinking or smoking more, but they were much more likely to use illegal drugs, including heroin. Across the UK as a whole since 1970 the level of unemployment has been mirrored almost exactly in its rate of increase by the levels of drug problems recorded by the Home Office. In any one year, if unemployment has gone up by two or three per cent so has the level of addict notifications and drug-related crimes, and this link is remarkable. It's a correspondence of more than ninety per cent.'

But while Martin Plant wouldn't underrate the consequences of taking hard drugs, he agrees that the problem must be kept in proportion:

'Every year in the British Isles about two hundred and fifty people die because of a misuse of illegal drugs, things such as overdoses and accidents that are connected with illegal drugs. Now many of those are also alcohol related, probably thirty or forty per cent involving intoxication. At the same time as you have two hundred and fifty people dying drug-related deaths, at least a hundred thousand die because of tobacco use and at least four thousand — some people have said the real number's perhaps twenty thousand — die from misuse of alcohol, principally through drunken driving accidents on the road. So, although we need to be very worried about illegal drugs, we should also remember that on any one night most of the National Health Service beds in Britain are taken up by people there through the misuse of alcohol, through tobacco and through overdoses. So keep it in perspective.'

Tobacco, alcohol, tranquillisers, hard drugs — a group of products which provide short-term solace, but lead to long-term problems. So what can be done about them?

The Scottish Health Education Group (SHEG) is the government-funded body with responsibility for informing the public about such dangers to their health. SHEG covers the full spectrum of health issues, working with an annual budget of £3 million — a pittance compared with the £200 million thought to be spent advertising tobacco and alcohol in the UK. But, according to director Stanley Mitchell, SHEG meets the glossy imagery of the industry head on.

'We know from our market research that people in Scotland don't like to be told what to do, and they certainly don't like to be told what *not* to do, and so we've got to use different approaches. What we've been doing in both smoking and alcohol is to speak to young people — nineteen, sixteen, that kind of range for the most part, and to some extent now to younger children. We're trying to use approaches where they're encouraged to feel that they have power in themselves to resist the kind of pressure that's put on them to smoke: where they can make their own decisions about life; where they feel powerful enough to make the health

Stanley Mitchell, Director of SHEG – *Scotsman Publications*

decision. It's an approach that's quite different; it's a lifestyle approach, not a hard-hitting fearsome approach.'

Research about how people respond to this type of advertising is vitally important. When SHEG were asked to tackle the hard-drugs issue, they and the government took different views of the approach required.

'They asked us to do a hard-hitting campaign and I suppose the problem for us was we didn't quite know what hard-hitting meant. We certainly thought it meant showing scenes of people shooting up drugs in closes or public loos and degradation and death or something like that, and that was not a very happy situation for us to be in.

'There was a fear that to take these threatening approaches might in fact make drug-taking more exciting, more adventurous for people who were on the brink, and we certainly didn't want to do any harm. So we went for trying to strengthen the resolve of non-drugs users and maybe that took us down a particular line which was not what the government expected, and maybe not what the police expected, because they could see a great crime-prevention issue there too.'

In that instance, the Scottish Office were persuaded to go along with a strategy different to the hard-hitting approach they originally preferred. But in England ad Wales the government took anti-drugs advertising out of the hands of the health education people, and ran a campaign designed to shock, despite evidence that such a strategy might have been counter-productive.

It was a riskier strategy than the damage-limitation exercise of the Scottish group. It also served as a reminder that health education must operate against a political background, in which demands for visible action assume great importance.

Tools of the heroin trade – *Scotsman Publications*

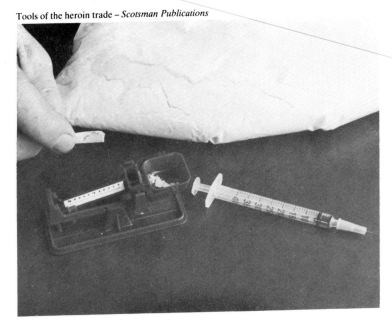

Increasing public anxiety also spurred the government to take action against the deadly virus AIDS. It's the most frightening disease to afflict the human race for many years. It's incurable and it kills. While well-known victims like Rock Hudson and Liberace hit the headlines, more than two hundred other Americans die of AIDS every week. In Scotland, however, while there's no cause for complacency, the number carrying the virus is still relatively small.

Dr Ray Brettle, a consultant at the City Hospital in Edinburgh, is a leading specialist in the disease:

'We're talking about an estimated thousand people in Edinburgh. The current figures suggest that we've identified eight hundred carriers of the virus in Scotland. Now these are only people who've come forward to volunteer for the test, so that there are obviously a number of people who haven't. It is a small proportion of the population, but of course they are young — their average age is twenty-five — so they're the future of the society, if you like. In England, sixty to seventy per cent of the people being detected with the virus are homosexuals — whereas in Scotland sixty per cent of them are drug abusers.'

While the capital city is the centre of the problem, Edinburgh's drug abusers are well travelled. A group of patients who admitted to sharing a dirty needle in order to inject drugs were asked where the incident had taken place. The answers ranged from Wick, through Glasgow, Liverpool and London, to Paris and Amsterdam. And every time a needle is shared, the risk of passing on the AIDS virus is at its highest.

As Dr Brettle explains:

'There is a drift out of this identified risk group — people who have abused drugs, or misused drugs — of about five per cent a year. If you like, the virus is spreading out into people who are not in that risk group, and that will continue unless the government's campaign persuades everybody that they must take sensible precautions.'

The voluntary group, Scottish AIDS Monitor, think that is unlikely. Their national organiser, Will Mallinson, believes the government's adverts are fine for those who understand them. But high-risk groups such as those under the influence of drugs need the sort of direct approach which AIDS Monitor's confidential telephone and counselling services provide.

'I don't think the people who need to be spoken to about the disease will understand the symbolism that's portrayed in the television adverts; and the government leaflet was much, much too wordy. Our information leaflet for the general public is a cartoon version which answers the question that most people will ask, and then it gives a route for further information — i.e. our phone lines.

'They've got to start putting substantial funding into the voluntary agencies like our own Scottish Aids Monitor and in England the Terrence Higgins Trust. These are the people who've been working in this field for four years now and giving a range of services that couldn't be provided in the statutory sector.'

But what about a potential cure? All the recent medical research has given Ray Brettle cause for cautious optimism.

'By comparison to six months ago treatment facilities are advancing at an enormous rate and we hope that in the United Kingdom there will be new drugs available before the end of this year so that people who develop AIDS will almost certainly have their lives prolonged. The most important thing, however, is to develop safe drugs for those people who are only infected with the virus now, so that we can prevent them from getting anywhere near AIDS. There is good preliminary evidence that when you give those drugs to people, their infectivity drops dramatically. If that's the case, then we can hope to see a limit to the further spread of the virus. That's much more exciting now than it was six or twelve months ago.

'A true cure — that is curing someone who's been infected with the virus — with, say, a two-month course of treatment, is a long way off. But one can foresee a vaccine being developed, though I don't foresee it being readily available for the next ten years. I think it would be about the year 2000 before we'd have an effective vaccine, although things are moving very fast in this area, and three or four years can bring dramatic changes.'

For the moment, however, education is the only weapon against AIDS, fuelled by public concern. But the power of public awareness should not be underestimated, as recent changes in Scotland's diet have shown. With all today's talk of healthy eating, it's hard to believe that until just four years ago, the relationship between sweet, fatty food and our bad health record was rarely discussed. Then, in September 1983, came a bombshell. A major committee headed by Professor Philip James of the Rowett Research Institute in Aberdeen, published a report which was highly critical of our eating habits.* The group was the National Advisory Committee on Nutrition Education, or NACNE. According to Professor James the NACNE report did lead to problems:

'For the first time it was set out in a very clear way that we had a national problem; we were not dealing with small groups within the community. Most, if not all of the population was affected, and we should be changing the national diet. We should be cutting down on the total amount of fat, cutting down on saturated fats in particular. We were eating too much sugar, too much salt. We should be eating more starchy foods, rich in fibre. These sets of recommendations were now put in quantitative terms for the first time.'

The discomfort caused by the report meant that to have it published at all was a considerable achievement. The food industry said it didn't tackle the real issues, nor did it accord with what their own experts were telling them. For their part, the government set up another committee to look at diet. That meant they wouldn't comment on NACNE's findings because their own report was pending. So, was the NACNE report being suppressed?

'Oh I think we can now recognise that the report was being suppressed. I was vaguely aware of that, and we now have evidence from other people that there was a systematic campaign to suppress the report. In the event it was very foolish, because the publicity that came from the sudden leaking of the report was so extraordinary that if I'd wanted to devise a way of getting across to the British public what a problem we had, I couldn't have thought of a better mechanism than actually having the report apparently suppressed to start with.'

*Health Education Council September 1983.

In the few years since the publication of the NACNE report and others like it, there's been a marked change in eating patterns. The consumer demand for information about healthy eating is overwhelming, and the food industry has responded well. Supermarkets direct you to eat meat with the fat cut off, the bakery turns out a selection of wholemeal loaves, and in some shops, sales of low-fat milk have actually overtaken those of full-fat milk. It's a first-class example of what can be achieved when enough people decide to put their health first.

But where does this new health awareness leave the National Health Service, the biggest employer in Europe, costing nearly £20 billion a year to run?

The NHS does a wonderful job. Thousands of patients are treated in hospital every day. Hi-tech medicine has led to major advances in treating diseased parts of the body. Transplant surgery, microsurgery and limb replacements are increasingly common. But increased demand together with the high cost of high-tech treatments puts increasing pressure on NHS resources — no less than 80 per cent of the health budget is spent on and in hospitals.

But hospitals can't provide the answer to Scotland's bad health record. Most of their effort is devoted to patching up people already suffering from disease. As Dr Alex Scott-Samuel says:

'We need to re-focus upstream. We're all too busy in the Health Service pulling drowning people out of the water and treating them, when we ought to be looking upstream to see who it is that's pushing them in.'

It's up to us to take steps now to avoid ill health in the future. The

The Good-Hearted Glasgow campaign – Lord Provost David Hodge setting an example – *Scotsman Publications*

NHS should be at the forefront of this movement — checking us for health hazards and advising us on preventive measures. Every year we take our cars for servicing in order to prevent major breakdown. If that's a sensible course of action for cars, why not do the same for our bodies?

A good structure on which to build preventive services already exists within the NHS. At well-woman clinics, for example, breast examinations are carried out, and cervical smears taken. These simple tests to identify cancers at an early stage save thousands of women's lives every year.

But preventive medicine needn't be restricted to special clinics. In Glasgow, a new screening programme to cut down coronary heart disease is under way, using the resources of ordinary health centres. The Good-Hearted Glasgow campaign invites patients who visit their doctors to take part in a series of tests covering risk factors such as weight, blood pressure and cholesterol count. And if the result is a shock, patients are given advice on diet and weight control, or are referred to specialist clinics. The programme is a major step forward. It's costing £8 million over ten years, but Greater Glasgow Health Board are convinced that it's money well spent, as the project's director, Dr Lindsay Davidson, explains:

A breathalyser with a difference – health testing while you shop – *Scotsman Publications*

'Forty-five per cent of Glaswegians die from heart disease and stroke; so it is a big problem. The scientific evidence is now very hard that if we can get individuals to reduce the major risk factors, we can reduce the effects of coronary heart disease — both death and disability — by ten per cent over ten years. We'll be able to achieve that if we can get Glaswegians to cut down their smoking, watch their diet, take a little more exercise and have their blood pressure measured.

'Once we've got these systems into general practice we can do all sorts of things, like provide screening for anything like cervical cytology, which is another important programme. The general practitioners in Glasgow are very enthusiastic about this because the new generation of doctors is being trained to be preventive.'

Major health centres are well equipped to carry out preventive work. They employ a broad range of professionals working together — doctors, nurses and health visitors. Better use of this kind of joint effort could help to relieve the time pressures facing GPs working on their own.

In recent months the government has been examining radical ways in which our primary health-care services can be improved. Dr Alistair Donald, an adviser to the House of Commons Select Committee on

Campaigning for better health – an anti-dampness protest outside Glasgow City Chambers – *Glasgo*

primary health care, sees better integration as a way forward:

'It involves quite a change in concept, developing a team of people to provide these services. The skills of the nurse and health visitor are developed as far as possible. A nurse is quite capable of screening somebody for blood pressure or even taking cervical smears. Health visitors visit elderly people in their homes to find out if they are lonely or showing early signs of illness – dementia, for example. The running of clinics in the surgery means more personnel, such as nurses and health visitors, more secretaries, more resources in the form of buildings.'

Dr Alex Scott-Samuel agrees that while Britain's primary health-care system may be the best in the world, being comprehensive and free, there is a great deal that could be done to improve it.

'We don't have nearly enough effective teamwork in primary health services. Better training of primary health workers, a common-core training for all health workers in the community, would go a long way towards breaking down the barriers between different hierarchies and getting them to understand each other's point of view.

'Another initiative which is well overdue is what I call neighbourhood prevention teams. The idea here is that all the preventive health workers combine in patch-based teams — based on a small neighbourhood — and work together to improve the public health of that neighbourhood. I'm talking about the three main full-time preventive workers in the community — the health visitor, the community health doctor who works in the child and school health clinics, and the environmental health officer. They could increase the team as appropriate with health education officers, community medicine specialists like myself, and a range of other health, social and community and voluntary workers, not least *users* of the services who would all be working together in these locally based teams.'

But better integration of services isn't enough. There must also be better access to them for those who need them most. As Alistair Donald said:

'I would like to see a system whereby doctors and nurses were not distributed simply on the basis of the numbers they're looking after but also on the needs of that population. The more affluent areas don't need quite so many doctors and nurses, the other areas need slightly more. We should get to a system where we deploy these resources according to population needs.'

Some feel even that's not enough. Linda Headland, of the Association of Local Health Councils, represents the patient's point of view:

'There's no reason on earth why doctors couldn't share premises with other people and other services. If we would really like to see the medical profession having something meaningful to say and contribute on health promotion then it would be very useful if they were to consider operating from a leisure centre where there is a swimming pool, where there are various activities available for people, which people actually use for health promotion. There's no reason why they couldn't operate from community centres, share premises with community workers and so on.'

Radical changes in primary health care are just one element of a strategy adopted in Finland. Fifteen years ago it was Finland, and not Scotland, which had the worst record in the world for coronary heart disease.

Among those most badly affected were the people of North Karelia, a province 250 miles to the north-east of Helsinki.

Dr Pekka Puska of the National Public Heath Institute in Helsinki initiated, and now heads, the North Karelia project:

'In a relatively small population of about one hundred and eighty thousand people in 1972 there were more than one thousand heart attacks, and many were fatal. Coronary heart disease caused a lot of premature deaths, a lot of invalidity and a lot of suffering. We realised that due to the chronic nature of the disease we had to go for prevention. You can of course save the life of an individual patient, but to tackle a massive epidemic you need mass action by prevention.'

A petition led to the creation of the North Karelia project — an all-embracing government-backed campaign to reduce heart disease. In schools, guidance on good health became part of the curriculum. Television series on how to develop a healthier lifestyle became a regular feature. And the food industry was transformed. Ten years ago farmer Pauli Kiiskinen began to grow berries, but for many years he struggled to sell the blackcurrant cordial he produced. Now the North Karelia project has endorsed his product by launching a berry campaign, and Pauli Kiiskinen can't grow enough. It's just one example of what has been achieved by the project's ambitious strategy. For Pekka Puska, the results are clear:

'The latest data show that the heart-disease mortality of men is declining in North Karelia so that over the ten-year period there's a thirty per cent reduction. And now data from our mortality statistics and from cancer registers show that cancer rates have also started to decline in North Karelia more rapidly than in the rest of the country. When we look at the overall mortality pattern of men below sixty-five we see that cardio-vascular mortality starts to go down, and when we look at all causes, all deaths, we see a great reduction.'

But while no one doubts the value of the North Karelia project, some people question whether it alone is responsible for Finland's improved health. In recent years the country's standard of living has risen considerably. Housing is good, and unemployment is comparatively low. Helsinki University's Dr Matti Rimpla says these could be the real reasons for the improvement:

'From the middle of the 1960s the standard of living has improved in Finland very rapidly. Of course we still have socio-economic inequalities, but compared to many other countries they are pretty small. And anyway social security has improved a lot during the last fifteen years.'

So while the campaign of intervention in Finland has been a success, many would argue that the main cause has been an improvement in general living standards. This view is endorsed by the World Health Organisation. In a report entitled 'Targets for Health for All'* they say that inequalities in health could be reduced dramatically by the year 2000 if the diseases related to lifestyles were reduced, if the health aspects of living and working conditions were improved, and if good primary health care were made accessible to all. This document is endorsed by the UK government.

Yet Scotland still has some of the worst housing in Europe, some of

*World Health Organisation 1985

the poorest and most decayed areas in Britain, and one of the worst unemployment rates in the country. Solving problems like these is a difficult and expensive business — no one doubts that. But if the evidence is that social conditions are a major influence on our health, and if the government signs a World Health Organisation document calling for a big reduction in inequality, surely they must initiate wide-ranging and radical action, involving everyone from the medical profession to the local authorities.

The cure for bad health can be found not at the operating table, but at the Cabinet table. This and future governments must have a co-ordinated health policy that will tackle effectively the main areas of concern.

It may seem an impossible dream, but if we could cut out smoking and drinking completely, at least a hundred and twenty-five thousand more of us could live to see the year 2000. Now isn't that worth working for?

PAST IMPERFECT, FUTURE CONDITIONAL

— *Margaret Macintosh* —

'Children of Scotland, it is a great thing to be a Scot and it is a great thing to be taught in our Scottish schools. We are providing better buildings, playing fields, gymnasia, playgrounds, pictures and music . . . you have inherited a great tradition; you must prove yourselves worthy of it.'
Sir William McKechnie
Secretary, Scottish Education Department, 1922-36

Sir William McKechnie's views were shared by most Scots. Most of us imbibed the belief that a Scottish education was the best in the world, if not with our mother's milk, at least with our third-of-a-pint delivered to us in its clanking crate each playtime.

This remarkable and rather innocent admiration for an education system which was firmly authoritarian and often cruelly harsh was embedded in two notions: its democratic nature and the breadth of the curriculum at the upper stages of secondary school. As to the latter, I wouldn't disagree. It has always seemed to me that there were indeed positive advantages in being able to maintain both science and arts subjects up the age of seventeen or eighteen while the English pattern of early specialisation was altogether too exclusive.

The much-lauded democratic features of the system, however, are more suspect. It is true, of course, that if you were clever, diligent, studious, favoured by your teachers and supported by your parents, you could make it to the top. This was the origin of the legendary lad o' pairts: the boy from humble background who through his own efforts and the patronage of the stern but kindly dominie attained university and eventually the top of his chosen profession. There are plenty of examples of these worthy fellows — Ramsay MacDonald, Sir Alexander Fleming and Sir James (or J. M.) Barrie.

And, on a more mundane level, there has been a steady trickle of boys and girls from modest backgrounds pushed and prodded through high school to gain Highers and entry to university and the professions.

This was always regarded as the pinnacle of achievement and the school curriculum has traditionally been geared to the academically able. For the rest, a good grounding in basic skills, a knowledge of the three Rs, leavened with a bit of history, geography and science, was regarded as a sound education equipping people for the world of work.

This proud tradition was a hierarchical, élitist system which allowed a select few to filter through while producing an obedient, modestly schooled workforce. The fact that a few always did get through fostered the conviction that it was egalitarian and kept alive the hopes of aspiring parents that their children would take advantage of this wonderful opportunity even if they themselves hadn't. So subtle was the system, so carefully set up and thoroughly taught and assimilated, that those who

111

Margaret Macintosh with some of her pupils – *BBC*

did not make it to the top — the vast majority — were usually convinced it was their own fault: they were stupid or lazy or both.

Sir William's grave admonition to the children of Scotland to 'prove themselves worthy' of the great tradition they had inherited encapsulated that attitude. This fine education which was generously being made available to Tom, Dick and Harry was something to be grateful for and certainly not something to be criticised or questioned. Children had to fit the system, not the other way round.

So long as there was work — and until the 1970s there had been — this arrangement seemed to serve our needs. People did not enjoy the experience but in their dour, Scottish, Calvinistic way they believed it was good for them.

Some people still hark back to the austere discipline of their own schooldays. 'It did not do us any harm' has a familiar ring. When things are not going well — and it is clear that they are not going well at present at many levels of society — the human reaction is to look backwards, to imagine that somehow things were better in the good old days. It is usually the same people who raise the cry 'back to the basics' who criticise

112

the comprehensive school.

In fact, however, in terms of exam passes, more people are leaving school with more qualifications than ever before. For example in 1965 more than two-thirds of school leavers had no SCE qualifications but by 1984 it was less than one-third. The level of qualification is also going up: in 1964–5 5 per cent of boys and 3 per cent of girls gained five or more Highers. By 1984 these figures had gone up to 11 per cent in each case.

Of course we can learn from the past but we cannot turn back the clock. In our schools as in society we are coping with very different problems from those of the 1950s or 1930s. Old answers won't solve these problems. We have to look forward and come up with new answers to meet the needs of people who are going to live most of their lives in the twenty-first century. In spite of efforts to change, Scottish education is lagging behind the changes that are taking place in society. It is out of step with the real world. Children see this with all the freshness of youth and many of them see the years spent in secondary school, especially the later years, as a waste of time. Frustration, boredom and alienation are the results.

The first day at school is a very important step for any child and its parents. The youngster does not know what to expect but parents hope that a good education will lead to qualifications and therefore a job. That is what we've been led to expect from an education. But is it enough, even if it does lead to a job?

'Hopefully she's happy at school; I think that's the best thing. If she's happy she'll get on.'

Perhaps this parent has glimpsed something else, something we too often overlook but which perhaps we should be giving more thought to.

Certainly children's happiness figures more prominently in nursery and primary education than at the later stages. The Primary Memorandum of 1965 transformed the early years of schooling and made them more child-centred. Now the rote learning and stern discipline leading to the qualifying exam are mercifully things of the past. In the 1980s the primary sector is more concerned with the needs of individual children, offering a greater variety of experience and a chance to develop at their own pace. Children get off to a good start.

It is the secondary school that parents and the general public are most concerned about and it is the secondary sector that is in crisis. The teachers' dispute of 1984–86 reflected the stress and difficulties which secondary teachers experience in their work. The job is not the same any more. Society is still expecting teachers to fulfil their traditional role of imparters of information and disciplinarians, preparing their pupils to pass their exams and turning out biddable, well-trained candidates to employers. But the reality is that many children reject this, and truancy increases as pupils move up through secondary school.

One person who recognises the way children's experience of school changes as they move from primary into secondary is Tayside's Director of Education, David Robertson:

'In a good primary school you have lots of activity, lots of enquiry,

Collaborative learning at Hilltrust Primary, Glasgow – *Glasgow Herald*

whereas in the secondary school there is more didactic teaching. The period between ages twelve and fifteen is when we can begin to lose pupils through the educational experience.'

And a pupil in Aberdeen has this to say:

'The teachers seem to prepare you as though you're going to get a job when you leave school and you're going to stay there until you retire. They don't seem to think that by chance somebody might be unemployed.'

'Preparing for jobs' has a hollow ring in an area like Possilpark in Glasgow. Eighty per cent of parents there are unemployed. And in any case, employers no longer regard paper qualifications as enough in themselves, as Bill Hughes, CBI education spokesman, makes clear:

'We're looking very much for personal skills. What we think is important today is good communication skills — that they can talk clearly, they can express themselves, they can make their point of view in an unconfused manner.'

Far too many young people regard their last year or two in school as a waste of time. Gow and Macpherson's wide survey of school leavers *Tell Them From Me* (1980) has some straight-talking comments from kids:

'I think the last year at school was not of any use because the teachers didn't bother about you because you were leaving school, so I played truant. I didn't like periods all broke up for different subjects. I think I would have been better off leaving school at fifteen.'

'Apart from the three Rs I thought school was a waste of time and did not cater for my needs, although some of the staff were helpful on a personal level.'

In *Future Shock* (1970) Alvin Toffler points out that 'mass education was the ingenious machine constructed by industrialism to produce the kind of adults it needed' and he suggests that even the structure of the school day is based on an industrial model. Children are the workforce, moving from one class to another, one job to another, at the ringing of the bell, whether the task is finished or not.

Being taught at St Margaret Mary's Secondary, Glasgow – *Glasgow Herald*

The handing on of knowledge and skills from teacher to taught, hierarchical structures, packaging of knowledge into separate subjects, rules and regulations, lack of choice and negotiation — all of these are patterned on a manufacturing model which is increasingly irrelevant. We are rapidly moving towards a less labour-intensive society thanks to the introduction of new technologies. Shorter working hours, job-sharing and early retirement are facts of life we shall have to get used to.

Whatever happens I think we can safely assume that work is not going to play such an important part in people's lives in the future. Maybe this is no bad thing; most of us would like some more leisure time. Over the centuries people have been burdened by a crippling load of work and that in itself has helped to prevent them from living the rich full life that is an implicit human goal. So some freedom from constant work is not necessarily an evil. What does it mean for schools though? Can we educate people in a different way so that their sense of self-worth and their feeling of identity is not so closely tied up with the job that they do or with how they perform in school?

Preparation for the world of work is still seen as the most important task of the school and yet it is only a small part of living and may well figure even less in the future.

I believe that the focus of the secondary school is wrong. Because of the demands of the universities for entrance qualifications and of employers for a yardstick to measure potential employees (even although they readily admit that they are looking for other things) we have lost sight of the real purpose of education, namely to enable people to realise their own potential, develop their rational qualities and have the means and the chance to shape and change their own lives for their good and for the general good of society. And while I agree that one's opportunity to achieve these things is severely restricted if one has little money, having a paid job does not automatically bring them about. Having a job is important but by making education serve that end we have failed people. Instead of holding fast to a vision of what really matters — our relationships with others, the quality of our friendships, our ability to be good parents, freedom to think for ourselves and to make choices, beauty, creativity, adventure, a sense of self-worth — we have lowered our sights and reduced education to an assembly line through which we process children with the ultimate goal of passing exams. What a travesty!

Training children to pass examinations never was a satisfactory form of education and it is even less appropriate now. Society has become immensely more complicated in the second half of the twentieth century. The family unit is no longer the stable institution it once was and the divorce rate has almost doubled in the last decade. The effect of television on attitudes is incalculable and consumerism and advertising have had a dramatic effect on values and aspirations. Unemployment and deprivation are not new phenomena but it could be argued that they are more intolerable in a society where materialism is blatant and encouraged. For the first time in history, too, we have a generation who have grown up in the shadow of weapons of such destructive power that the annihilation of life on this planet has to be seen as a distinct possibility.

And yet, in spite of all of this, in spite of the fact that our children are daily facing risks and coping with the problems of a complex and in many ways immoral society, we still put them through the same old process and watch them fall at the same hurdles we fell at. Passing examinations is what matters and if something cannot be examined and the answers written down on paper, it gets scant attention.

What makes matters worse is that many of the institutions which used to affect people's lives now have very little influence. In the view of Farquhar Macintosh, Rector of the Royal High School in Edinburgh and Chairman of the Scottish Examination Board:

Gluesniffers – *Scotsman Publications*

'No school operates in a vacuum. There are a host of factors outwith the school – decline in religion, break-up in family life, the breakdown in authority, certainly as that term has been understood in the recent past, the confusion about values. The net result is to alienate young people. The modern secondary school ought to be concentrating more of its time and resources on building up relationships in the school.'

Wester Hailes Education Centre in Edinburgh is one forward-looking school which has done just that — put the emphasis on relationships. One of the guidance teachers there, Sandy Peterson, says:

'Parents and society don't deliver to the school in the morning the same kind of kids that they did twenty years ago. They came to school then expecting to do what they were told and with no thought of questioning either discipline or what they were taught. That's changed.'

People are aware that everything is changing very fast and that the world is very different from the world we grew up in; and yet, somehow, there is an expectation that schools should still be able to cope. In the opinion of Julie Collis of the Scottish Parent Teacher Council:

'Society seems to expect an awful lot of everybody at the moment. We all expect everything to just sort of happen, but that doesn't happen. With the disappearance of the extended family I believe the schools could be at the centre of things, in community education and getting parents involved and accepting their responsibility.'

Parental attitudes reinforce the current system, as Farquhar Macintosh sees it:

'Parents everywhere wish the best for their children, and tend to see that in traditional academic terms, hence our exam-oriented curriculum with its emphasis on O-Grades and Highers. Admittedly a lot of our children do go on to university and higher education, but this sort of academic diet is not appropriate for the bulk of pupils throughout Scotland. Indeed I would go further: this sort of academic traditional curriculum is a factor in the disaffection and social alienation that is so manifest among young people today.'

Education, of course, has not been at a standstill over the past two decades. Far from it. We've had the much-disputed changeover to comprehensive schooling in the 1960s; the controversial raising of the school-leaving age to sixteen; investment in brand-new buildings (in some cases very poorly built); development of outdoor and environmental education; and latterly hardware for the new technology.

Schools have begun to edge into the computer age, but only so far as

Computing Department, Broughton High, Edinburgh – *Scotsman Publications*

limited funds will allow. Most schools have computer studies on the timetable and increasingly the computer is used as a vital tool in the teaching process. But lack of money still means that only the fortunate few have this privilege and there are, for example, business studies departments up and down the country where pupils are learning outdated skills on obsolete machines.

Some of the enthusiasm of the primary school is revived when pupils get the chance to go on field trips and outdoor educational excursions. Whey they leave school the outdoor experiences are the ones pupils remember long after they've forgotten nearly everything else they learned. And yet it is still often difficult to arrange such activities away from school, especially for older pupils, because the pressure to prepare for examinations is so great.

Most of these changes, however, are quite superficial, a mere tinkering with a system which remains fundamentally the same. In spite of the money which was spent on education in the 1970s the problems remained because of a failure to challenge the principles on which the whole structure rested.

What were these principles? Basically, that education is a process of fitting people into social roles. The hierarchical, authoritarian structure of Scottish schools where pupils learned to address teachers as Sir or Miss, to obey rules which were often unnecessary and arbitrary, where dialogue between teacher and student was discouraged, where all knowledge was assumed to lie with the teacher to be handed over to the passive learner — such a structure and system did nothing to develop an independent, creative and energetic people. The attitude was summed up by the teacher who reprimanded one of his bright scholars who had overstepped the mark, with the words: 'There is a gap between the rostrum and the benches, which *may* be bridged from the rostrum, but *never* from the benches.'

The hierarchy was evident too in the management structure, the autocratic rector, the powerful principal teachers and the rest. Until very recently few young or unpromoted teachers were able to contribute to school policy or development. Fortunately these attitudes are now going – but only slowly, and possibly too late.

Where education should have been providing people with an access to power over their own lives and over the circumstances in which they lived, it was doing the reverse. It was making them powerless, by discouraging spontaneous speech, by setting up hurdles for them to fall at, by teaching them to have low expectations and little self-esteem.

Recognition of the difficulties besetting schools in the 1970s led to the setting up of three committees who produced major reports. The Pack Report considered 'Truancy and Indiscipline in Schools' and had some very important things to say about the causes of these things. It tends to be remembered however, for its proposal of 'day units' for disruptive pupils — 'sin bins' as they came to be called.

The Munn Report on the curriculum of the third and fourth years of secondary education grasped the need to produce suitable courses for pupils of all ability levels. But while making a gesture in the direction of multi-disciplinary courses, it confirmed the subject as the basic unit of study, and emphasised breadth and balance in the curriculum. And the

Exam concentration, Broughton High, Edinburgh – *Scotsman Publications*

Dunning Report, 'Assessment for All', introduced the idea of the Standard Grade with its three levels and a promise of a certificate for everyone.

If teachers hoped the stagnating exam-bound system was to get the radical shake-up it needed through these reports, they were soon to be disappointed. Where the Munn Committee for instance had the opportunity for a complete re-think of the third- and fourth-year syllabus it failed to take it, so apart from advocating more skills-based courses for less-able pupils, it had little new to offer. It proposed that all pupils should keep a balanced range of subjects going right up to fourth year, but it failed to see that the balance which adults consider desirable may not motivate pupils.

Dunning could have got rid of exams and revolutionised the way we assess what pupils achieve in their school careers, but Standard Grade is only putting new names on old labels. Dunning saw what was needed, aimed for it, and missed. The Standard Grade won't motivate pupils any more than the futile pursuit of O-Grades, because once again the implicit message of the school will be that pupils doing Credit-level courses are more valuable and more worthy of teachers' time and attention than those doing Foundation courses.

The Head Teacher of Bankhead Academy in Aberdeen, David Eastwood, is even more sceptical of the Munn and Dunning proposals and thinks they completely missed the point:

'The Munn Report was on the whole the most philosophically inept report that has been published this century by the Scottish Education Department. It provides us with no basis for breaking the subject dominance which we have seen in secondary schools for so many years. We need to look at what's happening in the world outside, and there are things not bounded by subjects. We need to look far more closely at the whole approach of human beings to their environment and that means we need to teach much more integrated and thematic courses than we do at present. The areas exemplified by health education or technological studies show the sort of approach we need to adopt.

'The Standard Grade will only confirm the examination hold over the school curriculum. In spite of the argument that they would test the performance of youngsters against criteria, they will simply rank-order people; now when you embark on that strategy inevitably you tell half the population, "You are below average".'

Responsibility for the implementation of the report rests with the Scottish Education Department. But I suspect that senior officials at the SED seldom have any personal experience of the state system as either pupils or parents and don't understand the problems we are facing. The Scottish Office would not allow an interview with a serving official, but I spoke to the retired secretary of the SED, Angus Mitchell, who said:

'I agree that change is needed, and unless you get a fairly strong leadership from the centre I don't think it will happen as quickly as it needs to. It's got to be gradual, it's got to take account of the professionals in the field, and what resources you've got and all these things.

'The schools and the colleges can't move too fast ahead of public opinion. They have to take account of what their customers want and need, and society doesn't like rapid changes. Parliament would not sanction quick changes before the system is ready for it.'

But society is undergoing tremendously rapid change whether it likes it or not. Schools have to change more radically and more urgently than they are doing and I believe that Parliament will have to provide the resources to make the system ready for it.

While we fumble towards a solution we are in danger of losing a generation of young people.

We're not grasping the nettle of exams so they *continue* to dominate what goes on in schools, and people will go on learning to fail.

What's stopping us from finding a new, more flexible way forward to meet the needs of children instead of institutions?

Graduation from university is still regarded as the pinnacle of achievement. Our whole school system is geared to it and everything else takes second place. Because of their demands for entrance qualifications universities exert a disproportionate influence on the school curriculum.

So powerful is the system that those who don't make it at school are usually convinced it's their own fault. The fact that the system may be wrong doesn't occur to them. One man keen to change this is Dr Graham Hills, Principal of Strathclyde University:

'We could do what other countries do, which is to have a different form of entry to universities, essentially called Open Entry. It doesn't mean that everybody comes but that almost anybody who could benefit from university education will have a chance to start. So what you see there is not a high hurdle over which people have to jump but a step up which people are going to climb; you set as it were minimal performances and you say to students or intending students: "If you are good enough to go to the next stage then you are entitled to enter." That model of education is better than the one we have, which is a succession of hurdles where if you fail one you fail them all.

'By far the best method is for people to select themselves; only they know what's in their interest and in the end it will be a question of motivation. That's the most important characteristic a human being has, so I think we should be a bit relaxed about this; allow people to come and they must take the risk with their own lives and their own futures as to whether they can continue with the course or not.'

Can we dismantle the hurdles and replace them with steps? One attempt to do this is the Action Plan which, to be fair, is the brainchild of the SED. The Biotechnology Initiative at Possilpark in Glasgow is one example of these new courses.

The scheme has been prepared along the lines of the government's Technical and Vocational Education Initiative. It allows pupils to progress at their own rate, and in an area where school attendance is poor this course is having some success in motivating pupils in their final years.

The TVEI scheme running in many areas of England and currently being piloted in a few Scottish schools and which the government intends to 'replicate' in all areas, although with less resourcing than was given to the pilot schools, has much to commend it. Young people see the courses as relevant to the world beyond school.

Courses like this are not the whole answer because the emphasis is

Law Faculty Graduates, Edinburgh University, 1986 – *Colin J. Hall*

Practical Work, Smithycroft Secondary, Glasgow – *Glasgow Herald*

still on work and the skills required for work, but they do begin to break the mould of learning facts just in order to pass an exam. They help children to be self-confident and more responsible for their own learning. Why can't schools do more of this?

Sandy Peterson of Wester Hailes suggests: 'We need a certain amount of courage, a certain amount of risk-taking. For example, just to take one rule — most head teachers won't allow pupils to go out of school unaccompanied or unsupervised and yet the day after they're sixteen they're out in the world free to take all kinds of choices. A good exercise is to send a pupil, as I've done this morning, on a work-experience interview. He's gone on his own, he has to find an address, he has to ask for somebody to talk to, he then has to convince this employer to give him a three-week work experience. But officially, I've probably broken the rules.'

Someone else who broke the rules, working from a makeshift office he shared with a local taxi-rank, was Gordon Hamilton, a fifteen-year-old schoolboy. He single-handedly managed, wrote and edited *Eyecatcher*, an advertising free sheet.

Gordon's enterprise and initiative got him into trouble with his school when he took time out to attend to business, but he did not see the lack of qualifications as a possible disadvantage:

'I've got no qualifications at all. But I didn't really see it as important because I knew what I wanted to do. And I knew that I had the initiative to do it. I didn't see qualifications really as a major part of the business, because there's plenty people going out of school nowadays without qualifications and still getting a job and plenty with qualifications and not getting a job. I didn't see it as helping me.'

Most people now working in education did stay on at school, just as I did. The trouble is that those of us who benefit from the system then move back into it and keep it going, so we perpetuate an academically-biased type of schooling that is not educational in the true sense.

That apart, Scotland has always had an excellent well-trained teaching force and the quality of students coming into our colleges of education today is as high as ever. But I believe that after a couple of years' teaching their enthusiasm dwindles.

One person recently qualified and still enthusiastic is Marni Robertson, who teaches drama at Craigmount High in Edinburgh — obviously a committed teacher:

'There are many frustrations. Possibly the main one is just the amount of work you have to do, the amount of children you have in a week and the amount of time you have with them. I see something like four hundred children every week, and what can you achieve under those circumstances? No one is realising their potential. I'm not realising my potential as a teacher and the children are not realising theirs. It's rather sad, and very frustrating because there's a lot of ability.'

Marni uses real-life situations as the foundation of her teaching:

'What I'm trying to do here is encourage the children to think very seriously about the problems of a sixteen-year-old girl having an unwanted pregnancy. That would be a starting point. From there I would split the class into groups and they would take the parts of, say, the parent, the boyfriend, the doctor, and the girl herself, and they would act out a scene and through discussion would come to, hopefully, a better understanding of the problems.'

That's the kind of teaching that does prepare kids for life. But teachers of more traditional subjects entered the profession with different aims.

A group of teachers at Armadale Academy had this to say:

'Primarily I view my job teaching modern studies as one of getting as many pupils as possible through a terminal examination. But education should also be seen as covering the entire person, in as many aspects as possible; it should also cover a much greater range of pupil, not just those who can sit a formal academic exam.'

'Scottish education and teachers in general have been suffering from an exam-based system. The whole structure is based on the needs of the universities, which percolate down through the examination system and percolate into the classroom. The needs of the vast majority of children are in fact ignored in our modern Scottish education system.'

'All pupils will be assessed, once they leave school, in whatever setting they eventually end up in. Therefore we're failing as teachers if we don't assess the pupil, even if it means failing them.'

'It's a very alienating, very divisive system, drastically in need of reform. Unfortunatley, we don't have a curriculum in this country, we have assessment chemistry, assessment history, assessment geography, assessment maths. We don't have a real curriculum for folk, and we have to come to terms with that reality.'

'The pupils coming in from Primary Seven are so organised. They can do an awful lot more than you might think. We've incorporated this in our first-year course and let them do more for themselves, and they cope really well. If we just expect them to listen and then write down what

A field trip – planting trees – *Scotsman Publications*

we ask, we are turning them off.'

We need to encourage relationships of a different kind, both between pupils and between teachers and pupils. Traditionally competition has been encouraged — being top of the class, beating your neighbour, being better than the girls. When I challenge that, I usually get the reply: 'Life is competitive.' But is it? Many, many areas of our lives are far from competitive. On the contrary, they demand co-operation and collaboration. Family life, community life, the workplace, social groupings — these very important parts of our human existence are based on getting on well together. Indeed, competition can actually damage the most valuable, most worthwhile experiences of our lives.

Between pupils and teachers, an attitude of mutual trust and respect has to be built up over a period of time, with tolerance and patience on the part of the teacher to the 'childishness' of children. This is not easy to achieve when control and structured learning also have to be maintained. But it is certainly possible because many teachers, the best teachers, do achieve it.

For an outsiders's viewpoint of this relationship between teacher and pupil in Scotland's schools, I spoke to a teacher on exchange from Canada, Danny Coughlin:

'The biggest difference I've noticed so far is in the relationship between student and teacher. There doesn't seem to be that personal relationship as we would have — I'm just talking about my school in particular — between the teacher and the student.'

And can teachers learn from pupils? A boy at Drummond Community High found:

'In this school they've got good teachers and most of the subjects are really interesting and the teachers are sympathetic and most of them talk to you if you've got a problem. There are one or two teachers that I've had in previous years that aren't like that and they're not very good at explaining things.'

And from a girl at the same school:

'I think that some of the teachers teach something in quite a good interesting way. It depends what way their minds work in, and it just depends the age of the teacher, because if you've got a young teacher, his or her mind's more or less what your mind is.'

Yet another opinion:

'The younger ones are better, but. But the older ones are just strict and all that. Don't let you dae nothin'. Don't talk to you or nothin'. Just gie ye work and make you dae it.'

Tell Them from Me (1980) and its successor *The Best Years* (1984) should be required reading for all teachers, parents and policy-makers. Valuable educational research like this is constantly being done by universities and others, but much of it seems to end up gathering dust on library shelves. Certainly in my experience few teachers seem to be aware of it.

Sally Brown, Director of the Scottish Centre for Research in Education, discussed its uses and achievements:

'Very often research is expected to solve immediate practical problems and on the whole it isn't really well suited to that. Research is best suited to developing an understanding and to explaining why things are the way they are. It can identify the different courses of action that people can take in education and the implications of choosing one rather than another, but it really isn't well suited to making those choices for educators. Educators have to make decisions for themselves.'

And there's no lack of information to help them to decide. Recent reports offer a better way forward than Munn and Dunning. The 10–14 Report proposes child-centred education right into the secondary system; the Action Plan's modular courses cater for pupils and adults alike and break away from the pattern of 'grading' people according to performance

Margaret Macintosh and pupils planting a maple at Drummond Community School's new wildlife garden – *Scotsman Publications*

in a written exam, and Strathclyde's Under 5s Report outlines the region's commitment to pre-school education.

One way we are getting it right is by encouraging adults back into the classrooms. In increasing numbers they're returning to secondary schools and community education centres to take up the opportunities they missed or refused when they were younger. Jane Banks, an adult returner, has found this to be a good experience:

'When I think back I can't honestly remember ever being particularly happy at secondary — for lots of various reasons; but the over-riding feeling is that I couldn't wait to get away. It wasn't that I couldn't do it, but I was just frightened — not of all of the teachers, but frightened of a lot of them. If you didn't achieve then there had to be something wrong with you, you know. I did have difficulty with one or two subjects, in particular maths, and all that happened was the maths teacher that I had tended to leather . . . well, not leather, but you got the belt and I was always very frightened to go in. It was a vicious circle, because I made mistakes and I got the belt and the more I got the belt the mistakes compounded.

'Once I got the first Higher passes [as an adult student] and I realised they were good marks and I could do it, I got the confidence to see that there was maybe a bit more to life than actually having a job as such. With the atmosphere of being here, education suddenly wasn't just learning, it was exciting and I love it . . . really love it.'

And Jane Banks is going on to university this year. As she says, however, education isn't about 'just learning'.

Adults come to schools not only to pursue academic ambitions, but to use other facilities too — which more schools are making available to the community. And this is the way forward. With falling school rolls, we've a heaven-sent opportunity to open our doors to everyone to let people take part in a range of activities, from academic studies to recreational pursuits.

Not all schools can offer purpose-built leisure facilities, but many *could* provide the local community, young and old, with a more rounded, more relevant education – an enriching, life-enhancing experience, if only we could take down the barriers and stop thinking of school in narrow academic terms.

Removing the barriers means letting the kids out as well. Young people should begin early on to learn in an active way about the community they live in, how they can contribute to it and what their place is in it. Pupils from Deans Community High School in Livingston are conducting a survey allied to the Knightsridge Initiative, an officially-funded investigation into housing problems in the area. It's one of a choice of community activities open to pupils from third year upwards.

Many schools are doing things like this and seeing results in terms of increased interest and motivation; sadly, the more academic pupils rarely get these opportunities. However, instead of trying to evaluate the worth of such initiatives and giving them the support that's needed, people continue to hark back to more of the three Rs. Marni Robertson finds that suggestion naive:

'I don't think that the three Rs ever were sufficient, and today, when you consider the kinds of things that face teenagers, it's ludicrous to suggest that simply the three Rs are going to be enough. Obviously, children should be able to read and count and spell but there are many more things that we can be doing in school to help them and drama has a very important role to play. Education should be concerned with growing people, and we should concern ourselves with how they live their lives.'

David Robertson agrees: 'Every inspectorate report has said that too much time in Scotland is spent on the formal aspects of English and arithmetic and that the important way to teach these subjects is in context. This means that things like English and mathematics have to extend across the whole curriculum. Mathematics has to be taught by the business studies teacher. The social subjects teachers have to teach mathematics as well, in the context of their own subject, and English teachers have to develop much more language awareness and multi-cultural awareness.'

So the argument rumbles on — not enough time on the basics . . . too much time on the basics. Do other countries face the same questions, or have they followed different paths? In the opinion of Professor Nigel Grant of Glasgow University:

'Scottish Education was certainly ahead in the eighteenth and part of the nineteenth centuries. This is no longer so. We've been overtaken. I wouldn't think you can actually transplant the practices from one system to another – that's a bit like putting plants from acid soil into alkaline soil. But we can jolt our ideas of what's possible. This is the only country I know of where the planning of the curriculum of school policy for example goes in slices: one group looking at Secondary One and Two; other committees like Munn and Dunning reporting on Secondary Two to Four; another lot looking as Sixteen-plus. Now this, I think, is unique. Elsewhere it's taken for granted that you plan the whole system as one integral whole.'

How can we afford the changes that we need? Professor Grant says:

'We can't afford not to make them. We can't afford to run an educational system on the criteria of a chartered accountant. We are squandering or in danger of squandering the priceless source of human capital: a whole generation. At a rough guess, one of these nuclear submarines would pay for the entire higher education system in the UK for a year; a couple of them would do the trick quite nicely.'

It does seem that traditional Scottish education has failed most of the people it was meant to serve. I can't help thinking that the Scots have lost sight of their own culture and have found little to suit them in the academic, exam-oriented culture of the school. How long are we going to put up with this narrow view of education which classifies most of our young people as failures and destroys their ability to think for themselves?

Scottish people lack genuine self-confidence and are all too often inarticulate in a world where the ability to express ideas, argue a case, negotiate and persuade are becoming more and more important. The boorish, chauvinistic Scottish male and the burdened, docile Scottish female may be caricatures, but they are still around. Education must do more to help people to be in touch with and to express their feelings, regard themselves and others with respect and believe in their own abilities to achieve, to create and to be responsible for their own destinies.

David Eastwood says: 'It's a brave man who would predict into the future, but because society is changing, people will need to change, and we therefore need to prepare them to be adaptable. We need them to be self-confident as learners so they know what they can tackle, where they can find information and the sort of steps they can take to improve the quality of life for themselves. It will not be long before we have available to us a capacity for people to learn in their own homes in a way which has never been possible before. Yet we still insist on operating our schools system on the assumptions of the 1950s.'

We need to take a completely fresh view of the system. With a possibility of life-long learning, we don't have to insist on full-time schooling beyond the age of fourteen if this is not clearly benefiting people. We don't pay enough attention to emotional development, nor do we make allowance for different rates of maturation.

It should be possible to take a succession of short courses on a part-time basis alongside work or service in the community, and this might very well be a far more rewarding experience. Teachers and students together could plan a programme for each individual, and both adults and young people could dip in and out of the system, pursuing full-time education when they are ready for it, but learning in other ways when that is more appropriate.

An earlier end to compulsory full-time schooling is not the same as lowering the leaving age. I am arguing for a broader view of education, as a continuing process. Today's young children will be approaching adulthood in the year 2000. It is vital that they experience a more liberating education than their creatively-deprived and frequently inarticulate predecessors. We know they're getting off to a good start; we must build on this so that when they leave school they'll have the confidence and ability to meet the challenges of the twenty-first century.

If there's one thing we owe future generations of Scots, it's a constructive, relevant and fulfilling education.

MEDIA – WHOSE MESSAGE IS IT ANYWAY?

— *John Lloyd* —

We have always had media to bring us messages. Human societies have always depended on transmitting and receiving information: it is one definition of humanity.

The news came first to those who needed to know, carried from centres of power; between kings or chiefs; between merchants and their financiers. It was for the eyes of the élite only. The history of the media has been very largely one of spreading the word in ever-wider circles – from the élites to the masses; through the medieval town criers; through the first printing presses; through the first news sheets; to the eighteenth- and nineteenth-century newspapers, reflections of the political struggles of their days; and on to the creation of mass markets only a century ago, as reading skills took hold and state control loosened. Running through that history is the theme of *freedom* – freedom to publish; to argue; to oppose; a need born from the clash of religious and political principles, especially fierce in Scotland.

'The state,' said John Milton in his *Areopagitica* in the mid seventeenth century, 'shall be my governors but not my critics.'

John Lloyd – *BBC*

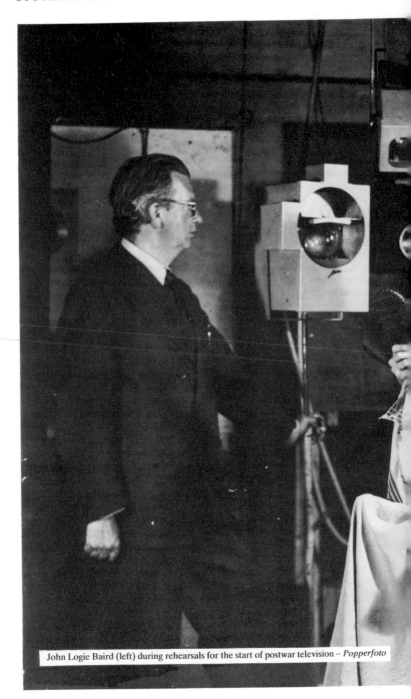

John Logie Baird (left) during rehearsals for the start of postwar television – *Popperfoto*

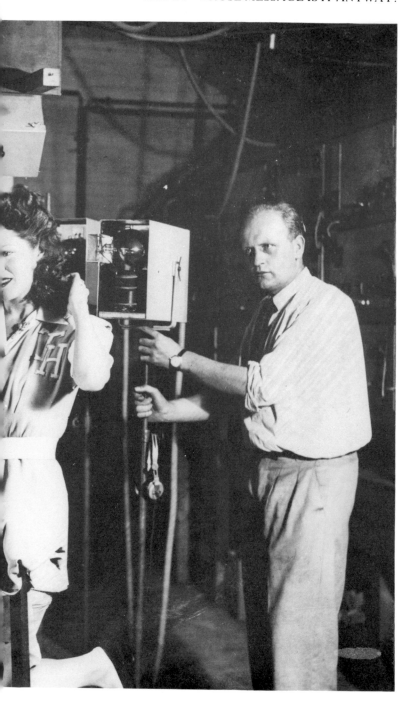

But what has today's press done with the freedom it has? What freedom has it? And what will new technology – and old money – do for press freedom?

How we communicate is a reflection of the development, the wealth and the political climate of our cultures; but so important have the *media* become in our own times that some believe they determine the way in which we view the world.

No one now seriously doubts that the media *do* shape our lives and experiences, and implant views in us about ourselves, our fellow citizens and our country.

But we are no longer sure that the ways in which they do so are always to our good. The media can do more than simply inform, enlighten and entertain – the functions they are *supposed* to perform in liberal societies like our own.

So what *will* the messages be which are carried into Scotland between now and the year 2000? How Scottish will the Scottish media be? How will they shape our ideas of what Scotland is, and what we are?

The future of the media in Scotland will only partly be in the hands of the Scots, though it may be no less so than at present. Scots have had an impact on the media out of all proportion to their numbers: John Logie Baird was the most famous, of course, with his huge contribution to the development of television. Fleet Street commonly has a number of Scots in editorial chairs and in other senior positions, while the BBC's most famous director general, John Reith was — and its most recent Alasdair Milne is — both Scotsmen.

But as these people have gone out into the world, so the world has gone into Scotland to own, if not usually to run, its newspapers and its radio and television stations. We have already a mixture of Scots culture and multinational capital – and we also have a mixture of multinational capital and Scots capital. That mixture can be a rich one, but there is a constant and reasonable alarm that the multinational side of the mix will swamp the national, because of the former's greater resources and greater pull over the attention of the mass of people. Schedule an episode of *Dallas* or *Dynasty* against the fine BBC dramatisation of Grassic Gibbon's *Scots Quair,* and see what comes out: we cannot afford to be over-pious about the dangers of multinationalism when people freely choose to watch its products.

Nor should we lie down before it, nor retreat into élitist disapproval. If Scots culture is to survive as a vital matter, it needs working at now as much as its past needs preserving or exhuming — more, since the past is beyond change while the present and future are in our hands. Gus Macdonald, new(ish) Director of Programmes for Scottish Television, put it like this:

'We've been battered by a very powerful culture — the English culture — for the last three to four hundred years, but we're still quite distinctively Scots. What I would hope to do is to play down that element of Scottish culture which was demoralised after the Clearances and after the Union — they went from demoralisation to Balmoralisation — and we were perhaps the only country in the world that turned its culture into a music-hall joke. So we've connived in a sense in being the Uncle Toms of the Western world, cavorting around for the amusement of our superiors. But there is a very strong indigenous culture here to which I am very committed in terms of traditional music, literature and song and so on, and which can be brought through and properly married with the more vivid modern forms to show that we have a future as well as a past.'

Can a highly-paid wholly modern TV executive who spent much of his career in England do for modern culture what the barefoot pibroch composers and monastic poets of the medieval period, the Enlightenment philosophers — to say nothing of Burns and Hogg and Scott (not much demoralisation evident in these, surely?) — did for their periods? Well, he will not do the same job, for sure. But he and people like him, whose art is in mediating between numberless strands of opinion, cultural ebbs and flows, current events and the rise and fall of personalities, can channel the surges which constitute modern culture, in Scotland as elsewhere.

The largest difference between now and the past is that culture will be created self-consciously — at least to some extent. Gus Macdonald talks of choosing between an old style of 'music-hall joke' and a new, 'more vivid, modern' style in a way which the shapers of culture could not do before. As we shall see, it is the most powerful of modern media — television — which can make and impose these choices.

Let's start, though, with the older form: newspapers. Scotland has had a lively newspaper culture for two centuries, as a look through the vaults of the *Glasgow Herald, The Scotsman,* the Dundee *Courier* and many other, more local papers will show you. It's vigorous still: indeed, Scotland is the only part, of the UK — with the possible exception of Northern Ireland — where a quite distinct newspaper culture exists, with upmarket and downmarket papers. They are not immune from competition from the London-produced national papers, of course, but the table below shows how successful the Scots papers have been in keeping the English at bay:

*Daily paper sales (Scotland)**

Sun	217,000
Daily Express	161,000
Daily Star	86,000
Daily Mail	30,000
Daily Mirror	18,400
Daily Telegraph	24,000
Guardian	14,700
Times	11,500
Today	9,000
Independent	9,000
Daily Record	757,000
Dundee Courier	125,000 (round Dundee)
Glasgow Herald	122,000 (round Glasgow)
Press and Journal	108,300 (round Aberdeen)
Scotsman	95,700 (round Edinburgh)

*Market Research Department, Scottish Daily Record and Sunday Mail (1986) Ltd.

But this dominance, while still firm, is threatened — by new technology. After a fierce battle, News International, owned by Rupert Murdoch, established a printing plant at Kinning Park, just off the M8 running through Glasgow. Editorial copy for the *Sun,* and other News International papers, is faxed up here; the papers are printed off and put on trucks on the motorway for distribution through Scotland and the north of England. Unlike the big, expensive plants which national newspapers used to have to run when they had editions printed in Scotland — as the *Daily Express* and the *Daily Mail* both had — this satellite plant allows low-cost 'local' production. Charles Wilson, a Glaswegian who now edits *The Times,* describes the changes:

'Many years ago the national papers served Scotland very well, because Glasgow was certainly the third if not the second major printing centre in the country. The *Daily Mail* was also printed in Edinburgh, and the Scottish reading public was then well served. But the economics of the 1950s to 1970s caused the close-down of the *Mail* and *Express.* The papers were then either served from Manchester or London, and I am afraid there was — and still is — a great deal of tokenism. *The Times* is currently printing in Glasgow, as is the *Sun.* We are gradually putting more and more Scottish content into the paper, certainly a lot more than there was even a few months ago. But it wouldn't be telling the truth to say that this is a paper with a strong Scottish flavour. It's really a London-based paper, as are all the nationals.'

Rupert Murdoch leaving Kinning Park, with escort – *Glasgow Herald*

Charles Wilson encapsulates both the opportunity and the threat for the Scottish press. The opportunity is to capitalise further on the inevitably London-based feel of the national papers (as the Scots press has done for decades) and to use new technology to extend their lead in their own market areas. Arnold Kemp, editor of the *Glasgow Herald* — in the happy position of seeing a steadily growing circulation — says:

'It would be hard to imagine that overseas-based papers would be able to penetrate the market, but London-based papers will continue to try to do so. I'm fairly confident we can resist that threat, because there is evidence of strong cultural resistance in Scotland to English titles. For example, when the *Record* went on strike earlier this year, people resisted replacing it with an English title. And similarly, the *Sun* since it opened printing in Scotland, has not managed to increase its sales significantly, we understand, because it hasn't made a similar investment in editorial content.'

Robert Maxwell – *Glasgow Herald*

All editors agree that editorial policy is decisively influenced by whether or not the proprietor is interventionist, and interventionism is now in vogue once more on Fleet Street. Harry Conroy, General Secretary of the National Union of Journalists, notes that the voice of Robert Maxwell, owner of the Mirror Group of newspapers (and of Scotland's *Daily Record* and *Sunday Mail*), is rarely muted in his Scots papers:

'There has been evidence of proprietorial interference in the editorials, in personal opinions and in the insistence that the *Daily Record* carry the same message as *The Mirror* when in fact it should be reflecting the voice of Scotland.'

And Charles Wilson admits that 'Rupert Murdoch runs the company [News International], without any question.'

Scotland's papers are largely 'foreign' (London or beyond) controlled. The *Record*, as we've seen, belongs to the Maxwell empire, whose ultimate holding company is in Lichtenstein. The *Glasgow Herald* is owned by Outram, now a subsidiary of Tiny Rowland's Lonrho group. *The Scotsman* and the *Press and Journal* are owned by Thomson Regional Newspapers — a subsidiary of the company founded by the Scots-Canadian Roy Thomson, who once owned Times Newspapers. By common consent, neither Lonrho nor the present Lord Thomson is an

'Tiny' Rowland – *Glasgow Herald*

intrusive owner. Says Charles Wilson, who edited three papers in the Lonrho group:

'I edited the *Evening Times* and the *Glasgow Herald,* then launched and edited *The Sunday Standard,* and I think I spoke to Tiny Rowland once. He rang me on some social matter. I had no pressure, no interference at all from the company, and the great advantage is the amount of financial backing there is for development.'

Arnold Kemp has worked for both Thomson (*Scotsman*) and Lonrho (*Herald*): 'The important thing is that papers should be allowed to have independent editorial content and judgements, and this has worked fairly well in Scotland. You could say that the proprietors ran them [*Scotsman* and *Herald*] as businesses and didn't interfere with the contents as long as they were doing a competent job and serving the interests of the community properly. In all these cases, the editor has very considerable freedom, and that's obviously very beneficial editorially.'

Once again we have both an opportunity and a threat. The opportunity is to use the access to large funds to develop and extend the newspapers in an atmosphere of some real editorial freedom which allows a diversity of views. The threat is that the piper, in the end, will call a harsher tune — as Maxwell and Murdoch already are doing — and that the Scots outposts of London paper empires will be told to toe a line which may be uncongenial. But in the end, the market is a restraint. If papers sell well proprietors tend to give editorial licence; it is most likely to be curtailed where losses are heavy.

The one indisputably Scots group is D. C. Thomson; it is also, by many definitions, the most successful publishing group operating in Scotland. D. C. Thomson publishes the *Courier and Advertiser,* one of the few daily papers in the UK still to have classified advertisements on its front page, yet still selling more copies daily than any other Scots-printed paper save only the all-conquering *Daily Record.* It also publishes the unique *Sunday Post,* read by some eighty per cent of the households in Scotland and consistently showing as the most popular newspaper in Britain. The group also publishes the *People's Friend,* which specialises in warm, couthy human-interest fiction and knitting patterns; and a range of brilliant comics, like *The Beano* and *The Dandy.* D. C. Thomson has resisted every trend and fad that has afflicted publishing elsewhere in the country; it has remained true to a vision of Scotland and of Scottishness which is full of stout-hearted straightforward lads and bonnie lasses. It has eschewed the coverage of sex, violence and most social problems for a resolute concentration on good news and conservative values (and this from a base in a city which has had the furthest-left Labour council in Scotland). It has never allowed its journalists to become unionised, in spite of a bitter campaign waged for unionisation by the National Union of Journalists (NUJ). It is a phenomenon, and one that likes to keep itself to itself. But popular? For sure. Alistair Clark, an Angus farmer, is a typical *Courier* reader:

'As a farmer I start reading it from the back. I read the agricultural adverts first and then I may turn to the farming and finance side of it,

D. C. Thomson's printing and despatch areas – *D. C. Thomson & Co.*

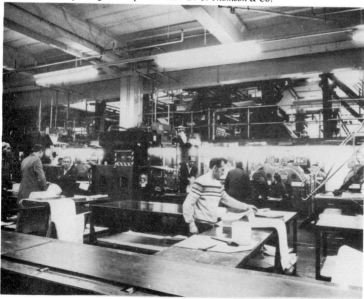

then on to the local news. Quite honestly the national coverage is the thing I read last, possibly because you get that sort of news on the radio anyhow. They cover things like the Women's Rural Institute very well, they cover the Young Farmers' Club, they seem to make a point of covering the local and social aspects of the community.'

Scott Smith, a Thomson writer and editor, gives his view of the D. C. Thomson appeal:

'Some people might think they're old-fashioned, and yet as far as the technology and printing are concerned they tend to leap out ahead of the field. We were setting material on film twenty years ago, Fleet Street is only doing it now. The unions were constantly trying to recruit Thomson personnel, but with very little success. Most of the people there were quite happy working without unions because they knew as far as getting a fair deal was concerned they would get it. I think D. C. Thomson must have a very good future because they're a fairly far-sighted company. Working in Scotland or based in Scotland they can take a detached view of London and they're a very independent company. They're beholden to no one and I'm sure they'll continue in that fashion.'

So there you have a modern, dynamic and entrepreneurial company which successfully markets a conservative view of Scots culture over in Dundee, while in Glasgow companies just as successful seek to market modernisation and cultural change. It would be a mistake — a common one — to see the first as 'essentially Scottish' while the second is seen as a foreign import. Scots culture has always been an open one, always been willing to import and to export. Its newspaper culture will reflect this in its future as well.

The possibility of an increased penetration by London-based journalism will depend on the market. When *The Times* and the *Sun,* and other papers who are likely to follow their example of establishing relatively cheap satellite printing plants in Scotland, begin to insert a good deal of Scottish editorial material and run genuine Scottish editions once more, then the domination the Scots-based papers presently have over the market will be threatened. That battle will not be long in coming.

Radio's been the neglected medium. It's had fewer feuds than television or newspapers and it appears to attract fewer of those who have to write their personalities and obsessions across the walls in huge characters. The very fact that it's treated like a water tap — turned on to flow, effortlessly, for as long as it's wanted — has meant it's taken for granted, heard as a background buzz while the listeners do something else — like drive, or work, or potter.

Yet it's very diverse, ranging from the BBC's World Service — paid for from the Foreign Office budget but still commanding a good deal of respect and attention worldwide as a relatively objective news service — through to local stations serving small communities. But it's real business, increasingly, is information and background entertainment. On a cold day last November, you might have turned on to Radio Clyde and heard this:

'. . . a couple of patience pills, I think, if you're heading that way. Coming in from Thornliebank on the M77, light traffic coming down and

Radio Clyde's 'Eye in the Sky' – *Radio Clyde*

joining on to the M8 motorway, but again on to the Kingston Bridge and you've got a slow congo line going across there. On the north side of the city, the M8 motorway coming in from the Edinburgh side, very very heavy traffic with a three-lane congo line stretching back from the Townhead interchange out towards the Cumbernauld on-ramp . . .'

That's Scotland's most popular independent radio station, and for a long time the only one in the UK that was making money. Clyde has done a remarkable job in combining information and pop with a bit of serious journalism and drama. The station's managing director, James Gordon, thinks radio will survive and flourish — but worries about quality in broadcasting:

'The future's bright — ninety per cent of the population listen to radio, whether BBC or independent, and I don't see that percentage dropping. Radio broadcasting costs a fraction of what TV spends, and I would have thought television programmes are under much greater threat than radio programmes. Radio really can operate on quite tiny budgets. I'd be particularly sorry if one saw a drop in the television standards by an erosion of income, wherever it might be. I hope that people will think twice before they alter the system of broadcasting too much.'

Scotland is rather well served by radio. It has its 'own' BBC — BBC Radio Scotland — which puts out twenty-five hours of original programming every day. It runs Gaelic radio — both through BBC Radio Highland and, right down to the closest focus on community, Radio nan Eilean, the station for the Western Isles, based on Stornoway. The spread

145

of community radio has been long mooted — but it's still a contentious topic, both as to how it will be funded and how it will be run. James Gordon wants an authority, like the Independent Broadcasting Authority or the much-battered BBC Board of Governors, to interpose itself between the government and community radios when licences are handed out or are up for review; while Pat Chalmers, Controller of BBC Scotland, questions where both the money and the enthusiasm are to be found:

'I don't believe they would actually provide the kind of service which we provide, which is a speech-based service — fundamentally oriented on news and current affairs. They would be radios with a local interest, but heavily sustained by disc music. So I would have thought there aren't too many people willing to take up that challenge. We certainly haven't been inundated in Scotland with people rushing to open radio stations in the more remote parts.'

Cable-laying in Glasgow – *Clyde Cablevision/Stewart Cunningham*

The future of radio will also contain decisions about whether or not Radios 1 and 2 — the mass-audience national channels — continue to be run by the BBC. And if they are to be hived off, what will be the fate of Radios 3 and 4, and of the regional radios, like Radio Scotland? For Pat Chalmers, radio in Scotland is about defining and describing and reporting on the country — not simply about filling the airwaves with sound:

'People do wish to be sustained by speech and by communication about Scotland, and that's what we do. We're increasingly trying to communicate in speech and not, as it were, filling up space with music.

Speech is what it's about.'

Radio for minorities, such as the relatively few Gaelic-speakers left in Scotland, is always controversial because it is often more expensive per head than mass radio. Pat Chalmers, a BBC man in his commitment to public-service broadcasting, falls back on that concept for defence of the service:

'Public-service broadcasting is not actually about majorities: it's the sum of minorities, and if public-service broadcasting cannot fund a service such as Gaelic — I'm not a Gaelic-speaker but I believe very much in its importance for the culture of Scotland — if you can't sustain these things, then naturally your culture begins to be dissipated, and I would find that very sad indeed.'

We see this again and again: the notion that the media, especially the broadcasting media, must play a role in the future, as they do now, in *protecting* Scottish culture by continuing to broadcast to minorities like the Gaelic-speakers, or by reflecting the country's traditional interests in output, or simply by insisting that much if not most material is originated by Scots in Scotland. Pat Chalmers is quite explicit about it:

'World media influences are constantly and increasingly undercutting a United Kingdom culture. I think, though, we're able to continue to defend and develop the Scottish culture. We're now beginning to use, increasingly, Scottish comedy. You don't have to be in Glasgow for five minutes to know that it's a very humorous city. We're beginning to export this kind of thing.'

Radio, with us for much of this century, is a familiar medium. The kind of defences which Pat Chalmers and his broadcasting colleagues describe are well known and, at the moment at least, command support. The taxpayers are willing to support Gaelic broadcasting, even if they don't listen to it themselves.

But the *new* broadcasting technologies, coming in under our feet or over our heads, are naturally less well understood — because they are recent arrivals, and because they have not yet been 'captured' by the BBC or the independent TV companies, and may never wholly be. They are thus seen as threats as much as opportunities, and they are held to be potentially more damaging than the established media for Scottish culture in the future.

Take cable: the transmission of a multi-variety of channels through broad-band networks based on cable, either using the existing British Telecom network or relying on a newly-laid fibre-optic network capable of carrying large numbers of new channels. And that's what cable will be able to offer: choice, in large measures.

Graham Duncan is managing director of Aberdeen Cable, which launched its service in May 1985 with *fifteen channels* on offer to its subscribers. In 1987, it offered twenty-five, including the four broadcast channels:

'Largely they're satellite-delivered services, specialised arts programming, movies, the blockbuster film of course, which everybody is really buying cable for at the end of the day. If you take a typical day's schedule of BBC or ITV, there's a bit of news, a bit of sport, a bit of general entertainment, some films and so on. What cable's all about, basically, is segmenting that. It takes the news, it takes sport, it takes the general entertainment and the films and it puts them on to individual channels.'

The cable operators are regulated by the Cable Authority. Set up under the 1984 Cable and Broadcasting Act, the authority has a similar function to the IBA. The Act regulates their operation, and broadcasting of indecent or other material is subject to the same laws as any other publication or broadcast. Graham Duncan believes that the future of cable is tremendously dynamic — but not just as a carrier of information and entertainment.

'Cable services have to establish their position, establish credibility in the marketplace — obviously get subscribers. But in maybe five years' time — perhaps longer in some cases, shorter in others — communications services will be developed and that may include such things as home banking and home shopping. Buying, booking and betting, basically, I suppose. And in the fullness of time it's not unreasonable to expect such things as video switching services, such as video libraries — so if you want to see a movie at seven o'clock at night, you press some buttons on a key-pad and lo and behold it comes up on your TV screen.'

Graham Duncan's vision — and the revealing throw-away remark that the blockbuster film is what 'everybody is really buying cable for at the end of the day' — conjures up a time when no one needs the BBC or independent TV companies any longer, and thus their efforts to defend Scots or any other culture will simply be by-passed by an audience which can exercise a huge choice.

But that's the pessimistic view — that the sum of the individual choices will add up to a massive vote for the latest blockbuster, and no one will choose community programming (however that is defined) or, for that matter, Jimmy Shand and his Band. Yet the experience of Sir Monty Finniston, Chairman of Clyde Cablevision — with some five thousand subscribers — has been that the *most* popular channel is that which provides a community service, even a community notice board. So again we have a dichotomy of view: again we can see that the technology can both encourage a local focus and open up a vista of international choice.

The problem for cable, though, is that it's terribly expensive to put into place. The vision of the wired society — where everyone, or most, have access to broad-band cable networks — is indefinitely postponed — and satellite broadcasting now appears a more likely competitor in the short term. Barry Fox, a magazine writer on TV matters, explains:

'The British government's dream about five years ago that the whole of the British Isles would one day be a giant wired society didn't happen — mainly because it costs a great deal of money to dig up a countryside. You can dig up cities reasonably cheaply, but Scotland, because you have a lot of space, is going to be very expensive to cable, so it's much more likely that satellites will be used for communication because there's no digging up when you have a satellite.'

It's satellite broadcasting where the interest is. Earlier this year the government awarded a franchise to a consortium of companies, led by Granada TV, whose aim is to offer three channels by 1990. Receiving the channels will require the purchase of a satellite dish, and the

Patrick Chalmers – *BBC*

consortium reckon they will attract 400,000 viewers in the first year. Some of the programmes will be paid for by advertising, some by subscription, and that means sets will have a decoder without which viewing the satellite programmes will be impossible.

You can readily see what this means. If it takes off, then people will switch away from the channels which are financed by a licence fee — that is, the BBC. Paying the licence fee — compulsory if you have a television — may seem less and less supportable. The BBC may be forced to compete in the same marketplace as the satellite broadcasters — that is, finance itself either by advertisements, or by subscriptions, or by both. This was foreshadowed by the Peacock Report on the future of broadcasting, published in 1986, and the choices will become acute by the early to mid 1990s. Rod Allen, London Weekend TV's resident satellite expert, believes satellites will come — but that they will bring great danger in their wake:

'The future of the licence fee is an entirely political matter and is entirely in the hands of politicians. The licence fee has always seemed to me an extremely good way of financing public-service broadcasting — but if you take the view, as the current government does, that broadcasting is not a cultural matter but a matter of trade, then clearly a compulsory

L/Sat telecommunications satellite – *Universal Pictorial Press*

tax is not the appropriate way to finance broadcasting. If you think broadcasting is a trade then the consumers should pay for it if they want it and have the opportunity not to pay for it if they don't, and that's entirely consistent with the current ideology of the government. I don't believe broadcasting is only a trade, it's an essential part of the cultural fabric of the country, and at least some part of it has to be funded in a non-commercial way. There has to be broadcasting in this country, there not simply at the whim of the marketplace and not simply dependent on the mass marketing that advertisers prefer. The only way that anybody has ever thought of to finance that kind of broadcasting is through a licence fee. That's not a popular or a fashionable view today, so it's quite possible that within ten years we will see the licence fee abolished and the BBC selling its wares either programme by programme or channel by channel to the public — and I think we'll be worse off for that.'

Broadcasters in Scotland, as well as elsewhere, are alive to the threat and hope to meet it. It raises all the questions — as Rod Allen says — of cultural protection with which they are familiar. William Brown, managing director of Scottish Television, says:

'We regard DBS (direct broadcasting by satellite) as a greater potential threat than cable. We're thinking ahead perhaps ten years, by which time we expect it to make inroads into our audience and perhaps into our income. It's also a challenge as well as a threat. It seems to me that there are two points that one ought to make about DBS. First of all there is the need for public-service broadcasting, and by that I mean what we and the BBC currently do. I think that will survive — but on two conditions: the first is that we are not regulated or legislated out of business, and that can easily happen. The second is that we — existing broadcasters — actually learn to use the new technology productively and efficiently. If we fulfil these two conditions we can meet the challenge of DBS for the foreseeable future.'

Gus Macdonald – *Scottish Television*

His colleague, Gus Macdonald, has a more mordant view of satellite and cable technologies: one which explictly reasserts the cultural place of the main TV stations. It is, essentially, a conservative view in that it prefers what is here to that which might come; but it is also a view which depends on a development of the present TV system in different directions than the free market would seem to dictate.

'One of the problems with satellite and cable is that it could so atomise human experience that people would have very little to share. Already, life is being privatised because the great collective experiences of work have been removed. People are left sitting in their houses watching Fiorentina playing Real Madrid at eleven o'clock in the morning, waiting to go to the broo. That's a dismal privatised culture that's growing up, and the battle for public-service broadcasting in Scotland will be a battle for national identity and may well revolve around questions of Scottish assemblies and so on.'

The Majestics, from the BBC Scotland series, *Tutti Frutti – BBC*

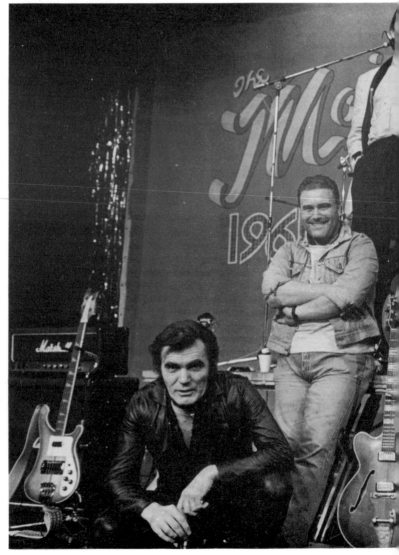

Gus Macdonald's vision is a radical one indeed — and perhaps slightly self-serving. He sees the main institutions of Scottish life decaying, or a good deal less powerful than they have been in the past, and sees the media, particularly television, as the replacement for the central cultural and political organising points of Scottish life. That's a very high claim indeed, but he makes it:

'Scotland can survive but it becomes much more problematic because Scottish capital has been grabbed and taken south. There is very little

Scottish control left in areas like manufacturing. The Scottish Labour movement, like the Labour movement in Britain, is in terminal decline and with that goes a lot of idealism and a lot of those elements of ethical socialism which helped make Scotland a bit special. The Scottish Church is still quite strong, the educational system still has its residual identity, we still have our football leagues — the importance of which is sometimes underestimated. But central to setting a cultural agenda for Scotland will be the media, particularly television.'

If this is in any sense true, and the media are either obliged, or take it upon themselves to act as a central cultural focus cum clearing house for the Scottish experience, then they clearly must be as independent as possible from ties to England. That is especially true of the BBC, which is controlled and run from London, and which gets most of its TV programmes from London. There seems little opposition to that state of affairs among the Scots public. But if the TV companies are to become more ambitious in their role within Scotland, then the tension between London and Glasgow will grow. Interestingly, Pat Chalmers recognises this tension — and is prepared to at least entertain the idea that it could be resolved by a greater independence of the limb from the body:

'We're five million people. There are many examples around Europe and elsewhere of populations of five million or so who run their own services. We raise something like eighty million pounds here in Scotland out of the licence system. If you were simply to say, "Could we live on that?" I think I could construct a formula by which we could. Things would be very different. We'd certainly co-produce an enormous amount with whatever came about in England — but yes, I could see that we would actually survive. Other countries have done it and I don't think the Scots are any less inventive.'

Pat Chalmers' ability to entertain that notion derives in part from his lower cost base in Glasgow compared to London — rent at £5-£6 a square foot against £25 is a large element in that — and from the conviction that he has, in some thirteen hundred staff, a base of professional expertise. He also assumes that there will be changes — any broadcaster who has not got that sense now is clearly not keeping abreast with the debate. The Peacock Committee's clear signal that the market must play a larger part in broadcasting is, of course, politically controversial. But few who interest themselves in broadcasting affairs expect that the Big Two — the BBC and the ITV stations — will simply continue to carve up the airwaves between them in a cosy duopoly for the foreseeable future. The success of Channel Four, relying on the work of independent producers working on short-term contracts, has put down a strong marker for the Big Two — and made the broadcasting unions fear for staffing and wage levels in an era of much greater competition. But if matters so fell out that the BBC were progressively split up, and forced to seeks its salvation in the marketplace — then Pat Chalmers, with some reservations, would be willing to find a new place as a cornerstone of a Scots 'national'. media:

'I would be quite interested in it, yes. A lot of people would be interested in it. There would be plusses and minuses, and many Scots would want to be assured that they weren't losing too much by such a thing. But I think there are plusses. And I suspect, in terms of the industry, and employment, there might be more plusses than minuses.'

This sense of national identity, and of identity of interest of broadcasters, is also true at Scottish Television. We have, of course, competition between the two: their news staffs regularly scan the ratings to see which of the Scottish news programmes gains the larger share of the audience — but at the same time, at the top, there is more and more talk of co-operation. Gus Macdonald, characteristically, goes the furthest in this:

'My view is that, because of the disadvantages Scotland has in television, I can take all the resources I've got for drama and just make some impact on the network with things like *Taggart* and *Take the High Road*. I've got nothing left for, say single plays. If BBC Scotland and Bill Bryden [BBC Scotland's head of drama] can make a dozen plays like the *Holy City*, then I celebrate that because people like Bryden are my mates. I might end up working for the BBC; they might end up working for me; we might end up working as freelances. It seems to me we are a community of interest. Any attempt to turn ITV against BBC is really divide and rule, and we shouldn't allow it; with our combined strength in supporting each other we might just about punch our weight in network television.'

Mark McManus, from the Scottish Television series *Taggart – Scottish Television*

This movement is, as Pat Chalmers and Gus Macdonald both stress, dependent at least in part on political developments. Yet, in the mid to late 1980s the political developments seem to favour a greater degree of Scots autonomy. An index of that has been the intense discussion around the so-called 'Doomsday' scenario — what would happen if the Conservatives again secured a government, with Scotland again showing a large, or even larger, majority for Labour and with a more substantial nationalist vote? For the moment, such theorising is no more than that. But the prominence it gained in 1986–87 showed that there is a feeling for devolution which is far from dead, and that the media have a certain interest in promoting it — even though it is also clear that, in many aspects, Scottish life, business and culture are less to be differentiated from England, or from any other advanced society, than they were, say, twenty years ago.

There is a harder-headed question, though: who is to pay for television if and when the present system — licence fee plus advertising for the independent channels — is to be dethroned, or is strained unendurably? The licence fee provided £81.4 million last year in Scotland. Scottish Television, and the smaller Grampian TV in Aberdeen, serving the Highlands, take £100 million between them, split two to one in favour of Scottish Television. That £100 million represents about forty per cent of the money spent on advertising in Scotland every year: and though it could rise, there will be some limits.

That's what the broadcasters are worried about. Cable — which presently attracts almost no advertising — and DBS, when it comes, will all want a share of the cake. It's possible that the BBC may be forced to privatise Radios 1 and 2 — and these, too, will be forced to look for advertising from the marketplace. That will mean a lot more competition — and competition is supposed to be good for consumers. Indeed, it can be exactly that, driving down the price of commodities and ensuring wide choice. But it isn't always and everywhere benign, and it could ultimately mean the creation of a media world worse, or at least no better, than the one we presently have. Rod Allen puts it this way:

'Although in the medium term it all looks terribly attractive as people jostle for viewers and so on, the outcome of a contest for viewers and revenue, in the purely commercial arena, is very very difficult to predict. Whoever's got the most financial muscle will win. If on the other hand you're interested in a wide range of programmes, it's very important to maintain a broad range and diversity of funding schemes, because that's how you have healthy rivalry for audiences without a damaging competition for a single source of revenue.'

We should not be too deterministic: the sheer spread of the uses of the media means for example that revenue for TV programme-makers doesn't have to come only from advertisers or from licence fees. More and more companies are interested in having in-house films produced for themselves. Malcolm McAllister, who runs the Glasgow production house SCOPE, makes an increasingly good living out of corporate video:

'What it means is making television for large institutions, for industry, for commerce and indeed small organisations; for people who want a video for, say, marketing purposes, particularly if they're marketing worldwide; for people who want videos for in-house training; and for organisations who have a problem in communication with their staff, particularly if they have a lot of offices throughout the world. There is a combination which allows us to make a programme which would be very similar to one you would make on the BBC.'

We should not forget, of course, that as well as having films made for large corporations, we can now make TV programmes for ourselves. Lightweight video cameras are now in the price range of the average family who want to take up video-recording as a hobby. Every family can now become its own soap opera, or situation comedy, or life-sized version of *Dallas*.

What we're seeing, then, is a series of developments, heavily dependent on technology, on finance, on political will and on popular taste, which together point to a multi-coloured future. We *will* get more concentration in media ownership, and that will mean more control from fewer centres. It will mean that a few very powerful individuals or corporations, or individuals acting through corporations, will be able to impose their will on what we see and read — that is, on our own view of our societies and of ourselves. Of course, there are all kinds of legislation governing this — ranging from the laws of libel or obscenity to the series of Acts governing broadcasting. But there is no legislation which prevents the owner of four UK national titles — Rupert Murdoch, with the *Sun*, the *News of the World*, *The Times* and *The Sunday Times* — from controlling his companies from New York. He is also wholly free to use these newspapers to attack the BBC — whose weakness or demise would be to the advantage of his extensive and growing interests in satellite television. Governments have greater control over the airwaves — which are a scarce resource — but where a government sees the market as holding the best solution to most of the thorny problems which beset broadcasting, as the present UK government does, then there is little defence in *legislation* against the break-up of the BBC.

Need this lead to a deterioration in what we are disposed to believe is the best media, certainly the best TV, in the world? Because the future seems to hold a demise or a very substantial dilution of the John Reith vision of a broadcasting service which would educate and uplift, is that any more than a recognition that tastes have changed, and that broadcasters would be élitist and irresponsible if they did not recognise the fact and come to terms with it?

The answer, we must hope — but we cannot be sure of it — must be no, it does not. The Channel Four 'experiment' has shown that it is possible to call into existence a host of innovative programme-makers with fresh ideas and new insights — and with a wide diversity of political viewpoint to set against the often rather bland neutrality enforced on the BBC and the ITV stations by the Broadcasting Act. Culture cannot, in the end, be protected as any more than a museum piece if it means little to citizens alive today, and if they themselves do no wish to carry the torch still. If Gaelic does not survive — to give an extreme example — there will patently be no need for Gaelic radio or television.

But most of life falls short of such an extreme. For the most part, the future of our media in Scotland depends on how far those who make it and those who view it are prepared to sustain newspapers and stations which are encouraged to define and explain the Scots national culture; how far such a culture, and such a sense of national identity, is seen as worth preserving. The issues of how such media are to be funded are of vital importance — but in the end, the availability of funds from any source is dependent on the willingness of the people to pay.

That depends, I think, on the development of an active relationship between the media and their audience — the kind of relationship at which a number of people whose views have been given above are hinting. There should be something of the old Reith formula left in the minds of most broadcasters: some sense that they are not paid merely to leave large numbers of people passive on the couch while a series of advertisements is wrapped in film or game shows. If a Scots media is to *deserve* survival, it must win its spurs on how far it can engage the active interest, whether it be the pleasurable or the angry interest, of people for whom it is an essential medium of definition and debate. That need not be done via some high-falutin series or documentary: it is as well done in entertainment, through a joke — in which, as Pat Chalmers remarked, we are rich — or through a local news item. It means that, in the future as in the present, the media will only benefit Scotland and the Scots if those producing the papers and the programmes have a community of interest with those they serve in understanding the world about them, and the world inside them.

WEALTH OR WASTELAND?

— *Tom McGrath* —

— What's this 2000 programme you're doing for television?
— It's about the future of the arts in Scotland.
— So what are you going to put up there? A blank screen?

Wealth or wasteland? The cutbacks of the past few years have led to a general feeling of insecurity among artists and arts administrators about the future of the arts in Scotland. At a time when major companies like Scottish Ballet have to drastically reduce their projected programmes because of chronic lack of funds, and Scottish Opera is reduced to making onstage pleas to its audiences for money, the future does not look bright. Yet the arts seem more alive now than they've ever been in modern Scotland.

The various efforts of funding bodies like the Scottish Arts Council, the district councils and private and business sponsorship — not to mention the initiatives of Scotland's artistic community itself — have led to a proliferation of arts activities throughout Scotland and a feeling of excitement about future developments.

In many different ways the arts are showing their worth. The integration of the arts as a necessary element in the overall social and economic strategies in places like Dundee and Glasgow, or in more rural areas like Dumfries and Galloway, indicates a growing acceptance of the arts as a necessary part of life rather than a rarefied extra. The achievement of our artists, in all fields of the arts, and the increasing international recognition they have earned, suggests that the arts also have a role to play in helping Scotland to relate to the rest of the world.

The arts are struggling to survive yet the arts are prospering. They could go forward from the here and now to play an important part in Scotland's future. Or they could go into decline. What is going to tip the balance?

There is no simple answer to that question. It depends on other social and political factors — the overall picture. What kind of Scotland is being planned for the future? Is it being planned at all? Are we simply going to muddle on into the future — allowing things to happen to us as they have happened in the past, or can we construct a model of what we want a future Scotland to be, and work towards it?

Who's we? Strip away the national myths and stereotypes and the identity of the modern Scot becomes a mystery to be unravelled and defined. This is where the arts, by their very nature an outlet for individual and social expression, have a crucial role to play.

The arts fulfil this role anyway. The difference lies in how conscious the rest of society is of this process and how much importance it is given. Though the arts have increased the number of people involved, as audience and participants, over the past twenty years, the fact is that barriers remain. Here I'm not speaking of the problem of relating the arts to the mass of the people. There have been inroads in that direction in recent years. The most urgent problem, as I see it, is to get the decision-makers, the opinion-moulders and educators to take the arts more seriously. I believe that the old world of industry and work ethic has gone for ever. Even a faith in technology rests on shaky foundations. If there is to be a positive strategy to give Scotland a viable future, then the arts must be given a central place.

So much for my assertions. How to approach putting across the arts? In what follows, I have largely concentrated on those areas of the arts of which I have a direct working experience in Scotland — theatre and the visual arts. At the same time I have not totally ignored the other art forms. Simply, there is so much happening in the arts in Scotland that I have had to narrow my focus in the hope that what can be found in detail in one art form might lead to generalisations which are valid for others.

I have also used an autobiographical approach. My justification for this is the strength and variety of my experience of the arts in Scotland and the fact that it has coincided with a major period of change in the relationship between the arts and society. At the same time, I have tried to reflect the various points of view existing in the arts in Scotland in the present day. But it's always good to tell a story.

*

Tom McGrath – *BBC*

My experience of the arts in Scotland began in the 1940s in Rutherglen, on the other side of the Clyde from Glasgow, when my parents took me regularly to the Ru'glen Rep to see a variety of theatrical fare. I remember being awestruck at the sight of Blind Pugh tapping his way across the stage in a production of *Treasure Island*. The power of the theatre impressed itself upon me.

Weekly visits to the Odeon cinema were also part of the cultural fare, as were musical evenings at home, with everything from Italian arias to Fats Waller jazz tunes on the programme. Those were the days before television when, as the cliché goes, folks made their own entertainment.

In the 1950s, my family moved to Glasgow where I got into the habit of going to hear Karl Rankl conduct the Scottish National Orchestra in the Saint Andrews Halls. There too I heard the big names of British jazz — Ted Heath, Ronnie Scott, John Dankworth. Protective measures by the musicians' union prevented American musicians performing in Britain. It was to take a few more years before I heard Louis Armstrong live at the Kelvin Hall, and the Stan Kenton Orchestra in Green's Playhouse (later the Apollo).

Now Saint Andrews Halls is a memory — it was destroyed by fire — the Apollo is shut down and the Kelvin Hall as a performance venue has been replaced by the massive Scottish Exhibition Centre. Accident and necessity have both played their part in making changes. Yet how basic have the changes been?

The Scottish National Orchestra has changed greatly since Karl Rankl's day, but it is the type of change that comes through growth and expansion. A major client of the Scottish Arts Council, the SNO is an important recording orchestra which continues to command large audiences wherever it performs. As for jazz, at the time of writing Glasgow is organising a major jazz festival which it is hoped will become an annual event. Though the Ru'glen Rep has long since disappeared, the Glasgow Citizens' Theatre Company plays to packed houses and international acclaim.

The underlying need for the arts and the response to them in terms of provision have not changed. What has changed is the level of ambition, the cultural sweep with which the arts are projected, the amount of money invested in them. In writing about the future of the arts in Scotland, I make no excuse for beginning with Glasgow.

Glasgow

A city which has suffered as much as any from the major collapse of traditional industries, it has struck back by asserting itself culturally. Now, with a Garden Festival pending in 1988, and a year of special status as European City of Culture in 1990, it has become a model situation, not just for Scotland but for the rest of the world to study. Art and culture, from having been viewed by the majority, and often by those in positions of power, as luxury items — the icing on the cake — in hard economic times begin to appear as a form of wealth.

Though Glasgow suffered for years from a bad reputation as a city of violence, those who lived in the city, or had become acquainted with it, knew differently. Yes, there had been the Billy Boy gangs and a hardman tradition in the hard-pressed segments of the population, but by and large the city was safe to walk in, and relax in, and the majority of the population were decent, friendly people with a quality of warmth and humour to them which was reassuring and attractive.

It was also a no-nonsense city which would not be easily fooled by artistic pretentiousness. Audiences at the Glasgow Empire enjoyed a fearsome reputation among visiting comedians, but, even in 'more arty' areas, such as painting and poetry, the strength of the local audience made for strength in the work.

It was possible to be 'pretentious' in Glasgow, however, and thank goodness for that. If people cannot dream and pretend a bit, chances are they can't develop creatively. The down-to-earth is a Scottish virtue, but things can become so embedded, they never grow. In the Sauchiehall Street cafés of the early 1960s (described so well by novelist Alasdair Gray in his book *Lanark*), Glasgow's Bohemian set gathered to talk of modern art and folk music and wag their beards over the latest piece of Italian artiness on show at the Cosmo cinema. The fashion then was poverty and unwashed intellectuality, but even so the seeds of enterprise were beginning to sprout.

I remember playing a small part in a film about the Scottish–German Centre, something that a budding director friend had landed as a job. In my scene all I had to do was walk, with a friend, to the door of the centre and ring the bell. The door opened and we walked inside. My co-star in the scene was none other than Tom Conti, who was then just finishing his training at the Royal Scottish Academy of Music and Drama. There was no doubt that the very presence of 'the Athenaeum' and the art school in the city created a pressure for an active cultural and artistic life. At the same time the juxtaposition of art and culture with the commercial life of the city gave things an exciting edge.

By the 1970s, however, regionalisation was under way. For better or worse we were going to have to think in terms of larger units of social organisation. It was apparent that cultural growth could no longer be left to find its own haphazard way, and art and culture in the city of Glasgow began to go public on a scale not seen before.

The key elements were co-operation between local authorities and national agencies, and a high degree of voluntary involvement from committed people who lived in the city. The Cosmo cinema became the Glasgow Film Theatre. Drawing support from everywhere it could, but primarily dependent on the Scottish Arts Council, Scottish Opera was established in the Theatre Royal. The Scottish Arts Council, which was then in the last phase of its pre-recession expansionism, established Third Eye Centre, an exhibition and performance space dedicated to the arts but with a populist approach in its location on a busy city street, and re-creating the café atmosphere of the previous decade.

There was a buzz to Scottish cultural life in the early 1970s. The MacRobert Centre in Stirling was new and active. The Eden Court complex in Inverness was just being established. Prior to Third Eye, the Fruit Market Gallery opened in Edinburgh.

Individual arts presenters such as Richard Demarco in Edinburgh were still highly active, though there were signs everywhere that increasingly art and cultural enterprise were being lifted away from private individuals

irl with catalogue at Burrell Collection – *Glasgow Herald*

into the public domain. Again I feel obliged to say: for better or for worse. There were many who felt that the new urge towards largeness was not an improvement, and smaller enterprise continued to exist or to come into existence even when the recession began to bite deep.

And bite deep it did. The mid 1970s ushered in a new era of insecurity in the arts which has not yet passed. Suddenly everyone was having to think about economies, belt tightening, even the prospect that their particular operation might suffer in 'the cuts'.

In this, of course, the people working in the arts were not alone. Every other area of public expenditure was under threat. I was director of Third Eye Centre at that time and I remember allowing the centre to be used as an outlet for a campaign in defence of an educational television service which was threatened with extinction. The campaign failed and the TV service went out of existence, putting several people out of jobs and leaving equipment abandoned and unused.

As the world began to collapse all around us it became clear that the arts would have an interventionist role to play, moving into gaps created by cutbacks and responding to sudden new needs. It was around this time that community arts began to take on a coherent form in Scotland. Despite everything, the arts continued to grow.

It was when I talked with regional and district officers and councillors, to try to interest them in sharing responsibility for Third Eye Centre with the Scottish Arts Council, that I first found out about the Burrell Collection. Then it seemed like a mysterious threat that lay in the basement of Kelvingrove Museum and Art Galleries, covered in cobwebs and going to wrack and ruin. There was no doubt that finding a home for the Burrell Collection was everyone's central aim. That they managed it is now history.

In its new home in the middle of a park in the south side of Glasgow, the Burrell Collection is now the major cultural draw in Scotland. In the context of thinking about the future of the arts in Scotland, it is a symbol of what can be done.

The Burrell does not exist in isolation but forms a centrepiece to an ongoing impetus in cultural and artistic activities in Glasgow, including the arts festival Mayfest, and, on a more directly commercial front, an emphasis on Glasgow style in fashion, pop music and film making.

The reputation of the architect, Charles Rennie Mackintosh, a child of Glasgow and a seminal influence on modern art, design and architecture internationally, has also been rescued from years of neglect and given its due status.

In the last two years a new bold breed of painters has emerged from Glasgow School of Art and established a strong position on the international art market. Art begins to appear not only as a form of wealth at home but also a way of relating abroad, something to export. But the success of the new Glasgow painters directly reflects the efforts made within Glasgow School of Art to attract good teachers and apply new thinking. Art rarely appears by accident. It has to be invested in and supported. You get out what you put in.

Edinburgh

The arts scene in Edinburgh is obviously dominated by the International Festival which is also a powerful factor in Scotland as a whole. The festival is international in its programming and drawing power and enjoys high cultural status. It puts Scotland on the world culture map and brings an international influence to bear which otherwise Scotland would not experience.

The festival is important to the city of Edinburgh because it is good for business. Once a year it fills the guest houses, crams the restaurants and makes every available hall in the city a desirable place to rent.

The Edinburgh Festival Fringe, which grew out of the official festival, enables new work to be originated and projected out to a wide potential audience. Other work which has been created in Scotland in the course of the year (e.g. new plays) can be presented in the festival to an international audience, including influential critics. The Edinburgh Festival, under the directorship of Frank Dunlop, has started to take more of an interest in presenting Scottish work. An example was the 1986 exhibition 'Scottish Art Today — Artists at Work', which was met with wide acclaim.

Wolfgang Fischer of the Fischer Gallery in London described it as 'a straightforward explosion of Celtic talent and Celtic energy, and it's really wonderful. But it's not really a surprise for me because I am Viennese-born, working in London as an art dealer for the last twenty years. I

Gordon Muir, Scottish Art Today, Edinburgh Festival, 1986 – *Sean Hudson*

Catalyst Performance Group – *Jan Stankiewicz*

have discovered that there is a straightforward connection between the Celtic energy and energies on the continent. I'd just like to remind you of Mackintosh from Glasgow, a great architect, who went to Vienna at the turn of the century and actually thought at one time to settle there . . . '

Clare Henry, art critic of the *Glasgow Herald,* is very optimistic for Scottish art in the future. 'In the last two or three years Scottish artists have had a lot of major exhibitions in North America, in Europe and in London, and they have been very well received. I'm very, very hopeful. They have all that artists require: the grounding of the skills, the good drawing that's taught here, the emotional fire in the belly that you need, and the guts and determination to go on. They're quite prepared for it. I think it's going to be great for Scotland.'

The Edinburgh Festival is a cultural asset which Scotland cannot afford to lose. When considering its future, the primary question — as with so many arts enterprises — is financial. Traditionally the festival is committed to presenting major musical events which are very costly affairs and grow more expensive by the year. The fear is that if the festival cannot afford to maintain its status in the music sphere, it may become less prestigious as a festival. On the other hand, international theatre presentations may show a way to the future.

In the early months of 1987 Frank Dunlop complained to the press that he was not receiving sufficient financial support from Edinburgh itself for the festival. The possibility of a Scotland without the Edinburgh Festival is in the realms of the unthinkable. The problem is continuing to afford it. The paradox is that the very existence of the festival is a creator of wealth.

For three to four weeks each year, Edinburgh is full of colour and events. Late-night venues and extended licensing hours keep the city buzzing well past midnight. Then, suddenly, the festival is over. The theatre groups, other visiting artists and most of their audience go away. The streets seem quiet. The people who work in Edinburgh's various art venues are exhausted. Yet life goes on, and the city must go on for the rest of the year.

Successive festivals have left their mark on the city. The Traverse Theatre and Richard Demarco Gallery are only two examples of organisations which draw much of their energy and significance from festival time. But Edinburgh's status as capital of Scotland, its intellectual and cultural history, the grandeur of its architecture, all of these give it a cultural assertiveness that is different from Glasgow's. With institutions such as the Royal Scottish Museum and the Museum of Modern Art, Edinburgh expresses a sense of national responsibility. Whether or not the rest of Scotland accepts such leadership from Edinburgh is another matter. There are those further north who see it as too anglicised. And Glasgow will not accept the lead from Edinburgh in anything. The general population of Edinburgh also seems unaffected by it all.

In the 1980s local authorities have taken strong initiatives in the arts in Edinburgh, giving them a much more central and active role in the scheme of things. They have established an Arts Outreach team, a writer-in-residence, an arts officer, and an annual festival, Spring Fling, which is intended specifically for the general Edinburgh population. All of this has led to widespread development of community arts but has also stimulated the conventional arts in general. If this trend were to continue into the future, the outcome would be a democratisation of the practice of the arts which could radically change both the content of the art produced and our overall view of culture.

Active involvement of local authorities in promotion of the arts is recent, however, and could be threatened by financial difficulties or political change. Much of the recent activity has been in response to severe unemployment. If fuller employment ever returns, there might be less interest in the arts as a substitute for work. The hope is, however, that the seeds sown now will continue to grow and that local authorities will also grow in confidence in their involvement with the arts and their appreciation of how much the arts have to offer to the community as a whole.

One teenager describes what her involvement in a Theatre Workshop drama group means to her: 'It brings out me, Jenny, the real Jenny that's inside me. Because I can come on stage and play my part and really let myself go. Really crazy and grotesque movements. But I know it's not just me, everybody else is doing it too. So I don't feel silly about it at all. It's really good fun, really good fun.'

Edinburgh and Glasgow! The closeness of these two contrasting and competing cities gives the central belt of Scotland a vitality which would be greatly weakened if either city went into decline. The competitiveness between them can sometimes be petty and unproductive, however, and there might be much to gain from more co-operation, not just between these two major cities but between them and the rest of the country.

When you work in the arts in Scotland, you have to be prepared to travel, and as you travel you get to know the complexity of the whole country, its potential and its problems.

Dundee

Even though you know it's there, it's a shock when you first appreciate that there is a whole other population living further up on the east coast, in Tayside Region.

Dundee, like Glasgow, has seen a collapse in its previous industrial base and is having to find new ways forward. Again the arts are seen as an essential part of the strategy. Dundee is a good place to study how the arts can work in co-operation with business and public initiatives. Public art works enhance and revitalise the environment. The work being done with video and computer technology in the college of art strikes an accord with the aims of the technology park. The new repertory theatre provides a varied programme which merges the conservatism of older theatregoers with the students' thirst for the new. A play about the city's past has been brought back several times. Each time it is shown, Dundee people fill the theatre. The Dundee Rep is helping the people of the place come to terms with their vanished past. At the same time, the very fact that they are going to the theatre could be the key to the future.

Good design is one of the factors which make the new repertory theatre a good place to visit during the day, but it is also a good place to eat, drink and relax. The arts do not exist in isolation but are seen as essential

They Fairly Mak Ye Work, Dundee Repertory Company – *Dundee Evening Telegraph*

in our approach to living, including in their scope everything from catering to town planning.

Within the art college, a training is given which co-ordinates hand with eye via different technologies ranging from pencil and paper to the latest computer. In textiles, jewellery, ceramics and graphics the students learn to be professionals with visual judgement, manual skills and, above all else, imaginative capability. With young Scottish designers in demand in other parts of the world, our artistic skills and creative resources begin to appear as primary assets.

Myer Lacome, principal of Duncan of Jordanstone College of Art, Dundee, believes it is wrong to concentrate on new high-tech industries whilst undervaluing the arts:

'If we look at the number of people who come to this country to see our theatre, our orchestras, our ballet, to read the books of our writers and poets, clearly, this is where we score. We seem to be a nation of idiosyncratic individuals. This is what is respected and admired throughout the rest of the world, and yet we're constantly trying to push out products related to science and technology when it's clear that we've already fallen so far behind and it is pointless to compete on those grounds. We should be building on our creative strengths.

'In everybody's makeup there is a desperate need for the arts. It isn't recognised perhaps in infancy, but later on, as people mature, they know there is more to life simply than earning their bread.'

There is a small airstrip in Dundee, with small planes taking off on regular flights both north and south, including London. There is something in their small scale and the brightness of their colours, their elegance of line, which gives a hint of at least one way towards a new style for Scotland.

Inverness

Go further north to Inverness and a new element enters the picture: the complexity of Scottish identity. It is present in any part of Scotland but becomes most marked once you traverse the divide between the north and the Lowlands. The people of the Highlands are *almost* a different people, and the great mass of land *almost* another country. Almost but not quite. Despite the differences between Highlands and Lowlands, there continues to be an allegiance to the idea of a Scottish identity held in common. Just exactly what this identity consists of is difficult to pin down.

Catherine Robins has been running the Eden Court Theatre in Inverness for two years. It is one of several major art venues established through Scottish Arts Council initiative in the early 1970s. The first problem she had to cope with was the fact of rural distances:

'We serve an area about the size of Wales and people will travel by ferry and coach and private transport, sometimes three or four hours, to come in here.'

Even within the north itself, she makes identity distinctions:

'Within the Highlands and Islands there are two areas. There's a divide in the type of people between east coast and west coast. There's also a big difference between the people who belong to the area and the people

The Crofting Act, Eden Court Theatre – *John Charity*

who have chosen to come and live in it.'

The Gaels, with their separate language and history of oppression, are a strong, if often silent part of 'the people who belong to the area', and an essential presence whenever one thinks of a Scottish identity. They have their own culture, traditions and sensibility which has expressed itself through poetry — as in the work of Sorley Maclean — but makes most immediate contact with the world beyond Gaeldom through music. Gaelic melodic lines — sad airs and rhythmic dance tunes — are an essential part of the atmosphere in the north where a new spirit of Scottish identity is being asserted. Now the old melodies of the islands are played on synthesisers as well as fiddles, the folk rhythms are merged with those of rock and jazz. Listening to some taped music in Eden Court Centre, I couldn't tell if the instrumental solo was being played on chamber pipes or soprano saxophone. But I did know, from the cadences of the melody and the very feel of the beat, that the music was what I would call Celtic.

The theatre show which Eden Court toured in late 1986 was produced to commemorate the passing of the Crofting Act 100 years before, and it was typical of Highland identity to get its bearings from the past. What was unusual about the show, however, was that the dramatic pictures it presented were of life in the north here and now.

One sketch used two languages, Gaelic and English. In it a psychiatrist pins various negative labels on the Gael, defining his identity. He is lazy, manic depressive, alcoholic, stupid, and so on. But the Gael, bound in a straightjacket, can take no more when it is suggested that he is sexually inhibited. This provides the energy for him to break free and start to establish a positive identity of his own.

Interestingly enough, the part of the Gael — a man with a bunnet — was played by a woman, the actress, singer and writer, Dolina MacLennan, herself a Gael. Catherine Robins, who directed *The Crofting Act,* is English. Others involved were Lowlanders. There may be a strong Celtic feel to the new sense of identity emerging in the north, but it is not necessarily exclusive to natural-born Highlanders.

As Catherine Robins puts it: 'This is the most dynamic area I have ever worked in. There is a tremendous spirit of growing confidence, of identity, of wanting to come back to live and work in this area, which is attracting a very lively bunch of people to come up here and join with the challenges. Some exciting developments are taking place, both in Gaelic culture and Highland culture generally. We're moving towards an explosion.'

What we have looked at so far is like a wedge cut out of Scotland to show different aspects of what the arts mean, and might mean, within the country as a whole. It is by no means the complete picture. In moving across the map from Edinburgh and Glasgow to Dundee, for example, we have ignored Stirling, Fife, Perth, St Andrews, and other places. The Arts in Fife group, which has been functioning for several years, servicing a rural area, is worthy of a study in itself. The Stirling Festival has its own qualities which make it more than just an adjunct to the Edinburgh Festival which it precedes. Anyone who has ever participated in the small arts festival in Pittenweem, on the Fife coast, will know the distinctive experiences which Scotland offers when the arts are linked to distinctive places. The MacRobert Centre, Stirling; Perth Repertory Theatre; the Byre Theatre, St Andrews; Pitlochry Festival Theatre; Aberdeen Art Gallery and Peacock Printmakers Workshop, Aberdeen, and many other venues and ventures, all combine to spread the impact and life of the arts in Scotland.

Moving down into the south of Scotland, the arts are not as well represented. Borderline Theatre Company has now been active in Ayrshire for several years and continues to grow, with new premises in the town of Ayr. As well as successfully servicing Ayrshire with a variety of theatre, the company also makes a strong, popular contribution to the national theatre scene. In Dumfries and Galloway a new arts association has just recently been formed and a strong arts initiative is getting under way.

In the far north, Caithness has long been impoverished in the arts. It is too far from any of the major cities, including Inverness, to be able to share in their cultural life, yet, until recently, has not had the resources to provide much in the way of arts facilities of its own. In all its vast expanse there is only one small arts centre. Yet the people of Caithness have not been slow to provide their own entertainment and it has been left to the amateurs — like the well-known Wick Players — to keep theatre going. One of Scotland's finest writers, the novelist Neil Gunn, came from Caithness and set most of his novels there. The area has a literary heritage which continues into the present. With Caithness becoming a focus for national attention because of the Dounreay enquiry into a proposed nuclear re-processing plant, there are signs that its writers, reflecting a sharpening of awareness in the area, are becoming more assertive.

Other communities, such as the people of Orkney, have made the arts an essential aspect of their identity. The novelist George Mackay Brown has, of course, become completely identified with the northern islands, and the composer, Sir Peter Maxwell Davies, has made Orkney his creative base over a number of years. Orkney's St Magnus Festival is an annual event which makes a strong contribution to mainland culture, particularly in contemporary music.

Many other rural areas have no arts provision at all and no way of raising money locally for what must seem like a luxury when other more basic matters — such as substandard housing — are in chronic need of attention. The gap between city and country in Scotland is a dangerous one. Over the past ten years touring theatre companies, mostly subsidised by the Scottish Arts Council, have been one of the main sources of contact with the far-flung communities and remote parts of Scotland. As well as taking entertainment and communication to such places, the theatre practitioners have had their own awareness changed by what they have seen and understood, and the people they have met on their tours. In keeping the country in touch with itself, the arts have an important role to play.

Supporting the Arts in Scotland: Subsidy and Sponsorship

That the arts should be subsidised at all is often questioned. If a thing is good, the assumption goes, then it should be able to pay its own way.

Scottish National Orchestra in the SNO Centre, Glasgow – *Joe Campbell*

In fact, the arts have always been subsidised one way or another throughout human history. Even when art is required for a religious ritual in an African village, special provisions have to be made both to feed the artists and to give them materials to work with. Great composers and artists worked usually for church or court. Also, down through the ages, rich benefactors have been the angels who made art possible. Either that, or the other traditional method for subsidising the arts would apply — the artists would starve. While this method could sometimes be successful with great novelists, poets, artists and other individual creators, it did not work well with opera companies or symphony orchestras. Some would say that it didn't ever work well, not even with individuals. The idea of the artist starving in a garret is a stereotype that creative artists still have to fight against. Many people think that artists should not earn at all. They are doing what they want to do and they should be grateful. Against this it is argued that the artistic labourer is worthy of his hire, but this is by no means unanimously accepted by the majority, whose view of arts subsidy has been for ever poisoned by the spectacle of two men who received a grant in the 1970s to walk around Britain with a pole on their heads. This happened, I hasten to add, in England.

In any Western society, of course, there are likely to be creative artists who are so successful that they don't need subsidy so much as secret trap doors through which they can escape the taxman. Such levels of success are rare in Scotland where there is not a big enough indigenous market to produce high levels of sales for books, and the like, and writers are at an initial disadvantage in relation to the cultural hoo-ha put out by other richer, more powerful nations when marketing their literary children. Many Scottish writers who have made large amounts of money have had to leave Scotland to do so. Often they have ended up writing films.

Many writers, artists and composers find Scotland a congenial country in which to pursue their art. It has a creative community, offers a variety of work situations and outlets for artists, and has at least a recent tradition of giving partial support to creative people so that they might continue with their work. This is a good system and it has often yielded good results. Writers subsidised by the Arts Council have gone on to write books which have both gained cultural recognition for Scotland and been best sellers. Film-makers backed by the Film Council have become very famous indeed. Playwrights working for subsidised theatres have produced works of important merit and, often, with wide popular appeal. The media have often benefited from developments which were first generated, nurtured and promoted within the field of the subsidised arts.

Most folk who work in the arts in Scotland know this phone number — 031-226-6051. It is the number of the Scottish Arts Council. Number 19 Charlotte Square, Edinburgh. Whether you're wanting to paint the roof of the chapel or walk around the country with a pole on your head, that's where you apply to get your dough. Of course you won't always get it. There are always more clients than there is money to go round. In the 1980s especially, things have been hard.

Supporting individual artists is only one small aspect of the Arts Council's function.

The Arts Council was set up after the war to give support to the

Don Giovanni, Scottish Opera – *Eric Thorburn*

development of major artistic endeavours. In Scotland it first developed in relation to classical music and opera, a history which continues to be reflected today in the way in which the Arts Council spends its money. But now it has departments to support all of the arts — drama, dance, literature and visual arts as well as music. If you call in at the Scottish Arts Council's information room you find an extraordinary array of arts events and initiatives on display, covering all of the arts, at every level, throughout the country.

The Scottish Arts Council received in 1986 close on fourteen million pounds, out of which it had to try to continue to maintain major enterprises such as Scottish Opera, Scottish Ballet and the Scottish National Orchestra, with contributions of £2,910,200, £1,148,200 and £1,250,500 respectively.*

Timothy Mason, director of the Scottish Arts Council, comments: 'If you are going to have an opera company, and an orchestra, and so on, you can't have them cheaply. They are extremely expensive because they employ a lot of people. The important factor for these companies is that we don't see them merely as Scottish national companies, we see them as Scottish touring companies — big ones, admittedly. And a lot of their cost is actually the cost of getting them around Scotland, so that you can see Scottish Ballet in Inverness, Scottish Opera in Aberdeen, you can see the SNO in those cities, and so on. That is expensive, but we believe it's very important that everyone in Scotland has a chance to share in the work of these companies.'

Timothy Mason has been director of the SAC since 1980 and has seen it through a most difficult time of economic recession in which government money has just not increased to match the ever-rising costs of the arts. At the time of writing, both Scottish Ballet and Scottish Opera have announced that they have severe financial problems. Can the Scottish Arts Council convince the government that it should increase its allocation of money to the arts in Scotland? Timothy Mason thinks it can:

'We've campaigned hard over the last forty years to increase the budget to what it is now, and I am sure we will continue to do that. It does depend on the political will — not just at central government but at local government level as well, and indeed on increasing support from the whole of the Scottish community.'

The arts represent a wealth to Scotland. We have a wealth of creative talent working in the land, and we have good buildings and resources for presenting the arts. The range of arts available to the public in Scotland in the course of a year is staggering. Though there continue to be barriers between the arts and the widest public, the actual attendance at art events is much greater than popular mythology would have us think. Ian Wooldridge, artistic director of the Royal Lyceum Theatre Company in Edinburgh, has this to say:

'The arts are incredibly cost-effective. They employ and they involve a lot of people. More people in this country go to see the performing arts than go to football matches.'

It sounds like an improbable statistic, but does become feasible if you consider it is all of the performing arts he is referring to — not just theatre

* Scottish Arts Council Annual Report 1985–86

— and take 'this country' to refer to Britain as a whole.

Ian Wooldridge's job at the Royal Lyceum is 'to fill this beautiful eight-hundred-seat Victorian theatre all the year round'.

But he has to do this and maintain high artistic standards. His aim is certainly to give people 'a good night out' but that should also involve, he feels, 'challenging their imaginations, challenging their ideas, challenging their perceptions of their world'.

Looking at the Royal Lyceum's auditorium, the challenge of filling it is certainly one worth taking on. It *is* a fine Victorian theatre and to ask if it will survive into the next century is to pose basic questions as to our sense of values as a society.

On what does that survival depend? Not just on attendance figures alone. Audiences are not generally aware that the money they have paid for their ticket really entitles them to only a portion of their seat. The real price of the seat is subsidised. It has to be. The costs of presenting theatre are now so high. Ian Woolridge complains that the arts in Scotland are 'grossly undersubsidised, compared with our European counterparts', and that 'we need more money from central government to enable us to carry on addressing that huge audience who participate in the performing arts'. Otherwise, theatres like the Royal Lyceum will become 'the bingo halls of the future'.

Responding to this, Timothy Mason comments: 'Certainly one doesn't get the feeling that there is a real political will in Britain to see the arts as a very important part of our life. There is a will to support the arts but not to raise that level of support. If you look across the Channel at what happened in France with the previous government, you can see the kind of impetus that a really dramatic development in the level of government funding for the arts can give. We are talking about relatively small sums of government expenditure anyway. I mean, the fourteen million pounds which the Scottish Arts Council gets to distribute would be a large sum if you and I received it as a cheque in the post, but in fact, in terms of central government expenditure, it's not large. And, if we saw, say, a twenty-five per cent increase in that, we could see a fifty per cent increase in activity.'

The magic word from the government in the past few years has been 'sponsorship', and almost every arts organisation worth its salt has had a go at finding business sponsorship to help fund activities. Timothy Mason refers to it as the 'white knight on a charger' expected to ride in and save the arts in distress. But, though sponsorship 'has been very valuable, it certainly has not provided the kind of relief that perhaps the government expected it would. In Scotland now we're getting about one and a quarter million pounds a year from sponsorship for the arts. Compare that to about thirty-eight million pounds which is being spent by central and local government in Scotland. The difficulty in Scotland is that the number of big sponsors available is small. There aren't a lot of large companies based in Scotland. So we've been encouraging arts organisations to look more locally — to local firms, local businesses and so on. But of course they are not extremely wealthy and can only contribute comparatively small amounts. Five hundred pounds, a thousand, fifteen hundred. Which does help. But it will take a long time before that kind of resource, at that kind of growth rate, will do anything

Ane Satyre of the Thrie Estaites, Scottish Theatre Company 1984 – *Sean Hudson*

to relieve central and local government from their responsibility to provide core funding for the arts.'

Even so, there can be no doubt that private sponsorship has been a boost to arts organisations just at the time when it was most needed. Graham Vick of Scottsh Opera goes so far as to say that 'without private sponsorship the nature of opera in Scotland would change completely. There would be a lot less. The general artistic climate in Britain, let alone Scotland, is becoming more and more reliant on private sponsorship.'

Graham Vick's daring productions have given Scottish Opera's output artistic edge in recent years. There is no doubt that his output has done much to subdue criticisms from other performing arts organisations who have always tended to complain about the funding money consumed by opera. Now Graham Vick is leaving Scottish Opera just at a point when his innovations have been justified by audience support. The tendency, he feels, is towards conservatism in artistic output and this is directly related to the increased reliance on private sponsorship:

'Not surprisingly, the people who tend to give money — commercial companies, corporations, insurance companies, banks, whatever — understandably want something out of it in return. It isn't pure altruism. They want a certain kudos, a certain respectability, and the danger is that it will move the artistic life more and more into a middle-of-the-road, safe world where risks can't be taken.'

The Scottish Arts Council receives its funds from the Arts Council of Great Britain, based in London. One possible way forward would be to devolve the Scottish Arts Council so that it is the responsibility of the

'We've talked about it very often here. The Scottish Arts Council is part of the Arts Council of Great Britain. Together with the Welsh Arts Council, we receive a percentage share of funds from the Arts Council of Great Britain. Once we've got our money, we are, to all intents and purposes, independent in the way we wish to spend it. But one of the difficulties we find is that arguing a particularly Scottish case in the British context is not easy. Certainly the Scottish Arts Council has felt in the past that it would like to be devolved to the Scottish Office, and receive its government funding in that way. The main advantage in that is to be part of a much wider policy for arts development in Scotland across a whole range of organisations — the galleries, museums, film council — and to feel part of that, rather than feeling a little on the edge of ministerial thinking in Scotland for arts development. That would put the arts much more in the centre of a whole range of other policy development, like education and so on, which is important.'

John Myerscough has been responsible for important studies of arts funding in the United Kingdom and in Europe, on behalf of the Policy Studies Institute. He cautions that higher levels of expenditure on the arts in Europe cannot be directly compared with what is spent here, but does say: 'One does get a distinct impression, across the whole of continental Europe, that the arts hold a firmer position in the public scale of values than they appear to in this country. You commonly feel when you talk to arts administrators in Britain — even in Scotland — that they live in a perpetual state of anxiety and nervous apprehension about the continuity and security of their existence, that they might not be there next year. It's not true — they will be there next year — but

Young artist at Burrell Collection, Glasgow – *Glasgow Herald*

you never get that feeling on continental Europe.'

It is likely that the Arts Council and public subsidy will still be a feature of the arts in Scotland in the year 2000, but unless the present financial strain is somehow eased it is possible that there could be a catastrophe with regard to at least one of our major artistic organisations. This would not only be disastrous to the organisation concerned but would have a strong negative impact on life in Scotland as a whole.

Individual Artists and Artistic Innovation

Over the past twenty years creative artists of all kinds have been well integrated into mainstream Scottish life. Beginning in the 1970s efforts were made — mostly by the Scottish Arts Council — to 'place' artists in contexts where their particular skills and insights could be of direct social use. Artists now work in the community, are attached to educational organisations, operate as animateurs to entire cities, and so on. Utilising various Arts Council support schemes, writers are able to read their work in schools (an activity which had to be curtailed during recent disputes over teachers' pay) and travel the country to give readings. Book fairs, dance workshops, talks and exhibitions, all of these help artists to make contact with people in the world at large. To a large extent the image of the artist as someone who inhabits an isolated ivory tower has been replaced in Scotland by a practical engagement between artist and society.

Poets such as Edwin Morgan exemplify the type of creator who achieves an international standard in his work yet is known and understood throughout his native land. The Glasgow-born composer, Edward McGuire, though he knows all the subtleties of modern music, has this to say about himself:

'I act in the community. I play with the Whistlebinkies folk group, which gets me out to all sorts of corners of Scotland. This effectively breaks the composer as an isolated individual. I think that's essential: to write good music you've got to know what society's up to — to know what they're struggling about, what the latest fight is about. You've got to reflect that in music.

'More and more these days there's a crossover between my popular work with the Whistlebinkies, in folk music, and my "art music", so called, and I would like to give the impression that there's beacons within my composed music that can attract people into the middle of it. When they're in the midst of their musical experience, they can be taken further and explore new languages and new sounds that I might conjure up for them.'

New languages, new sounds. We cannot assess the value of artistic innovation. Today's innovations often become a standard part of the vocabulary of tomorrow's popular music. But, beyond that, the discoveries made by artists in their works are the products of deeper levels of brain activity than ordinary reason. They are ahead of their times and, even when they are not clearly understood, they can stimulate others. This level of work deserves to be supported in the same way as scientific research. McGuire comments:

'Basically the music that I'm writing is not a commodity. It is a reflective type of music, it's music that will stimulate further thought about emotions

Phil McCall as Argan, with Cherubs in
The Hypochondriak, Royal Lyceum Theatre Company
– David Liddle

and social behaviour and what's going on in the world today. It's music that people should definitely think about and not just let wash over them. Though there is an aspect to music, it's got to be first of all attractive in a sense to make people's minds open to the experience. Modern music shouldn't be ugly because then it creates an immediate barrier to anyone who listens.'

Unfortunately, in the course of the recession, the Scottish Arts Council has withdrawn some of the support it had previously given to new music. It is now much more difficult, for example, for anyone to commission a composer like McGuire. Whereas in the 1970s composers were given a full grant from the Arts Council to enable them to buy time to create a new piece of music, now the person doing the commissioning must find a percentage of the fee. The violist James Durrant, who frequently performs McGuire's work in public, stresses that the amounts of money involved can be substantial:

'If you're commissioning a large work for three or four thousand pounds, it means that the player is responsible for finding perhaps over a thousand pounds from his own resources, or writing lots of letters to try to get sponsorship. This is an area which worries me, because composers have a tough enough time as it is. And this just makes it less likely that players will commission new works.'

As a playwright I noticed that coincident with the recession was the development of an extreme conservatism in the programming of our theatres. Fewer theatres were interested in commissioning new plays. Perhaps it was simply that with money so tight they could not run the risk of failure which a new work always involves. But it seemed to me to lie deeper than that. The 1980s have shown an obsession with the past, the classical, the tried and tested, which is perhaps a need to be comforted. It can also create — or aggravate — a sense of inferiority. If all the great work was done long ago — and usually in other countries — where does that leave us?

Hector MacMillan's successful *Hypochondriak* — a Scots version of Molière's *Le Malade imaginaire* — is a case in point. But it had a host of positive factors in its favour, such as the exuberant production created by co-directors John Matthews and Gerry Mulgrew. In talents like theirs lies hope for the future, especially Gerry's sense of commitment:

'There's no tradition of theatre in Scotland, so why not make one? It's a great opportunity to create something which is unique, a Scottish theatre that could be recognised the world over. I see this as a beginning, if the actors and directors and people who care take responsibility for making it happen.'

Looking into the future, I hope I can see a Scotland which takes pride in its promotion of the new. That is, at least, an identity worth striving for. Perhaps the year 2000 will produce a few commissions. If we ever get there, we'll be needing to celebrate.

*

My arts manifesto for the future is as follows:

1. The arts to be used as a central resource in Scotland — a form of national wealth which helps the whole country to keep in touch with itself and maintains its self-respect.

2. People of exceptional artistic abilities to be given high social status whether or not their work is seen to be directly socially useful.

3. The arts to be given a central position in education, allowing for a much greater interplay than hitherto between 'artistic' thinking and other disciplines.

4. Scotland to pursue a future based on its creative and design prowess rather than trying to compete in the technological stakes.

5. Scotland to use its achievements in the arts as a point of active contact with the rest of the world. Maximum attention to be paid to the promotion and marketing of Scottish arts abroad.

6. The development of the arts at a community level to be taken much further so that the arts become as familiar a part of social and individual activity as sport.

7. Scotland's pride in its achievements as an artistic nation to be extended to cover the basic quality of life with regard to architecture, town planning and environment.

8. An emphasis on modernity in the arts, even if at the expense of the classical.

9. Imagination to be regarded as quite as important as analytical reason and salesmanship.

10. Art to be regarded as central to the development of the self-expressive and creative potential of every individual.

Utopian? I hope not. I think it's realistic. If all the points above were to be implemented, Scotland would be moving in a positive direction — creative rather than reactive. Don't tell me that we can't afford it. We can't afford not to.

Rev Stewart Lamont – *David Richardson*

THE BURNT-OUT BUSH

— *Stewart Lamont* —

Genesis. The moment of conception deep inside a woman's body when two particles collide. Fusion and fission occur, following the chemical choreography of DNA. Cells multiply and produce the mystery — or should it be the miracle? — of life.

We can reduce the human embryo to a recipe book of the laws of chemistry and physics. Science has split its atoms of knowledge into seemingly watertight compartments — disciplines like biochemistry, mathematics or zoology — but when we add up the sum of human knowledge there is more than the parts. A human baby is composed of millions of cells which multiply in accordance with a coded message contained in its original single cell. Alternatively, we can say that the baby is composed mostly of water — which is chemically correct — but few would pretend it is the whole story. The invisible 'spirit' remains a profound mystery to scientist and theologian alike. Atheists deny it exists at all except as an abstract idea with no meaning in reality, but even they cannot deny that there is something essentially different between the ovum which rolled down its mother's fallopian tube and the bawling infant which emerges at the parting of the waters.

If the science textbooks cannot capture the paradox at the heart of human life, poetry and parable reach closer. 'And the spirit of God hovered over the surface of the waters . . .' It is as poetry and parable that the book of Genesis ought to be seen and not as history or science textbook. Its view of humanity as part of the created order and unspoiled by self-awareness is another way of saying that humanity is shaped and influenced by the environment in which it lives and moves and has its being. It evolved from the seas to the land, from amphibian to mammal and from monkey to man. The challenge which Darwin's *Theory of Evolution* posed to religion last century resulted in a costly battle which has left its scars on the intellectual respectability of religion. Determined to prove that they were not descended from monkeys, churchmen hurled themselves over the cliff of reason like demon-possessed swine impelled by their pride and ignorance.

Nowadays, a large number of Church of Scotland ministers, to my personal knowledge, do not believe the Genesis story as literally true, nor do they believe in the Virgin Birth as an historical fact. They tend not to air these views, least the old controversies burst into flame again.

But one of the positive things to come out of the battles between science and religion in the nineteenth century is that neither has a monopoly on truth or on beauty. The biblical account of Creation in Genesis is poetically true, but not the whole truth. Science has beauty in its awesome account of a single cell multiplying into a complex embryo and ultimately a human being. Although the scientists can dissect this complex organism, they cannot put Humpty Dumpty or Homo sapiens together again. The whole is greater than the sum of the parts. Nor can they explain why suffering and love seem inextricably bound together.

189

It's at this point that the logic of science ends and the mystery of faith begins.

Although the logical positivists may argue that religious statements have no empirical meaning, not everything can be verified in this way. If we take a strictly materialist view of life then the haunting and melancholy first movement of Elgar's *Cello Concerto* is cat gut being scraped with horse hair, or the stirring echoes of the *Trumpet Voluntary* is wind whistling down a funnel.

My thesis is that there is another, non-material dimension to life, but that fewer and fewer people are now aware of it, because of a spiritual crisis in the Western world of which the decline of institutional religion is but a symptom.

The century that has passed since those battles between faith and reason, between mysticism and materialism, has produced a new synthesis which enables the theologian once again to talk about the ghost in the machine. Matter is now thought of as energy and the laws which govern the old atomic billiard balls have been replaced by the gospel of probability.

That does not mean the model of a godless machine has been replaced by a diffuse anarchy, a flush of entropy in which events run chaotically out of control. It was Einstein, the founder of modern physics, who said, 'God does not play dice with the cosmos.'

Darwin's theory of evolution is only partially able to explain the facts. Waterbound reptile forms have been shown to have developed the techniques and physical attributes they would need for survival on land

Adam and Eve in the Garden of Eden, by Rubens and Jan Brueghel – *BBC Hulton Picture Library*

aeons before they needed to use them. Similar proof lies in the knee of the camel. (The calluses which camels have developed on their knees in order to kneel, resting, on rough ground, were acquired after generations of camels had developed them in life, and were encoded into the genetic make-up so that baby camels are now born with the calluses already on their knees.)

So if Darwin doesn't have the whole truth neither does Mr Noah. Self-awareness for humanity means no more Garden of Eden innocence but it also means the ability to create new species. It is a two-way influence. Man influences his environment for good or ill, and in its turn the created world shapes and influences humanity.

The embryo of religion in Scotland is the standing stones at Callanish in Lewis — a kind of neolithic cathedral built by prehistoric peoples more than four thousand years ago to appease the forces which shaped their lives and, intriguingly, built in a cruciform shape. 'The fear of the Lord,' said the psalmist, 'is the beginning of wisdom.' Whether or not it was fear that caused these prehistoric people to sacrifice there, undoubtedly in their lives was a profound sense of the numinous, the mystical, the transcendent. The standing stones remain as a monument to the religion of the ancients, linking them in harmony with the earth and the stars.

When Christianity came to Scottish shores it travelled east across the Irish Sea to the bleak remoteness of Iona and Whithorn, the places where Columba and Ninian started their churches. As it spread through Scotland in the Dark Ages, Scots Christianity remained ascetic and rugged. Behind the wind and the weather was an equally powerful dominant God whose

Standing stones at Callanish, Isle of Lewis – *British Tourist Authority*

temples dominated the landscape as far north as the Norse territory of Orkney. But by the medieval period the ecclesiastical capital had settled in the eastern extremity in St Andrews. The tower of St Rule's monastery church affords an angel's-eye view of the cathedral begun in 1178 and consecrated in 1316 with King Robert the Bruce attending. It was the centre of life in the medieval town, fulfilling the role of cinema and supermarket rolled into one. Its environs were used for trade, the produce coming straight up the hill from the harbour, whence it had come across the North Sea from Germany and the Low Countries.

Along with the produce were pamphlets, hot from the Gutenberg printing press, containing the sermons of Martin Luther, and later John Calvin whose ideas of the sovereignty of God and the rule of religion through theocracy and democracy were well suited for transplantation to St Andrews.

When George Wishart was burnt outside Cardinal Beaton's castle home, the torch was put to a religious revolution which became the Scottish Reformation. Its leader was John Knox, trained at Geneva under Calvin – but not the autocrat of the Scots Kirk, more its architect. Legend portrays him as harsh and humourless, bombastic and iconoclastic.

John Knox – *BBC Hulton Picture Library*

Certainly a few images were pulled from the cathedral, but its decay was from neglect rather than vandalism. Knox himself did not think women monstrous — he enjoyed the company of women, even taking his mother-in-law on honeymoon. A widower at fifty-four he married a seventeen-year-old-girl. His latter years were spent in quiet retirement in St Andrews and on his deathbed he ordered a butt of wine to be opened at his funeral. It was the successors of Knox who gave Scots presbyterianism its harsher image.

After the Reformation there was only one Church — and it was Presbyterian. Although the eighteenth century brought tolerance, the Presbyterians remained dominant. Their uncompromising style did not make it easy to effect a compromise when a Church-State conflict grew up in the mid-nineteenth century over the issue of patronage — effectively whether the landowners and the law had the right to tell the Kirk whom to appoint as its ministers and how to do it. It led to the Disruption of 1843 when a third of the Kirk's ministers and members walked out to form the Free Church of Scotland. Their patriarch was Thomas Chalmers, a distinguished evangelical whose maxim — 'You cannot preach the gospel to those with empty bellies' — sprang from a social conscience.

The first General Assembly of the Free Church of Scotland, 1843. (From an original painting by D. O. Hill) – *BBC Hulton Picture Library*

The Disruption divided the Presbyterians into three tribes all roughly similar in style of worship and doctrine. There was the Established Church funded by endowments and taxes on heritors or landowners; the United Presbyterian Church, which was originally a collection of congregationalist churches whose members raised their own funds; as did the new breakaway Free Church. They were not poor, these churches, and their top ministers were paid as much as today's Harley Street specialists. Today the average kirk minister gets around nine thousand pounds per annum.

But the Victorian Church has left one legacy to the present Church of Scotland — its buildings, which hang like millstones round the neck of a Church trying to shake off its Victorian ethos. Reunions of 1900 and 1929 brought most of the Victorian churches into a unified Kirk (with a strong fringe group in the West Highlands remaining independent). Instead of large full churches, the proud congregations cling to their bricks and mortar as if they were consecrated ground and continue to worship in sparsely filled temples which are full of heat but not a lot of light at the end of the tunnel. Such blinkered vision not only wastes the resources of the Kirk but makes mockery of all those pious pronouncements about seeking church unity.

In Edinburgh's West End the trinity of St Cuthbert's (Auld Kirk), St George's West (Free) and Palmerston Place (ex United Presbyterian) sums up the problem. Presbytery attempts to rationalise the 'plant' have so far failed and membership is withering away. Topping up with finance is frequently required. St Cuthbert's have just committed a fortune to a roof repair.

Historically St Cuthbert's had two ministers but in fairly recent history they didn't speak to one another, preferring to pass notes instead. In Busby they have two churches, the East and the West. The East have their service at twelve noon, the West at half-past-ten, but here's the catch: they share the same minister, who walks the few hundred yards from one to the other to deliver the same sermon. As far as one congregation is concerned, the other congregation lives on the wrong side of the tracks, for the railway literally runs through the House of God. Now, these people have defied every attempt by the Presbytery to unite them. They share the same hairdressers, they get their newspapers delivered by the same newsagent, they even (as someone has pointed out) attend the same Christian Unity services, but Christian unity seems to be all right as long as it's not in the same denomination.

Unity has been one of the recurrent themes in postwar Christianity and since Victorian times there has been another ecclesiastical tribe in Scotland, the Roman Catholic Church. The oft-quoted Jesuit dictum 'Give me a child before the age of seven and he is ours for life' usually refers to the apparent ability of the RC Church to retain lifelong influence on those baptised into it. Catholic schools bolster that view and understandably the Roman Catholic Church does not want to give up the right to have state schools for its children, instituted in Scotland under the 1918 Education Act, whose passing was thought to be a reward for loyalty to the British Crown during the Great War.

The Catholic community in Scotland was mostly Irish in origin, having come to Presbyterian Scotland during the nineteenth-century Irish famines. They landed at the Broomielaw Quay in Glasgow, sometime jokingly referred to as one of the prime religious sites of Scotland. Today, the Archdiocese of Glasgow is building prestigious new offices alongside its cathedral there. It has a higher profile now than in the days when chapels were deliberately sited in side streets with modest facades lest they attracted anti-Catholic vandalism. Catholics lived in ghettoes on the edges of the cities and were treated by their Presbyterian neighbours as second-class citizens.

Prejudice and persecution cut both ways, and account for the paranoia of many Catholics who still see Orangemen under the bed. One often hears tales that the Labour Group controlling Glasgow's Council now make up for decades of discrimination by doing a little in the opposite direction. Perhaps they are encouraged by the offensive language and thuggish antics of the Orange Order.

Today the Orange Order is hardly a religious body. Indeed the links between the Reformed Church and the Orange Order are virtually non-existent. However, their bands make a lot of noise. Orange candidates are to be fielded at a general election in an attempt to bring Irish issues to the fore in Scotland. Most people inside and outside the churches do not think they can succeed. Mutual respect between the Catholic and Protestant churches has risen too far for that but there is still suspicion over many matters such as mixed marriages and Catholic schools. The Roman Catholic Church will not give up the latter without a huge fight, as Archbishop Thomas Winning, leader of Scotland's Catholics, readily agrees. One has to ask how long the anomaly of Catholic schools can be maintained now that in every other respect the education system takes a neutral or even pluralistic approach to religious issues. Until then, Catholics are making the most of their stronger position. The official statistics of baptised Catholics are now over eight hundred thousand and on paper the RCs look set — especially with their legendary birth rate — to overtake the Presbyterians in numbers. Well, not quite yet. That figure includes babes in arms and lapsed Catholics and so it does not correspond to the real attendance figure at Mass. Archbishop Thomas Winning does not see that breeding an attitude among RCs of being the Shadow Establishment:

'I look on that kind of attitude and stance as very old-fashioned. We're not really in the numbers game. The Second Vatican Council has given us a new historical expression of the Church and it's not so much counting heads as having people live according to the teaching of Christ. So I don't think we — or anyone — would take any pleasure out of the national Church diminishing in numbers. It's quality that counts. We've been told, over and over again by theologians like Rahner, that somehow or other the Christian Church will decline in this period but the quality will probably be much better, because people will be asked for a personal commitment and take personal ownership of the faith, rather than be supported by a very influential institution.'

If proof were ever needed of the growing influence of the Catholic Church in Scotland it was provided on 31 May 1982, the day the Roman Catholics of Scotland came of age. The Bishop of Rome had come to bless them at Bellahouston Park and to invite them to walk 'hand in hand' with their Protestant brothers. Viewed in the light of past religious conflict, that is progress. But at present the romance stops short at holding hands and is unlikely ever to reach the altar.

Theology has been taught at my own University of St Andrews in St Mary's College since before the Reformation. Now after centuries of hostility Roman Catholic students sit side by side with would-be ministers of the Kirk. But, despite such harmony in the doocots of Academia and dove-like performances between the churches over the issues of nuclear weapons, Catholics and Protestants still cannot share or break bread together — the one liturgical act that they have in common. Presbyterians have an open table but the Catholics cannot, nay, *will not* participate and as long as the Body of Christ is thus broken, it is little wonder that many people regard the institutional Church as an obstacle to faith.

Centuries of suspicion do not disappear overnight. Scotland's Catholics willingly gave up their Latin Mass and they have been equally docile over birth control and women priests, and never flutter even the occasional dove in the theological doocot. There is one Tridentine Mass Church in Glasgow, an exception which proves the rule of conformity among Scottish Catholics. But it is not the temple to which the most reactionary elements are drawn. Many would say that the Vatican is the Kremlin of the Western World. The treatment meted out to gifted theologians like Kung, Schillibeeckx, Boff and Curran in recent years does not give much encouragement. Most ecumenists seek not so much church unity of an organic nature (what someone once called 'ecclesiastical joinery') but at least a recognition that Catholics and Protestants belong to the same religion. In Scotland there are still many old guard parish priests who view requests for dispensation for a mixed marriage as some sort of disgusting perversion. Despite the power of an archbishop who wants to implement a Renew programme, that dead weight of conservatism still provides a counterbalance to the intolerant wing of the Kirk.

Archbishop Winning concedes that not all the backwoodsmen are Protestants:

'There's no doubt that a minority is always on the defensive and closes ranks against the more powerful forces. So we have suffered to that extent. But every negative has positives. You could say that the community gained strength from feeling pressurised, it kept them close together. If anyone is attacked the natural thing is to oppose or to resist, and maybe to counterattack, and there's no doubt that has happened. If somebody expresses in some way that he dislikes you, then — unless you're a very exceptional Christian — you'll probably come down to his level and say "I dislike him" as well.'

In 1986 the Kirk's General Assembly made a noble gesture by publicly dissociating itself from the clauses of the Westminster Confession of Faith which describes the Pope as the antichrist. But there are many who complain that it has now reached a point where there are no distinct doctrines left. Fortunately the Bible-bashers have not yet reached sufficient numbers in the ministry to force through fundamentalism, although there is some evidence of a rise in the number of candidates for the ministry from fundamentalist congregations which could tip the balance. It is the heavyweight theologians who are lacking these days. Scots used to be far more conscious of theological issues than their Sassenach Christian neighbours. But in recent years it has been an academic-turned-bishop who has been making the running in theological debate in Britain. Dr David Jenkins, Bishop of Durham, pinpoints 'the dark night of our institutions' in a forthcoming book. He makes a distinction between faith and optimism:

'I'm not optimistic about the immediate future of the institutional Church in Britain; I think it is, on the whole, regressing into defensive nostalgia and not facing the questions. I am optimistic about the future of the real Church because I think the real Church is on God's wavelength and God will do something about it.'

Dr Jenkins also addressed himself to the doctrinal issues of the Virgin Birth and Resurrection. Unfortunately the public debate concentrated

Pope John Paul II at Bellahouston Park, 1982 – *Popperfoto*

on the question: Does he — or doesn't he believe? It missed the rather more important and universal issue of importance, namely that *we* don't in general believe what we did about these doctrines. The decline of the institutional Church has a philosophical basis. It wasn't Darwin who did it, or the literary detective work which has opened up the Bible to forensic examination, or the devil, or even second-rate preachers who did it. It has come about because of a crisis in Western thought. Protestant theology has suffered 'a radical disjunction between faith and reason'. In other words we believe what we can verify, like good scientists. All the rest we put in the attic of the mind where myth and symbol are stored in our subconscious, and forget about it. When it comes to knowing if it is there, like those treasures in the attic, we are not quite sure.

When I inteviewed him, the Bishop of Durham put it thus:

'There has been a sort of combination between conspiracy, collusion and comfort. One of the parts of religion is to give the people the comfort of the knowledge, of the presence and the grace of God, but people have colluded in a comfortable comfort instead of a realistic comfort.

'It's precisely because people have built up separate religious enclaves

198

where you go on worshipping in the Christian tradition, but keeping worship apart from the real events, from the sciences and nuclear war and all the rest of it. So there's a break between religion and the world which is false to the biblical God, because he is responsible for the whole world and is met through the world.

'I am quite clear, though it is a matter of faith and not of proof, that we are not alone; that there is a power, presence, promise within things and beyond things and he has specially made himself known, or she or it has made herself or itself known, through Jesus for the sake of the whole world and the whole of history.'

Catholics suffered less from this disjunction because of their sacramental theology which fuses myth and matter (e.g. transubstantiation in the Mass). One sign of this missing dimension in Western Protestantism is the number of Church of Scotland congregations who are celebrating Communion more frequently. The old-style worship centred round a preacher in a pulpit has been wittily described as a process in which the word was made flesh but then turned back into words again. The preacher, no matter how hot his gospel, finds it difficult to compete with the hot medium of television.

The Bishop of Edinburgh, Richard Holloway, a high-church Episcopalian, comes from this sacramentalist tradition and has written several influential books on theology. He has ministered in Glasgow's East End, Edinburgh's city centre, fashionable Boston USA and a prestigious Oxford college. From that global perspective he agrees that we are experiencing an eclipse of the sunny days of Western Christianity:

'There has been a growing crisis of belief in our highly sophisticated, technological culture for about a couple of hundred years — it's well documented. We've crowded out the transcendent; a sociologist describes it as a process of disenchantment. We no longer think there's anything out there, you know, we're in the plane on our own. There's so much noise and pressure in our culture that (if I can be corny for a minute) you can't hear the still small voice. If you wander about with a ghetto-blaster up against your ear, you're not going to hear anything, including a cry for help.'

The statistics to go with that analysis are not hard to find in Scottish terms.

Adult members of the Church of Scotland still outnumber Roman Catholics two to one, but over the last twenty years the Kirk's membership has sunk from 1.2 million to well below the million mark. From a gentle 7 per cent decline in the 1960s the rate of fall in membership increased alarmingly to 18 per cent in the 1970s.

	Membership	Communion Attendance
1957 — 1967	− 7%	− 9%
1967 — 1977	−18%	−41%
1977 — 1987	−16% †	−24% *

† projected   *estimated decadal decline

For those who say that it is active members who count, the figures are even worse. Attendance at Communion has sunk dramatically and on present trends will hit bottom by the year 2000. And the source of new members through baptisms and new communicants has slowed to a trickle. The figures are striking. While 75 per cent of baptised children attended Sunday school in 1962, the figure in 1982 was 43 per cent. While 74 per cent of baptised children came into full membership in 1962, only 27 per cent were admitted in 1982.

The Church of Scotland performs the majority of the rites of passage for the Scots population still — funerals, baptisms and marriages — and while there's been no drop in funerals in recent years, there has been a downturn in the number of church marriages, and indeed in the number of baptisms. While 80 per cent of the Scots population say they believe in God, only 10 per cent still go to church, and if downward trends among the young continue, then the Church of Scotland will literally be a dying institution and the hymn most appropriate at the funeral will be that well-thumbed favourite in crematoria hymnbooks, 'Abide with Me', which contains the line 'Change and decay in all around I see'.

Can we identify reasons for this decline? There are plenty of suggestions: Too much change or not enough of it. Too much adherence to outdated Bible stories and historical conflicts or not enough Bible-based belief and orthodoxy. The yearning for more sacramental worship is said by diehard Kirk conservatives to weaken Protestantism, to which one might remark that it appears to be doing quite a good job of undermining itself without enlisting high-church moles. Indeed, I would argue that many of these alleged causes of decline are symptoms rather than diseases. I want to examine a number of these symptoms, some of which are expressed as reactions against the larger institutions by groupings outside it. But first, three factors at work inside the Kirk — Sexism, Ageism and Neuroticism.

There is often confusion in the public mind between the Mother of God (an alternative term used by Roman Catholics for the Blessed Virgin Mary or BVM) and the Motherhood of God (used to describe the feminine attributes of the Godhead in addition to its qualities as God the Father). Paradoxically, the Roman tradition stresses the former but denies the preisthood to women (the Pope has justified this on the ground that there was no woman present at the Last Supper). Protestants play down the BVM factor but have been more open to ordaining women in their churches.

The Church of Scotland has had women elders for a generation and women ministers for over fifteen years. At present there are sixty ladies among the Kirk's fourteen hundred parish ministers, not many of them ardent feminists. But there are some who argue that this 'inequality' is diminishing the Church. Mrs Anne Hepburn was a missionary in Africa when she met her husband who was also a missionary and is now a parish minister in Braco. In recent years her mission has been to project the issue of the Motherhood of God before the Kirk. As National President of the Woman's Guild she caused a stir by using the phrase 'O God our Mother' in a prayer. She remains adamant that a dimension is missing if feminine elements are excluded from the worship and organisation of the Church:

'We need in the Church to have images of God that reflect the whole of human life, not just one half of humanity, not just men. In our worship and in our hymns we use male metaphors, although there are female analogies in the scriptural tradition. Patriarchy still rules. The very fact that there was a row over "God the Mother" showed that in the Church a lot of men and women accept that male is norm. That's what patriarchy purveys: to be male is the norm, and that leaves women either abnormal or subnormal. When I talk about patriarchy I mean domination by men and subordination of women. It goes right through our society and right through the Church, and it is oppressive to women. What I want is a community of women and men; it is a wholeness that I want in the Church. Domination and subordination do not result in wholeness — that is sinful, and what we want is wholeness.'

It has been unkindly said of the Church of Scotland that it is a body of middle-aged women led by old men. While agreeing with the need to have a male and female component in our view of God, I cannot help but feel that the plight of Presbyterian women is not that desperate. After all, a constitutional equality exists in the courts of the Kirk, even if there is not a groundswell to support more female involvement. But far more urgent in my view is the domination of those courts by the geriatric grenadiers.

General Assembly of the Church of Scotland, 1986 – *Glasgow Herald*

The Kirk's presbyteries send nearly thirteen hundred Commissioners to the General Assembly each May (ministers and elders in equal numbers). But elders would also be a highly appropriate word to describe many of the ministers in each presbytery. What other body would allow retired members of the profession to exercise a deliberative vote, after their retirement? The Kirk *does,* and an attempt to remedy that situation a few years ago was defeated by — yes, you've guessed it — the votes of the retired ministers. Who can blame younger elders who don't want to give up an evening at dreich presbytery meetings? Indeed, one minister used to say that to prove he was a Presbyterian he went to presbytery once a year; and to prove he was a Christian he stayed away the rest of the time.

Ministers used to be inducted to parishes 'ad vitam aut culpam' and unless they died or committed a grave sin, many went on well beyond seventy. Now it is compulsory to retire at seventy, but increasingly there is evidence that fewer are living to celebrate their Biblical span of three score years and ten. A form of nervous exhaustion, sometimes called 'burn-out', is apparently taking its toll of ministers. Rev. Dr John Cameron of St Stephen's in Broughty Ferry, whose relaxations include regular rounds of golf over the Old Course, has done a study of the causes of this syndrome. He identifies one principal reason as the difficulty of job specification for a minister. The symptoms of burn-out are not hard to find:

'Either odd behaviour or just sheer physical and mental exhaustion which at times can end the minister up in a hospital — and on some occasions in a psychiatric institution. It sounds as if the ministry today are a bunch of crocks, but this is part of the problem because the tendency has been to take the view that there has been individual weakness. When industry is looking at a similar problem of people in trouble they look for points of stress within the structure rather than looking for individuals, trying to find out if there are "areas within this job which are burning out our salesmen, burning out our men in marketing".'

Maybe the answer does lie partially in the structures of the Kirk but there again RC priests have shown many of the same symptoms and the Glasgow Archdiocese has a confidential report which parallels many of the Kirk findings. Another antidote to the 'structural' solution of reorganising the churches is that this has been tried — remember the heat and light of the Committee of Forty? — and failed. It is not sexism or ageism or neuroticism which is the problem. They are the symptoms. We come back again to the conclusion that the problem is a spiritual crisis of our epoch, with clergy as the Middlesex Regiment in the front line.

We can get another perspective on the plight of institutional religion by examining those groups which have reacted against trends of the age. The old maxim of the preacher was 'argument weak here, so shout louder'. There has always been a tendency when faith was under attack for one group to reassert dogma more dogmatically. It happened last century when the Darwin controversies were raging. Moody and Sankey came over from America and found ready customers for their Bible-bashing brand of conservative religion. It also found a willing soil in the bleak Isle of Lewis where the tide of secularism has not succeeded in breaking down the dykes of Calvinism built last century when the Free Church

Free Church Congregation – *David Richardson*

was founded. Uncompromising to the last, the Free Presbyterian Church and then the Free Church erected their bulwarks as the secular tide rose further. It has resulted in a strong and distinctive ethos, which even today is undergoing one of its periodic revivals.

Is it something deep in the soul of man which responds to stern admonition and Gaelic psalms, or is it a whale of religion beached by the tide in the Western Isles in whose stomach modern man could not live, except as a refuge from reality? We city slickers may act as if it were the latter but, while we might not swallow all that the more authoritarian churches preach, we should not deny them their impressive witness. The young people who throng the Free Kirk at Stornoway on a Sunday night grew up to hear psalms in church but pop music from the radio. Today's version of Ira Sankey, the Victorian evangelist, would be Cliff Richard or one of the other Rock Gospel artists who preach with a guitar. They are perhaps not everyone's glass of beer but they do reach parts that conventional religion does not. But the drawback of the Rock Gospellers is that most of them are selling the authoritarian version of religion which takes the Bible literally and that means they must, in my mind, despite their modern clothing be relegated to our past rather than our future.

Television has proved the most influential medium of modern times and is likely to remain so. Religious broadcasting has, because of the ground rules which govern it in Britain, tended to preach to the already converted, and there is no evidence that it has led many to religion who were not practising it already. But this is not so in America where the Electronic Church puts God in a box and markets him on as many TV stations as it can buy. Or to be more accurate, the preachers ask for money which is used to enlarge their empires. It is certain that, when satellite TV has become firmly established in Britain, we will be able to sample the delights of Rex Humbard, Jimmy Swaggart and Moral Majority leader Jerry Falwell. Already the Cable Authority has ruled that the Worldwide Church of God, publishers of *Plain Truth* magazine, have as much right to air time as they do to sell their magazine. Yet the WWC of God has been rocked with scandals of incest in its leadership and is clearly as undesirable as cults like the Moonies or Scientologists.

It is easy to sneer at the Electronic Church. In some ways it is not so much our tomorrow as our yesterday, a kind of televised Moody and Sankey, offering the old-time religious formula of certainty and sentimentality. In that way the responses of authoritarianism or revivalism will always have a market, but they do not have enough breadth or depth to appeal to sufficient numbers to make them a significant force in society. Having said that, it is only fair to say that the Damascus road experience is still a startling reminder of how lives can be changed for the better by a sharp, sudden conversion. Many such people were 'born again' during the Billy Graham Crusade of 1955. But Dr Graham would agree that despite their testimony faith is like health and requires to be sustained and is not like inoculation against disease, effective for all time.

But the growth of many evangelical churches contradicts the overall decline of the larger denominations. The fastest-growing denomination in the world is the Pentecostal Church which clings to the pattern of the early Christians when gifts of the Spirit and healing miracles were looked for as signs of God's blessing.

Despite declining mainstream churches and widespread unemployment, the tiny independent Pentecostal congregation in Motherwell built the King's Centre complex for £300,000 and are growing fast under the pastorate of Hugh Clark, steel executive turned preacher. They use glossolalia (speaking in tongues) as part of their ecstatic praise and can claim many healing 'miracles' at their services.

Undoubtedly this is one area in which the larger churches could learn to use the beneficial effects of what is sometimes called parapsychology. There has been an irrational fear of such phenomena by churches. They have been imprisoned in the laboratory or the occultist's tent for too long — or left to the fringes of religion — whereas they are potentially a force to link the trinity of mind, body and spirit and the systems of psychology, medicine and religion.

More adapted to the New Age of Aquarius are the various forms of personalised religion, in which psychotherapies now must be included. They teach, through textbooks and tutors who double as therapists, a gospel which is written inside oneself and which consists of finding a way by which the imprisoned splendour may escape and wholeness may be found. This primrose path appealed to the flower-power dropouts who shunned conventional religion and found transcendence in other ways. Sometimes they found it through drugs or meditation, and many found their way into cults, some of which used meditation as a mind-bending drug.

There is no doubt that meditation can relax the mind and release it for greater potential. Machines like the mind mirror can monitor through EEG waves the state of mind which produces the most alpha waves, the ones which predominate during relaxed meditation. You can buy flotation tanks, fill them with Epsom salts and warm water, blank out your eyes and pipe 'white noise' (produced electronically or by recording a waterfall) through your ears. You have created the conditions of sensory deprivation where your mind will be able to dissociate itself from your body. Truly transcendent. But by definition it is themselves that they find or lose, not God. Or if it is a God, then it is one made in their own image, in the hall of mirrors that is religion in the television age. The more unfortunate reach for the Valium bottle (for if religion was once the opium of the people — Valium is now the Valium of the people). They try to turn their doctor into a confessor, a quack priest, little realising that their psychosis is the symptom not the disease.

Mainstream churches used to rely on yuppie families as the lifeblood of recruitment to their leadership. Now these social groups are by-passing the churches and when they drop out of the rat race, they go to the so-called New Age communities. One of the best known is at Findhorn in Moray, where the RAF Nimrods roar overhead through the magic meteorological window in the clouds known as the Findhorn Gap. Huddled in their caravan home, two middle-aged dropouts worked their own piece of alchemy, charming young people to share their community — an oasis of spiritual communion, growing forty-pound cabbages and eight-foot delphiniums, animated by angelic force.

The Findhorn Community has evolved in its quarter century. The Universal Hall is a symbol of the permanence and the professionalism they have brought to the task of running an alternative 'church', which is the Ecology Party at prayer.

There are those who would say Findhorn is a low-grade cult which will never replace conventional religion. The poor, the ignorant and those who do not share their doctrines have no place here. But they do share some things with their brethren, the monks at Pluscarden Priory which nestles just across the hill.

Gardeners 'attuning' in the herb garden before starting work – *Findhorn Foundation*

At Findhorn there is a link between the sanctuary and the land, between altar table and kitchen garden. But there is something else peculiar to a religious community. The yuppies of Findhorn learn to attune with the earth spirit. The novices at Pluscarden learn to listen in silence for the still small voice of God. Both are concerned to give something in prayer which cannot be touched, felt or smelt or measured by a meter.

Writer Jeremy Slocombe was a rising young advertising executive in Australia before he became a member of the Findhorn Community. He sees the pattern which they have developed being replicated worldwide, but instead of being seen as itinerant hippies they will build on their foundations at Findhorn:

'Now that we've been here for more than a couple of decades and as the mean age of community members is getting older, with young dependants, we're really pining to put our roots down and become responsible citizens of Scotland along with everybody else. That involves developing businesses, developing new housing schemes and the rest, so that we can demonstrate a lot of our ideas in a more concrete and permanent form.'

At Findhorn they stress the inter-dependence of life on our planet, and that we were created by one God — and created equal.

Man, says the Book of Genesis, is made in the image of God. The problem about the reactions to decline which have just been looked at is that they create God in the image which we need. The authoritarian father figure of fundamentalism; the jumping jack flash of Rock Gospel to excite us; the Merlins of meditation; the cult gurus, who initiate us into the mysteries of the occult. They spring from our need rather than a reality which we can prove scientifically.

When the monks pray they sometimes do so through an image, the Blessed Virgin Mary. You don't need to be a psychologist to suspect that there may be an element of need in this too, in a community of celibate men, revering a divine virgin; but that does not make it meaningless. Prayer goes *through* a saint, not to a saint, and it doesn't matter whether the saint was a real historical figure. The crux of the matter is whether there is anyone listening — and whether it does any good. That brings us back to the crisis in belief for modern man and the fundamental question of whether God is a reality.

Failing to respond to the authority figures of the past and emotionally unmoved by much of what conventional and unconventional religion has to offer, modern man chooses to respond in a way that Darwin would have recognised as familiar. He channels his activities to the survival of the species.

The nature of Bob Geldof's appeal for the famine victims of Africa, and the unprecedented response to it, was not a religious event. It was moral, humanitarian, but it did not mention God or need to. It relied on the fact that vast numbers of people are agnostic about God but prepared to have faith in their fellow men. Thus God has become de-mythologised.

In that situation the commandments of religion and the doctrines of the churches are transformed into social and moral codes and the vehicle for action politics, not religion.

It is all too easy to accuse churches of meddling in politics, the business of the State. But we should not forget that throughout history the State has encouraged and underwritten a political role for the Church. There was the official role first given to the Christian Church by Constantine in AD 312. There was the two-swords doctrine of the medieval world. There was the theocracy of Calvin's Geneva. And in Knox's Scotland there was the General Assembly — which, since the dissolution of the Scottish Parliament, has played a symbolic and influential role in Scottish life. Rev. Dr Finlay McDonald, Vice-Convener of the Business Committee, defines its role thus:

'The General Assembly is like a parliament; but it's not elected democratically the way a parliament is elected. However, the people who sit in the General Assembly come from every part of Scotland, and they represent in many ways the life of the nation. The ministers of the General Assembly are people who work day by day, week by week, in parishes, with the concerns of people; the elders are men and women who have different occupations within the life of the nation, and to that extent it provides a real national forum for debate. The General Assembly has differing functions; it has a judicial function, the hearing of appeals from the lower courts of the Church; it has a legislative function, determining church law; it also has a policy, determining the Church's views on various social, moral issues; and of course, through the Church and Nation debate, it allows ordinary people, the ministers and elders of the Church, to

The Moderator, Rt Rev Dr Robert Craig, visiting
Faslane Peace Camp, March 1987 – *Brian Averell*

express their views on a broad range of issues, and it's well known that Members of Parliament and others pay great attention to what is said in the General Assembly on Church and Nation day.'

That is a different matter, of course, from heeding the advice. But is it such a bad thing to have a parliament without power — in which spiritual power is the driving force? Is this not just a revival of the medieval idea of the two swords — one restraining the other from doing violence? One of the key debates at the General Assembly for the past two decades has been on the question of the nuclear deterrent. As a veteran of fourteen assemblies I have noticed a decided shift in the position of the Kirk and other churches, from acceptance of the nuclear deterrent to outright opposition to the Bomb as 'evil' and retaliation strikes as 'becoming Satan'.

One of the amazing things about these quotations and the Ban the Bomb stance of the Kirk is that their leading proponents are former Moderators and holders of the Military Cross. Opposition to nuclear weapons these days crosses age barriers and denominational barriers — a little group singing in the rain outside Faslane nuclear submarine base may look like the wholemeal and sandals brigade — but they are representative of a growing caucus of all ages in the churches, who see Christian witness in political statements. But are they not selling their religious heritage for a mess of political potage? Rev. Maxwell Craig, Convener of the Church and Nation Committee, rejects the charge:

'I don't have any problems with that criticism because it seems to me that Jesus Christ was crucified not on a shining altar between candlesticks but on the city's rubbish dump between two thieves, and the incarnation puts the Bible and all our faith right into the heart of the daily life of men and women now.'

Inevitably many of the churches are being drawn more and more into political protest of a kind that is verging on the illegal, such as cutting of the fences at Faslane, for instance. This was supported by a lot of churchmen and in the eyes of other people seemed to be making the Church into a kind of civil disobedience society. Maxwell Craig argues that the Church should be selective about those issues which have spiritual content and should act as much as possible within the law. In this he does not go as far as some radical British churchmen who already see some laws as requiring disobedience — a potentially explosive situation which draws on the kind of liberation theology in which power is substituted for prayer.

It is yet another example of the disjunction between the politically possible and the heavenly ideal. But not all Christians who practise rather than preach are political. There are a vast number whose spiritual hero is not Gandhi or Martin Luther King, but the Good Samaritan.

The Church of Scotland Social Responsibility Department has an annual budget of £12 million and employs 1250 people across a spectrum of care — homes for the elderly, the mentally handicapped and addiction centres. The more old-fashioned and down-and-out hostels have been upgraded in an attempt to provide more appropriate care. Drug addiction centres like Spectrum at Haddington, a former List D School, are an attempt to keep pace with social problems. Rev. Frank Gibson, the Kirk's Director of Social Work, says it is aptly named:

'We've a spectrum of care: homes for the elderly, homes for mentally handicapped, mentally ill, those with epilepsy, List D Schools, all of that — more homes proportionally than the Salvation Army have in the United Kingdom. Quite extraordinary, and as well as that, a budget of ten to twelve million pounds a year, and all of that caring in Christ's name for folk in need. We feel we've got to do it, because Jesus said: "As you care for the least, you care for me." And that's why we're here in Spectrum, and that's why we're doing this work, and we give God thanks for the opportunity to serve society in it.'

I invited Frank Gibson, whose drive has resulted in the expansion of many areas of caring work, to make a prophecy as to what might be the key areas towards the year 2000:

'There will be more elderly people because folk will live longer, and we believe more people will have senile dementia. That's an area of expansion in which we are beginning to have a considerable expertise. Taking people out of mental hospitals, and bringing them into their own communities and to be cared for, is another area which will increase. And I'm sorry to say that the hostels for the destitute and homeless are still needing to be better. It's tragic, says something about our society. But I fully believe the Church must look again at its own structures, because the less the Church looks at its structures, the more it will prevent the expansion of work in caring for folk.'

So far we've looked at a number of ways in which religious groups have been scoring successes against a background of decline: the caring work that's undertaken over a wide range of social problems; the esoteric appeal of communities like Findhorn; political lobbying on social and moral issues; the biblical certainties of the Free Church in Lewis; or the appeal of the Electronic Church in its 'prime time' religion; or that of charismatic congregations such as the King's Centre in Motherwell. Yet in none of these instances is the Church occupying its traditional role at the centre of the community, and the medieval cathedral which was the centre of work as well as worship has long gone, except pehaps in Buckhaven in Fife, where it has been revived with exceptional success.

Buckhaven was a thriving fishing village until its harbour silted up. Its mining economy declined. It became a slag town — literally and metaphorically. Now, thanks to multi-million-pound investment from the Manpower Services Commission and Fife Region, a giant conjuring trick has saved Buckhaven from the death of a thousand cuts.

They even have their own workshop for making conjuring tricks, known as the Miracle Project. It's one of many craft projects. There are dozens of workshops making everything from garden furniture to stained-glass windows and candles. They have their own small TV studio and boat-building shed. And soon they'll be able to launch their boats in the harbour they're reclaiming. The workshops producing theatrical costumes, props and scenery don't have to look far for a home. A theatre project will be opened this year.

The impresario, pied piper and entrepreneur behind this venture is the parish minister, Dane Sherrard, who says that one of the aims of his community programme is to find jobs for the long-term unemployed:

'In that term our success has been phenomenal; four out of every five people who have come on to our programme have moved into permanent

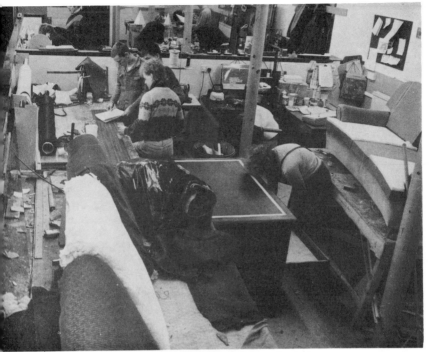

Buckhaven Community Project Workshop – *Buckhaven Community Project*

employment during the course of the year. To put it another way, more than eight hundred people who have come through our scheme were long-term unemployed and now have permanent jobs. That's colossal.'

I put it to Dane Sherrard that perhaps it's not the job of the minister to be running a complex like this, that he should be visiting hospitals or writing sermons.

'We're very anxious not to say that what we are doing is necessarily the right thing for everyone else. We *are* saying that we are part of a small community with a wonderful God-given opportunity not available to anyone else within our particular community. People have said, "Why hasn't it been something like a Chamber of Commerce running a scheme like this?" Well, the answer is that in Buckhaven there is no Chamber of Commerce. In Buckhaven there's nothing except the Church. We are the kind of community where the doctors, the social workers, the bank managers, and so on, come in during the day and go out at night. The only organisation, the only resources on which the community was thrown back were the Church and its people. They are wonderful resources, available throughout the whole of Scotland.

'The second part of your question related to people's expectations of a minister. One of the things that started everything off in Buckhaven was the union of the churches — there used to be three, now there's one. Obviously one person could not do what three were doing before. I believe very, very much that in Church of Scotland unions at the present

Christening service in Buckhaven – *Buckhaven Community Project*

time we're seeing the liberated spirit of the Holy Spirit. It's helping us to go back to what a church is meant to be. It's not a minister-centred thing, it's people-centred, and in my church, a whole number of people are caring for those who are sick, those who are elderly. We employ somewhere around fifty people who are involved in caring work within our parish. We now have a cosy corner, to which old people of church membership, and also non-church membership, are brought in to share in warmth, friendship and food. Many people, I believe, are being kept alive by that facility. That couldn't happen if I was trying to operate on my own.'

Despite its success in fulfilling a role in the total community, the church at Buckhaven does not hold itself out as a model for others. With the irony (and perhaps the jealousy) that comes with the success it stands alone in the declining industrial and church scene in West Fife. But undeniably it has given new life and hope to thousands of people.

So has my second model of church success against the prevailing trend. It is mirrored in the double life of Anna Murphy.

Anna Murphy practises what she preaches and preaches what she practises. Her double life consists of being a consultant in renal medicine at Yorkhill Hospital by day and living in the pastoral centre of Glasgow Archdiocese in Newlands by night. There is nothing particularly new about a person with a religious vocation practising medicine — medical orders of nuns do it all the time. Nor of doctors seeing their work as a vocation; most do anyway. But the link between Anna Murphy's two worlds is an interesting model which is taking root both in hospital medicine and in church evangelisation.

The kidney unit which she runs jointly deals with the most heart-rending cases — the children who face the prospect of death from kidney failure unless they can obtain dialysis or, better still, a kidney transplant. The difficulties — the high cost of dialysis, the availability of machines and skilled operators, the tense wait for a kidney to be donated and the even tenser wait to see if the transplant has worked — these all demand a greater involvement by the staff, and the Yorkhill unit is no exception. The emphasis is on treating the child together with his family. By private donations the Yorkhill unit has built up a complex of rooms in which families facing the tragic possibilities can share their experiences helping one another through in conjunction with the medical staff. Flats are built into the unit so that parents who come from a distance can stay with their children and help them through the experience.

But the help is not a one-way street. The doctors are not there, Anna Murphy says, to play God and decide who can or cannot have dialysis, they are also there to learn. 'I remember one fourteen-year-old boy who had a transplant. It was my decision and he died. I couldn't cope. Then there came a letter from the parents saying that Malcolm would have wanted me to go on transplanting so that someone else might be helped. If we could capture that kind of self-giving spirituality in the Church we would really be going somewhere.'

The Renew programme which centres around the Archdiocesan Pastoral Centre is designed to apply the same kind of group ministry as the group medicine at Yorkhill. Parishioners come in for residential courses and share their experiences. Anna Murphy sold her house and lives in the Pastoral Centre and has become an integral part of the programme set in train by the papal visit of 1982. 'We're asking for a turnabout from the priests who've been raised to tell people what to do. Leadership is to do with witnessing to others. It's to do with what you are and how much space you have for people to invade,' she says in her soft-spoken way. 'As a Church we haven't exploited the potential of human beings.' She disclaims that she is a nun in street clothes and a doctor's white coat. That kind of way of viewing vocation is not relevant for her. 'Everyone has a vocation and the potential to practise what they're preaching.' Anna Murphy accepts that her role within the pastoral programme was made easier by her status as consultant, and that her commitment is facilitated by having no family at home. 'I come from a large family with its roots in Ireland and I was in the right place at the right time when the Yorkhill unit was being set up in 1972. It's like having children of my own, and I feel very much part of families. You see them coming together to combat the illness of their child.'

While some might see it as the tail wagging the dog, policy is sometimes determined by the needs and wishes of the families. For instance the doctors were inclined to favour more dialysis, but it became clear that the vast majority of families saw a transplant, despite the risks, as the preferred solution. Dr Murphy has learned not to have low expectations of what the families can achieve:

'One day I came to the staff here and said, "Do you know there's a

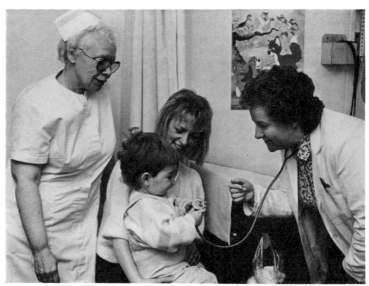

Dr Anna Murphy with young patient at the Renal Unit, Yorkhill Hospital – *BBC*

family here with three children who've got renal failure? I don't know if we can help them." And the staff said, "Very difficult, they'll crack up." The family came back to me at the clinic two weeks later, and the dad said to me, "Dr Murphy, please, these are our children. Could you do what you can for them?" I said, "Okay, we'll try." And we tried.

'Within one month the whole neighbourhood was helping these children, and a little neighbourhood group was born. Within that group you couldn't get more fundamental Christian values — anywhere. And that's how Renew is bringing life to the people of Glasgow. That's how Renew and renewal will transform society, because deep in the hearts of all of us is the wish and desire to help others. It's like the blind man and the Gospel. God has given us these sick and suffering children in order that he can use us, and in order that we can grow, in love and care and understanding. Now in that neighbourhood where those children were treated, they're continuing to fund-raise, and tremendous generosity is coming from one of the poorest areas in the city. We're seeing the same thing in the Church.'

The twin examples of Buckhaven and Renew demonstrate committed Christianity at work in the community. Who can tell what could happen if there were more people and communities in which worship and work were more intertwined? The Christian churches have thousands of highly placed 'agents' in influential posts in our society. A hostile foreign power would find it easy to conquer us with that kind of ally. Perhaps we do not work enough on the inside of society — preferring to be the outsiders, calling for this or that political action. Who can then complain if we are treated as marginal?

There is no doubt that church pronouncements on social and political issues attract attention. There are plenty of them and they often make helpful contributions to debate. It would be absurd to separate Christianity and politics. They need each other. Politics ought to be an outlet for the moral impulse and for the social expression of spirituality. Perhaps the fault of the churches has been to hunt with the hounds which have pursued the stench of racism, militarism and capitalism so that their voice has become one with the baying pack, not offering anything distinctive.

Or perhaps their mistake has been to hunt with the hounds when they should have been guarding the chickens. Politicians of all parties encourage us to turn to them for salvation — and perhaps it is no surprise that they cannot deliver Utopia. But the present government has done something new in its term of office. It has held out our salvation as something we can work for. It is attractive, just as it was when it was first coined as a heresy 1500 years ago. By moving whole areas of public agencies into private ownership it transferred the responsibility, it appeared, back to the people. It held up figures like Richard Branson, the transatlantic jet-setter and proprietor of Virgin Records, as the kind of chap we might emulate. But we can't — and many of us don't want to. In a terrible way that condemns vast numbers of people to fail before they begin. If not believing in the Virgin Birth is the unspoken heresy of many churchmen, then refusing to concede that vast unemployment is here to stay is the heresy of most politicians. Yet if it is — where does that leave the gospel according to Thatcher, of self-help and journeying to the promised land on one's bike? In short, it condemns whole areas of the country to despair.

Slums and poverty are supposed to be things of the past, of the Victorian era when, contrary to myth, the vast majority of the Scottish population didn't know what the inside of a church looked like. A century later, the story is much the same. There are ghost towns on the outskirts of our cities which are euphemistically described by the bureaucrats and the sociologists as 'part of the outer estates'. 'Scottish Soweto' would perhaps be a better description of these monuments to the folly of the 1950s and 1960s. But it almost doesn't matter who was to blame for the planning of these nightmares. The fact is that tens of thousands of people live in these urban deserts, starved of the resources of shops, banks and post offices which we others have come to take for granted.

There are schools, there are churches, welfare agencies, all trying to irrigate the desert and doing a job that outsiders like me can only admire; likewise the courage of many of the people who live there. But it's neither patronising nor is it political to say that the long-term effect of living in these places is liable to corrode the human spirit and destroy faith in a creator God. Bad housing doesn't make for bad people, but it doesn't make the good ones any more Godly and, in that sense, there are many places in Scotland today that could indeed be described as Godless.

Where then shall we find God? Whither shall we look for him? Richard Holloway, Bishop of Edinburgh, tells a story that is a kind of parable of modern man's search for God.

'When I lived in Oxford, I used to walk a lot, and one of my favourite walks was across Port Meadow into the village of Wighton, a little thatched village that nestled up against a wood. There was an old medieval church called All Saints, with a seventeenth-century Flemish stained-glass

Back courts in Blackhill, Glasgow – *Scotsman Publications*

window, and I used to go in there with my dog and just sit. You couldn't tell what the window was like from the outside; it looked rather dirty, dusty and dull. But from inside, the thing was illuminated; it was a gloriously simple golden kind of window. That's a kind of parable in a way: you can't actually tell what faith is like from outside; you cannot tell what the Church is like from outside; you can never objectively assess faith from the exterior. It's always surprising, it's always bigger on the inside, as C. S. Lewis used to say, than on the outside.

'I used to sit in that church and look at the light streaming in the window, and see it as a kind of parable of the mystery of life. At the heart of all religion is the thing call Revelation. Is there anything in the universe other than us? If it exists, is it getting in touch with us? If it is getting in touch with us, how can I make myself available to be got in touch with? And one of the classic ways is by finding space, by finding silence, by stopping, by sitting, by listening, by breathing deeply. In a rushed culture it's not surprising that not only God but lots of other precious things are being crowded out, lots of other kinds of intimacies. One American sociologist describes us as a kind of lonely crowd – we're all rushing together, but we've never been more isolated. So, people who are genuinely wanting to get in touch with transcendence have to find space, and silence, and stillness, and emptiness in their lives. And that can be quite frightening.'

But is it more frightening to contemplate the fact that there might be nothing there?

'Yes, yes. Dostoevsky said that if there is no God, all things become possible, because God is the thing that concentrates our moral and spiritual attention, makes us pin the enterprise of our lives on some kind of meaning, on some kind of discipline. If that goes, if there's no overarching meaning, if there's no God, no purpose, then we just roll our own philosophies, our own moralities, and if I'm a Hitler, and want to roll a Holocaust, what's to stop me? What absolute objective authority is there to say that I can't be a monster if I damn well want to be one? And that's the hideous thing about our culture, a culture that's become completely disenchanted. There's no reason why anything shouldn't happen, and a lot of unthinkable things have in fact happened in our century, I think no accident either.'

Now is the time for stripping the spirit bare,
Time for the burning of days ended and done,
Idle solace of things that have gone before:
Rootless hopes and fruitless desire are there;
Let them go to the fire, with never a look behind.
The world that was ours is a world that is ours no more.

These words were written by the same poet, Laurence Binyon, whose words about 'they shall not grow old as we that are left grow old' are read each Remembrance Day. The First World War poet who saw the war to end all wars was right — the world that was ours is a world that is ours no more. There have been wars and rumours of wars but never before has mankind possessed the means to wipe out all life on earth. It would be as easy as pressing a button. Genesis has turned into Nemesis.

Stewart Lamont and doves, St Mary's College, University of St Andrews – *David Richardson*

If some argue that this will lead to greater co-operation between nations, there is little sign of it in the year of our Lord 1987. The fact that such annihilation is possible has an inevitable effect on our state of mind. Little wonder that those who have never had it so good, in a material sense, have never had so many anxieties. Life is a bed of neuroses.

We anaesthetise ourselves against reality in so many ways, partly because reality hurts. That's why the churches find it so difficult to face up to the changes they have to make to adapt or die. The reason I do not finish on a totally pessimistic note (nuclear accidents apart) is that I believe that Christianity can offer a way forward for modern man because it integrates the God of the numinous, the transcendent, the mystical (whatever you care to call it) with the aching, lonely and bewildered mammal, Homo sapiens, and somehow manages to create something better and higher, a new creature.

As a snowflake becomes a drop of water, our existence may be fleeting and brief before we are absorbed back into the ocean which gave us consciousness. Because we are trapped by time and space, we cannot *know* with certainty but can live by faith without mocking ourselves or God. Those who have tried it make as many mistakes as anyone, suffer just as much, but in my view they are possibly, no, *probably* in the scientific sense, much closer to reality.

'The fear of the Lord is the beginning of knowledge but fools despise wisdom and instruction.' That text from Proverbs is the very first text I ever preached from, eighteen years ago in a wee country kirk in Angus. I doubt if I said anything very memorable and I doubt if the four people who attended the service thought it memorable either, but I do remember the text, 'The fear of the Lord is the beginning of knowledge.' The fear referred to is not fear of a tyrant or a bully, although the Church throughout history has sometimes adopted that role, forcing conformity upon its flock. Fear here means awe and wonder. Whether it's the grim realities of life in an urban 'desert or the sterile satisfaction of consumer society or the threat of nuclear annihilation, people don't seem to act as if there were awe and wonder in their lives. The real threat is that people are wandering around in an arid desert where their only spiritual experience is a kind of mirage made in the image of their own needs. They don't have their complacency challenged; they don't climb above themselves to seek the mountain of the Lord. Were they to seek it, they would need to expend energy, be dynamic, not passive, expend love that might not be returned, suffer in a way that, really, might not be justified at all. And when they reached that mountain top, they would have a peace that passed understanding. But it would be the peace of a roaring and powerful waterfall, not the peace that is found, too often, in too many churches — the peace of the graveyard.

APPENDIX

BBC Scotland commissioned System 3 Scotland to conduct a survey of public attitudes to accompany the *Scotland 2000* series. Around nine hundred Scots were asked a total of sixty-two questions about the eight programme areas.

To ensure that the sample was representative of the adult population in terms if age, sex and class, it was weighted to match JICNARS population estimates from the National Readership Survey of January to December 1983.

I. POLITICS

1. Respondents were shown a prompt card listing fourteen different possible courses of action that might be undertaken by a British government and asked to rank in order of priority the six they felt to be most important to be tackled. The following table summarises the frequency with which each was ranked first, second or third, and also at all within the first six.

While the first three priorities were somewhat predictable, it was less so that they should be followed by cutting taxation, coping with AIDS and setting up a Scottish Assembly, all of which emerged considerably ahead of both nuclear and defence issues. Indeed the remaining eight courses of action all received relatively sporadic support from no more than one in four of all respondents.

	First (%)	Second (%)	Third (%)	At all (%)
1. Cutting unemployment	58	15	9	94
2. Increasing health and social security spending	13	22	15	78
3. Increasing education spending	7	12	18	74
4. Cutting taxes	4	12	15	68
5. Coping with AIDS	3	10	11	62
6. Setting up a Scottish Assembly	5	9	9	51
7. Scrapping British nuclear weapons	3	4	3	26
8. Closing US nuclear bases	1	2	4	24
9. Cutting public expenditure	1	3	5	22
10. Introducing proportional representation	*	3	2	22
11. Ending the civil nuclear programme	1	2	3	18
12. Re-nationalising British Telecom	*	1	2	15
13. Increasing defence spending	1	1	2	13
14. Re-equipping the navy with Trident missiles	1	1	2	9

(* = Less then 1%, but not zero)

Not surprisingly there were some differences in opinion according to political party supported, mainly on party lines — Labour supporters in favour of increased public spending but not on defence, and the reverse true of Conservatives. The following table summarises the percentages rating each issue in the top six among the various party supporters:

	Conservative (%)	Labour (%)	Alliance (%)	SNP (%)
1. Cutting unemployment	93	94	98	96
2. Increasing health and social security spending	70	84	80	72
3. Increasing education spending	70	77	83	66
4. Cutting taxes	75	65	60	67
5. Coping with AIDS	75	59	67	51
6. Setting up a Scottish Assembly	42	51	45	81
7. Scrapping British nuclear weapons	8	39	20	22
8. Closing US nuclear bases	8	34	20	29
9. Cutting public expenditure	36	17	14	19
10. Introducing proportional representation	23	13	43	25
11. Ending the civil nuclear programme	5	25	19	18
12. Re-nationalising British Telecom	7	19	14	15
13. Increasing defence spending	24	8	11	17
14. Re-equipping the navy with Trident missiles	23	5	11	7

Interestingly, for all the partisanship of party politics, the same six issues emerged to the fore in each case.

2. A further prompt card was then shown listing six groups of potential opinion-formers, and respondents were asked to rank these in order of importance as sources of advice in making up their own minds on major issues.

	Most important (%)
1. Family and friends	38
2. Newspaper columnists and editorials	24
3. TV commentators	16
4. Local councillors	6
5. Government ministers	9
6. Other MPs	2

There was thus a tendency to put little store by the views and opinions of politicians, whether MPs or local councillors. Overall, most preferred to rely on their family and friends, followed by newspaper columnists and editorials. The contribution of the latter assumed greater importance up-market.

3. Whether or not they themselves were in favour of devolution, respondents were then asked which party they thought it would be best to vote for to achieve a Scottish Assembly. They had already been asked which party they intended to vote for in a general election, and these results are the basis of the comparisons outlined here.

	General Election (%)	Scottish Assembly				
		Total (%)	Conservative (%)	Labour (%)	Alliance (%)	SNP (%)
Conservative	17	4	16	—	2	—
Labour	42	24	8	46	11	4
Alliance	13	11	16	5	31	6
SNP	14	49	42	42	52	88
Other	*	*	—	—	—	1
Uncommitted/ Don't know	15	12	19	6	4	2

Whilst recognition of the SNP as the party to vote for in this situation was not unexpected, it is interesting that 42 per cent of Labour supporters saw the SNP as a better bet for an Assembly than their own party.

4. However, opinion was evenly divided on the likelihood of a Scottish Assembly actually being established by the year 2000, with those aged under forty-five less confident than older respondents.

	Total (%)	Conservative (%)	Labour (%)	Alliance (%)	SNP (%)
Very likely	16	11	19	9	29
Quite likely	33	29	37	35	32
Not very likely	36	37	34	41	31
Not at all likely	15	23	10	14	8

There was clearly some uncertainty about the likelihood of this happening, with the majority preferring a lukewarm rather than definite response. SNP and Labour supporters remained more optimistic than those of the Conservative and Alliance parties.

5. Even if an Assembly were to be set up, views were again divided on how effective this might be in pursuing policies very different from those of the government in Westminster. The likelihood of the Assembly being able to follow a separate course was thought to be:

	Total (%)	Conservative (%)	Labour (%)	Alliance (%)	SNP (%)
Very likely	15	7	18	8	29
Quite likely	31	25	33	26	45
Not very likely	37	43	35	52	21
Not at all likely	11	21	6	11	3
Don't know	7	4	9	2	2

Once again there was a difference of opinion according to party supported, with adherents of the SNP in particular, but also Labour, more convinced that any Scottish Assembly would be able to pursue separate policies, and Conservative and Alliance supporters considerably less so.

6. The final question on politics concerned an issue of education — namely how important respondents thought it was that the Scottish education system should begin with Scottish history and culture, before broadening out to cover the UK, Europe and the rest of the world. As indicated below there was quite a strong measure of support for this approach:

	(%)
Very important	36
Quite important	31
Not very important	26
Not at all important	6

Over 60 per cent in all demographic sub-groups thought it at least quite important to proceed on this basis.

II INDUSTRY

1. Respondents were asked whether they thought that the following groups of people were becoming more or less confident about Scotland's future prosperity:

	More confident (%)	Less confident (%)	Neither/ no change (%)	Don't know (%)
1. The government	17	54	23	6
2. UK companies or investors	23	55	14	8
3. Overseas companies or investors	34	41	14	11
4. Employees	14	69	9	7
5. Management	23	52	15	10
6. Trade unions	17	58	13	12

The results make fairly depressing reading, presenting a pessimistic picture for Scotland's future prosperity. The only signs of confidence were thought to lie with overseas companies or investors, with the majority of respondents perceiving a growing lack of confidence in all sectors on the domestic front.

2. Continuing in a similar vein, respondents were then asked to rate the prospects of success in Scotland for a variety of manufacturing industries.

	Very/Quite good (%)	Very/Quite poor (%)	Mean score
1. The steel industry	20	76	−0.91
2. Electronics	86	8	+1.09
3. Shipbuilding	15	82	−1.17
4. Chemicals	63	20	+0.57
5. Coalmining	25	72	−0.74
6. Arts and crafts	63	21	+0.54
7. Machine tools	54	33	+0.22
8. Oil industry	62	33	+0.40

There was thought to be little future for the traditional heavy industries of steel, shipbuilding and coalmining, although all others had reasonable prospects for success. The brightest future was clearly thought to lie in electronics. As far as the oil industry is concerned, whilst higher ratings of success might have been recorded eighteen months ago, it is interesting to note that the majority still had confidence in its future in Scotland.

Respondents living in the central belt were generally less optimistic than those in the north of Scotland.

3. When a similar question was repeated for a number of service industries, the following picture emerged:

		Very/Quite good (%)	Very/Quite poor (%)
1.	Hotels or restaurants	85	11
2.	Retailing	80	15
3.	Tourism	85	13
4.	Leisure or recreation	79	16
5.	The media and communications, such as newspapers, radio and television	86	10
6.	Financial services like banking and insurance	89	8

The situation on the service side was thus much brighter, with four out of every five respondents rating the prospects of each of the service industries mentioned as at least quite good. Financial services in particular scored very highly, marginally ahead of electronics in the manufacturing sector, but the future of all of these was viewed with some optimism.

4. The greater potential perceived in the service rather than manufacturing sector was confirmed when respondents were asked where they would prefer to invest their money, if they had the resources to start a new business in Scotland. Given the choice between a manufacturing business or a service business, respondents opted two to one in favour of the latter (62 per cent) rather than the former (30 per cent) — a preference in evidence across all sub-groups.

5. In the situation where respondents were generally aware of the decline in Scottish traditional industries such as shipbuilding, they were shown a prompt card listing seven factors possibly contributing to this and asked to rank these in order, in terms of which they regarded as most responsible for this decline.

		Most responsible (%)	Second (%)	Third (%)
1.	Government policies	38	13	11
2.	Foreign competition	22	22	17
3.	Uncompetitively high manufacturing costs	10	16	19
4.	Failure to modernise	9	13	15
5.	Poor management	7	15	13
6.	Resistance to change	6	10	12
7.	Trade unionism	8	10	10

Overall, then, government policies were identified most often as mainly responsible for the decline in Scottish traditional industries, followed by foreign competition and, allied to this, uncompetitively high manufacturing costs. The responsibility was thus mainly ascribed to 'outside' forces rather than to any problems within the industries themselves and their methods of operation.

There were, however, some quite significant differences of opinion according to political affiliation — most notably between Conservative and Labour supporters.

Fifty-three per cent of Labour supporters held government policies to be mainly responsible. Conservatives, on the other hand, attached greater responsibility to trade unionism and resistance to change — by far the least contributory factors from the Labourite point of view!

6. When respondents were asked how well they thought the Scottish educational system equipped people with the skills and knowledge they require to meet the needs of employers, results were:

	(%)
Very well	10
Quite well	45
Not very well	34
Not at all well	7

On balance, then, the system was thought to perform reasonably well in this respect, although it was noticeable that those who emerged most recently from it, the eighteen to twenty-four age group, were the least impressed. Of these, the majority (52 per cent) opted for a negative rating.

7. Finally, in the industry poll, a five-point rating scale was employed to investigate respondents' views on how the Scots will be faring in the year 2000. The note of pessimism detected earlier was again in evidence in the stronger tendency to see Scots as being worse off rather than better off then than they are today, although opinion overall was quite widely spread:

	(%)
Much better off	3
A little bit better off	25
About the same	32
A little worse off	22
Much worse off	14

Perhaps significantly, prospects for a better future were rated positively only by those aged fifty-five and over, with the outlook of those younger tending to be more gloomy on balance. Views were also somewhat class-related, with optimism declining down the social scale.

III LAND USE

1. Respondents were asked initially how important they thought it was that remote communities in Scotland should survive. There was considerable strength of feeling that they should continue to do so:

	(%)
Very important	68
Quite important	27
Not very important	3
Not at all important	*

(* = less than 1%, but not zero)

Support for the survival of remote communities was unanimous across all sectors of the community, albeit marginally less so among those under, rather than over, forty-five. Interestingly, support was as strong in the more heavily-populated west as in the north.

2. Asked whether there should be any restriction on the amount of land owned by certain categories of owner, respondents' views were:

	Yes (%)	No (%)	Don't know (%)
Any single individual	63	31	6
Anyone who isn't Scottish	58	37	5
Any company or institution	58	33	9

With 77 per cent in favour of restrictions on at least one of these categories of owner, there is quite clearly considerable support for some measure of control on the amount of land that can be owned by any one individual or institution. Indeed the overall majority (at a similar level) on each question indicates that this should operate on a general level, irrespective of the origins or status of the landowner in question.

Younger respondents were less interested in seeing restrictions than were the older age groups, and support for these also declined slightly down the social scale.

Conservatives were less likely to favour restrictions than were the supporters of other parties — particularly as far as any single individual was concerned.

3. A prompt card was then shown listing four possible uses of land in Scotland and respondents were invited to rank these in order of perceived importance:

	Most important (%)	*Second* (%)	*Third* (%)	*Least* (%)
Farming	75	17	6	2
Forestry	8	50	23	19
Wildlife and nature conservation	13	22	42	22
Recreation	4	10	28	57

The overwhelming view was, then, that the land should be put to productive use — primarily for farming, but then for forestry. Use of land in Scotland for recreation was by far the lowest priority, surpassed even by wildlife and nature conservation. These views were expressed consistently throughout the sample.

4. This situation was confirmed when respondents were asked directly whether they regarded nature conservation as more or less important than, firstly, increasing farming developments in Scotland and, secondly, increasing leisure-based developments such as skiing. In relation to increasing farming developments, nature conservation was thought to be less important by the majority (53 per cent), and particularly so by respondents in the north:

	Total (%)	*West* (%)	*East* (%)	*North* (%)
Nature conservation is . . .				
more important	30	31	32	25
less important	52	47	51	66
neither/don't know	17	22	16	9

Those perhaps least affected by this issue (in the west, which is more industrial) were less committed in their views.

Overall, however, when the issue was one of nature conservation against increasing leisure-based activities, the situation was reversed, with support firmly in favour of the former:

	Total (%)	*West* (%)	*East* (%)	*North* (%)
Nature conservation is . . .				
more important	61	58	63	62
less important	24	23	23	28
neither/don't know	15	19	14	10

5. Respondents were generally of the opinion that farmers were doing a reasonable job of conserving the countryside at present, as indicated

when a four-point rating scale was used to investigate views on this subject. Those living in the north of Scotland were marginally more critical in this respect than those based elsewhere:

	Total (%)	West (%)	East (%)	North (%)
Very good	18	16	21	17
Quite good	57	59	54	55
Quite poor	13	12	14	15
Very poor	5	3	5	7
Don't know	8	9	6	6

6. In the situation where Scotland is well-suited for growing trees, respondents were asked how much of the country they thought should be used for forestry:

	Total (%)	West (%)	East (%)	North (%)
Much more than at present	10	11	8	13
A little more than at present	25	25	20	31
About the same as at present	52	49	58	46
A little less than at present	6	6	6	4
Much less than at present	3	3	4	1
Don't know	5	5	3	6

If one adopts the slightly cynical view that a reasonable proportion of respondents would be unaware of how much of Scotland was used for forestry at present, then the fact that 52 per cent opted for 'about the same' represents the 'safe' answer. On balance, however, opinion was weighted towards an increase in the use of land for forestry, and again, this was stronger in the north, which might be the area most affected by any developments in this respect.

7. Finally, respondents were asked in which generation their family had last worked on the land, for example on a farm or in forestry. Approximately one in four claimed a connection of this sort either in this or their parents' generation. Not surprisingly, links were much more immediate in the north, with a higher proportion in the west and east unable to give a definite answer:

	Total (%)	West (%)	East (%)	North (%)
Current generation	9	7	7	16
Parents' generation	15	12	14	24
Grandparents' generation	16	15	17	19
Great-grandparents' generation	7	8	8	4
Earlier	5	7	3	2
Never	31	32	30	29
May have done, don't know	17	18	21	6

In terms of age, a slightly higher proportion of older respondents (29 per cent of those fifty-five and over) were likely to have had a connection with the land within their immediate family.

IV HEALTH

1.   Respondents were shown a prompt card listing five factors possibly contributing to Scotland's extremely poor health record and asked to rank them in order of responsibility.

		Most *responsible* *(%)*	*Second* *(%)*	*Third* *(%)*	*Least* *(%)*
1.	Bad habits such as smoking or excessive drinking	49	29	14	3
2.	Bad social conditions, such as poor housing or high unemployment	29	29	16	4
3.	Bad diet	13	24	33	8
4.	Lack of exercise	4	10	29	20
5.	Insufficient medical services	5	7	7	65

Virtually half the sample ascribed the poor health record in Scotland firstly to the bad habits of the Scots themselves (in their smoking and excessive drinking), followed by bad social conditions. Although acknowledgement of the former was general throughout, bad social conditions emerged more strongly in the west of Scotland than either the east or north.

2. Respondents were then asked which of the following groups had greatest responsibility for trying to improve the health of people in Scotland.

		Most *responsible* *(%)*	*Second* *(%)*	*Least* *(%)*
1.	The government	51	28	20
2.	Individuals, through self-help	43	35	21
3.	Doctors and nurses	5	36	57

Responsibility was thought to lie quite squarely in the hands of both the government and individuals themselves, although the order of these is interesting in view of the previous findings. For although individual bad habits were seen as the main cause of damage to health, it was more the job of the government than the individual to put matters to rights, and this might suggest that some saw these bad habits themselves as a consequence of bad social conditions.

3.   Overall, there was a high level of satisfaction with the National Health Service in Scotland, both in hospitals and in the GP service.

	In hospitals	The GP service
	(%)	(%)
Very good	43	39
Quite good	43	48
Quite poor	8	9
Very poor	3	3

Although positive throughout all sub-groups, levels of satisfaction increased with age. If it is the case that involvement with hospitals and GPs also often increases with age, then older respondents may be answering more on the basis of personal experience, and their higher ratings reaffirm the quality of service provided.

4. Whilst the overall service provided by GPs was generally thought to be good, views were more divided on the extent to which they were involved in *preventing,* as opposed to actually *treating,* ill health:

	(%)
Very involved	8
Quite involved	34
Not very involved	41
Not at all involved	9
Don't know	8

Thus half the sample felt that GPs were not particularly involved in preventing ill health. However interpretation of these results depends on one's point of view as to whether doctors *should* be involved in prevention rather than cure, and it is noticeable from the earlier findings that doctors and nurses were seen as least responsible for improving the health of people in Scotland, after the government and individuals themselves.

5. Although doctors themselves might not be particularly involved in preventing ill health at present, it would appear that the general public might be receptive to any moves in this direction. For, when the proposition of a full medical each year, including whole-body scanning to detect early signs of serious illness, was put to respondents, reactions were very enthusiastic, with a high level of keenness being expressed to take advantage of such a facility if it were offered:

	(%)
Very keen	67
Quite keen	25
Not very keen	5
Not at all keen	2

Responses were extremely positive across all demographic sub-groups.

6. When respondents were asked whether they had in fact made any significant and lasting change to their lifestyle — either diet or amount of exercise taken — in the past five years as a result of anything read or heard about health issues, exactly one in three (33 per cent) claimed to

have done so. However the likelihood of having done so was much greater up-market, and also among the twenty-five to forty-four age group than other groups.

Whether changed

	Age						Class			
	18-24	25-34	35-44	45-54	55-64	65+	AB	C1	C2	DE
	(%)	(%)	(%)	(%)	(%)	(%)	(%)	(%)	(%)	(%)
Yes	21	42	42	32	33	31	51	36	32	26
No	79	58	58	68	67	68	48	64	67	74

7.   Finally, views were sought on cigarette advertising and sponsorship of public events by cigarette companies. In each case, a prompt card was shown presenting a range of alternatives, with respondents being asked to select the one which best matched their own opinion.

	(%)
Cigarette advertising should be banned completely	40
Cigarette advertising should be restricted to places where cigarettes are sold	26
Present restrictions on cigarette advertising are adequate	29
Present restrictions on cigarette advertising should be relaxed	3

There was thus two-thirds support for a further tightening of present restrictions, if not actually a complete ban on cigarette advertising.

Women (44 per cent) were more in favour of a ban than men (34 per cent), with the latter slightly happier with the status quo (23 per cent as against 35 per cent respectively).

Although the majority in all sub-groups supported a further restriction, strength of feeling on this matter was distinctly class-related.

	AB	C1	C2	DE
	(%)	(%)	(%)	(%)
Banned completely	49	47	39	32
Restricted to places where sold	28	22	24	28
Present restrictions adequate	20	27	29	32
Present restrictions relaxed	2	2	3	6

The question on sponsorship produced similar results:

	(%)
Sponsorship of public events by cigarette companies should be:	
Banned completely	37
More tightly controlled in the amount of publicity the sponsors get	27
Allowed to continue as at present	33

Again, women were stronger in their support for a tightening of restrictions than men, with ABs also tending to be more extreme in their views than any others (47 per cent favouring a complete ban, as against 32–37 per cent for other socio-economic groupings).

V EDUCATION

1. Respondents were initially asked how good a job they thought Scottish secondary schools were doing in general, putting aside any particular effects of the recent teachers' dispute. As indicated below, the majority felt that they were doing at least quite a good job, with no significant differences of opinion across the sample:

	(%)
Very good	13
Quite good	51
Quite poor	20
Very poor	7
Don't know	9

2. A number of alternatives were then put forward as priorities for education in Scottish secondary schools, with respondents being invited to rank these in order of importance. The percentages ranking each of these within the first three and also least in the order of importance are shown below.

		Most important (%)	Second (%)	Third (%)	Least (%)
1.	Teaching pupils the personal and practical skills that will help them to get a job	42	27	16	4
2.	Giving pupils a broadly based education for its own sake	24	19	24	13
3.	Preparing pupils for adult life	20	28	22	16
4.	Teaching pupils specialised knowledge in two or three subjects	7	12	19	28
5.	Getting pupils as many examination passes as possible	7	12	16	39

Quite clearly, then, the priority was thought to lie more in training pupils in skills for their future employment and life ahead than in education for education's sake, particularly if the latter were reduced to specialisation in a few subjects, contrary to the traditional Scottish system, or geared solely to passing examinations. A broadly based education was seen as a better preparation for the future.

3. Although the majority had earlier expressed themselves as satisfied with the job being done in Scottish secondary schools, when respondents were asked how well informed they felt they were about the methods used to teach children at secondary schools and assess their progress, a similar majority admitted to being relatively ignorant in these matters, even those with children of school age!

	Children of school age		
	Total (%)	Any (%)	None (%)
Very well informed	6	7	5
Reasonably well informed	25	31	23
Not very well informed	41	45	40
Totally confused	3	5	2
Don't really know much about it	20	9	25
Don't know	5	3	5

Only the ABs professed to being knowledgeable to any extent about methods employed in secondary schools (47 per cent at least reasonably well informed), and it would appear that either not enough effort is made to advise parents of developments in the education system, or parents themselves are not interested enough to find out about or take note of these developments.

4. As far as their personal situation was concerned, respondents were generally confident in their own level of education, with four out of five regarding themselves as at least 'fairly well educated'. Although social class was a discriminator in this respect to some extent, it did not distort the overall levels of confidence throughout:

	Class				
	Total (%)	AB (%)	C1 (%)	C2 (%)	DE (%)
Highly educated	7	19	8	3	5
Fairly well educated	73	74	79	75	68
Not particularly well educated	16	5	11	19	20
Not very well educated	4	2	2	2	6

5. When asked to compare the education being offered in Scotland today with the schooling they themselves received, respondents were evenly divided in their views.

School today is. . .

	Age						
	Total (%)	18-24 (%)	25-34 (%)	35-44 (%)	45-54 (%)	55-64 (%)	65+ (%)
much better	19	4	9	22	26	32	24
a little better	18	13	22	24	20	15	13
much the same	22	55	29	14	14	7	9
a little worse	24	19	23	27	19	24	30
much worse	13	6	11	9	16	7	18
Don't know	5	2	7	5	6	6	6

As age increased, so respondents became more convinced that education had changed, with views polarising accordingly. It then became a matter of whether it had changed for the better or worse, with no unanimity on this. Those in the thirty-five to sixty-four age group were more inclined to think that education had improved, as were those actually with children of school age at present.

6.   Perhaps not surprisingly in view of the overall confidence in their level of education, when respondents were asked whether, on leaving school, they felt they had in general terms been successful or not there, 66 per cent thought that they had indeed been successful, as against 31 per cent unsuccessful.

Likelihood of having been successful (in their own estimation) was greater among those aged over forty-five than under forty-five and also declined down the social scale:

	Age					
	18-24 (%)	25-34 (%)	35-44 (%)	45-54 (%)	55-64 (%)	65+ (%)
Successful	58	65	60	71	69	75
Unsuccessful	38	32	38	25	27	23

	Class			
	AB (%)	C1 (%)	C2 (%)	DE (%)
Successful	78	71	68	57
Unsuccessful	21	26	30	38

7.   Following on from this, respondents were invited to rank in order of perceived responsiblity five factors to which their success or lack of success might be attributed.

		Most responsible (%)	Second (%)	Third (%)	Least (%)
1.	Teachers	41	28	19	3
2.	Own motivation	28	27	24	5
3.	Parents' attitude	21	26	21	7
4.	The courses followed	8	14	25	14
5.	Attitude of fellow pupils	1	4	10	70

For 41 per cent the most important factor in their success at school was their teachers, although it is interesting to note that credit to teachers increased with age: indeed younger respondents ascribed at least equal importance (even more among the eighteen to twenty-four age group) to their own motivation. Courses followed were also rated more highly among younger age groups.

As far as reasons for lack of success were concerned, the corresponding picture was:

		Most responsible (%)	Second (%)	Third (%)	Least (%)
1.	Own lack of motivation	56	19	10	3
2.	The courses followed	11	25	26	5
3.	Teachers	17	17	25	12
4.	Parents' attitude	8	13	10	34
5.	Attitude of fellow pupils	3	16	17	36

A clear majority of those who felt they had been unsuccessful at school placed the main responsibility for this on their own shoulders, with less than one in five blaming their teachers as the primary cause. Interestingly, although the attitude of neither parents nor fellow pupils featured strongly, the role of the former increased with age, with the reverse being true of the latter. If parental attitude was a problem for older generations, then the attitude of fellow pupils was a more disruptive influence nowadays.

8. Finally, there proved to be overwhelming support for the practice of adults returning to school to pick up on their education — 84 per cent regarding this as a good idea, as against only 13 per cent who were opposed to it.

VI THE MEDIA

1. Respondents were asked initially whether they would like to see more or less Scottish control of each of the three main media — television, radio and newspapers.
Results were:

	Television (%)	Radio (%)	Newspapers (%)
More	60	46	60
Less	6	5	4
Stay the same	31	41	33

There was, then, majority support for increased Scottish control of both television and newspapers, but with views more evenly divided in this respect as far as radio was concerned. With the latter, there was a higher level of satisfaction with the status quo.

Interestingly, there were some marked variations in opinion according to area, with respondents in the west of Scotland least satisfied with the current situation on all counts and those in the north most so:

		West (%)	East (%)	North (%)
Television:	More	68	55	51
	Less	4	8	6
	Stay the same	24	34	42
Radio	More	52	44	37
	Less	6	5	4
	Stay the same	34	41	54
Newspapers:	More	68	54	52
	Less	5	4	1
	Stay the same	24	39	42

2. A comparative rating was then sought of coverage of Scottish affairs by the Scottish-based, as against London-based, productions of the various media:

	Very well (%)	Quite well (%)	Not very well/ Badly (%)
1.) Scottish newspapers	16	60	22
2.) National newspapers printed in London	1	16	76
3.) TV programmes made by BBC Scotland, Scottish Television and Grampian	12	60	25
4.) National TV programmes broadcast from London	1	21	75
5.) Scottish radio stations	15	58	14
6.) National radio stations broadcast from London	2	17	65

Overall, there was a clear division irrespective of media, with Scottish-based operations thought to be performing reasonably well in their coverage of Scottish affairs and their London-based equivalents generally poorly. Views were consistently in accord on this throughout.

3. Asked how reliable they thought each of the main media was in its reporting of the news in terms of truthfulness and accuracy, respondents' views were:

		Newspapers (%)	Television (%)	Radio (%)
Very reliable	(+2)	4	13	12
Quite reliable	(+1)	40	68	65
Not very reliable	(−1)	42	15	11
Not at all reliable	(−2)	12	3	2

There was thus considerably greater faith placed in the broadcast, as opposed to the printed, word, with the majority (54 per cent) actually regarding newspapers as not very reliable in their reporting. Whilst it might be argued that this may depend on the individual newspapers referred to, it is significant that this opinion was expressed by all demographic sub-groups — including both up-market and down-market, whose reading habits were likely to be diametrically opposed in the choice of paper.

Television and radio emerged similarly positively in terms of reliability in this respect.

4. Views on the relationship between the BBC and government, in terms of government control, were:

		(%)
BBC is . . .	not independent enough	34
	about independent enough	38
	too independent	17
	Don't know	11

Overall, one in three felt that there was thus too much government control over the BBC, with marginally more regarding the relationship as about right. However it should be noted that this poll was conducted before the recent controversy over the Zircon satellite programme erupted fully. Support for a greater measure of independence for the BBC was stronger up-market.

The situation according to political party supported was:

	Conservative (%)	Labour (%)	Alliance (%)	SNP (%)
Not independent enough	30	39	32	41
About independent enough	50	30	51	32
Too independent	14	20	13	15
Don't know	5	12	4	12

Conservative and Alliance supporters were thus likely to be happier with the current state of affairs than those of Labour and the SNP, each of whom favoured greater independence more strongly.

5. When asked whether they would be for or against a system where the television licence fee were scrapped and instead viewers had to pay a small charge each time they watched a BBC programme, the majority (53 per cent) were opposed to such a system, although 37 per cent were in favour. Support was stronger among those aged under forty-five than among older age groups and, not surprisingly, also increased down the social scale — reflecting viewing patterns between BBC and commercial stations:

	AB (%)	C1 (%)	C2 (%)	DE (%)
For	22	33	41	42
Against	69	59	49	47
Neither/Don't know	8	8	10	12

If such a system were to be introduced, 28 per cent thought that this would result in their watching BBC programmes less than at present, whereas the viewing habits of 65 per cent would remain unaffected in this respect; (2 per cent actually thought that this would increase their viewing of BBC!) This pattern was similar across the sample.

6. Opinion was widely spread as to the effect that a considerable increase in the number of television channels might have on the general standard of television compared to the present, although the balance was towards a deterioration in this respect:

	(%)
Better than at present	27
About the same standard	30
Worse than at present	37
Don't know	6

There was a significant difference of opinion demographically, with expectations of better TV declining with age but increasing down the social scale — perhaps in line with propensity to watch television:

	Age					
	18-24 (%)	25-34 (%)	35-44 (%)	45-54 (%)	55-64 (%)	65+ (%)
Better	41	33	29	26	19	13
About the same	27	30	25	29	33	39
Worse	25	37	41	40	42	38
Don't know	7	*	5	5	6	10

(* = Less than 1%, but not zero)

	Age			
	AB (%)	Cl (%)	C2 (%)	DE (%)
Better	12	25	32	31
About the same	27	26	36	30
Worse	57	46	28	30
Don't know	5	3	4	9

7. A prompt card was shown listing a range of types of television programme and respondents were asked firstly which of them they would like to see more of on television, and then which less of:

	More (%)	Less (%)
Documentaries	51	6
Feature films	45	4
Comedies	28	6
News and current affairs	28	5
Quizzes	25	19
Sports	22	31
Plays	22	6
Chat shows	16	21
Soap operas	14	39
Arts programmes	10	16
Religious programmes	8	14
None of these	11	7
Don't know	3	1

Documentaries and feature films were thus the most popular candidates for increased airtime, with the former in particular quite widespread in their appeal. Demand for more feature films declined with age.

The two most controversial were, clearly, sports and soap operas, where the request for reduced coverage actually exceeded that for an increase. In the case of sports, this was largely due to strong resistance among women (44 per cent), although 16 per cent of men also thought there was too much of this at present. With soap operas, however, which tend to have greater appeal to women, the fact that 27 per cent of these favoured a reduction, as against 21 per cent an increase, in programmes of this type may indicate that saturation point has been reached.

8. When a similar measure was repeated for radio programmes, results were:

	More (%)	Less (%)
News and current affairs	19	5
Talk programmes	19	10
Weather, traffic and other information	18	3
Documentaries	16	3
Pop and rock music	16	22
Plays	14	8
Classical music	9	11
Jazz	4	14
None of these	22	31
Don't know/no answer	17	18

The lower figures generally for the various programme types, and also the higher ratings for 'None' and 'Don't know' compared to the equivalent on television may indicate the lower interest in, and involvement with, radio.

Again, there were considerable differences of opinion demographically, not surprisingly most in evidence in relation to age on pop and rock music. That apart, interest in hearing more of virtually all other programmes mentioned increased with age.

9. Finally, respondents were asked to identify from a prompt list the extra services which they might expect to make use of through their TV in the future, with the following outcome:

	(%)
Rented or bought videos	24
More teletext-based services	22
Satellite programmes	19
Cable programmes	18
Home banking by TV	11
Shopping by TV	11
Voting by TV	10
None of these	27
Don't know	10

Sixty-three per cent of all respondents thus expected to make use of at least some of these services, although expectation of doing so declined quite sharply with age — from 86 per cent of the twenty-five to thirty-four age group to only 22 per cent of those over sixty-five. The relatively low levels recorded for each, however, may be more indicative of a general lack of awareness or understanding of the technology and implications of these than of selectivity among respondents.

VII THE ARTS

1. Respondents were asked to indicate from a prompt card any of a range of events that they had been to in the last three months:

		Class		
	Total (%)	AB (%)	C1 (%)	C2 (%)	DE (%)
A dance event	22	23	22	24	19
The cinema	20	25	29	18	14
The theatre	18	33	22	15	12
A musical concert	13	23	17	11	8
An exhibition	11	31	15	9	3
Any other artistic event	2	4	4	2	1
None of these	46	27	40	47	57

Thus almost half the sample had not attended any of the listed events within the stipulated time period, and likelihood of having done so was strongly class related, particularly in respect of the 'purer' art forms.

The cinema, above all, attracted a younger audience (51 per cent of the eighteen to twenty-four age group), and indeed age was a discriminator, too, as far as attendance in general was concerned — declining as age increased. However 'musical concerts' and 'dance events' were perhaps open to a broad interpretation.

2. As far as reading was concerned, 'consumption' of the following in the last month was:

		Class		
	Total (%)	AB (%)	C1 (%)	C2 (%)	DE (%)
A novel	45	61	53	42	35
An arts magazine	7	13	8	5	4
The arts pages of a newspaper	26	44	33	20	18
None of these	42	25	33	45	54

Novels were, not surprisingly, the most popular, with arts magazines in particular not widely read. Readership of all three was again strongly class related.

3. Participation in artistic events was very much for the minority, with three out of four never having taken part in any of the undernoted activities. Levels of participation were:

		Class		
	Total (%)	AB (%)	C1 (%)	C2 (%)	DE (%)
A musical performance	14	27	21	9	9
An amateur dramatic performance	12	25	16	9	6
An evening class on an arts subject	9	19	14	5	4
Some kind of arts workshop	5	12	6	3	3
None of these	72	49	61	78	83

The already familiar patterns in relation to social class were again in evidence.

4. As if to confirm impressions from the previous findings, when respondents were asked directly (using a four-point rating scale) how significant a part the arts played in their lives, only one in four rated this as at all significant, with almost 40 per cent regarding the arts as having no significance at all:

	Total (%)	AB (%)	Class C1 (%)	C2 (%)	DE (%)
Very significant	7	15	9	3	4
Quite significant	21	32	23	15	19
Not very significant	34	32	37	37	30
Not at all significant	39	21	31	44	46

5. In spite of the apparent lack of personal interest or involvement in the arts, however, there was some recognition of their value shown in two ways. Firstly, when respondents were asked, from a prompt card, how high a priority they thought should be given to the arts by television, radio and the press, there was a feeling that these were, if anything, under-represented at present:

	(%)
Higher than now and similar to sports coverage	11
Higher than now but less than sports coverage	27
About the same as now	37
Less than now	9
Don't know	15

Secondly, a similar situation emerged when the question was then posed as to how much public money from the government and local authorities should be spent to support the arts. Although 37 per cent were happy with present levels of expenditure, a similar proportion thought that this should be increased, with only half that number advocating a reduction:

	(%)
Much more than now	11
A little more than now	27
About the same as now	37
A little less than now	9
Much less than now	9

Support for a fairer deal for the arts was in evidence across all sectors of the population.

6. If such financial support were to be increased, the main candidates for this from a prompt list were:

	(%)
Community arts	28
Amateur dramatics/operatic groups	25
Film-making	24
Arts workshops	18
Writing	13
Painting and sculpture	11
Professional drama	11
Classical music	9
Dance	9
Professional opera	7
Jazz	5
None of these	18
Don't know	13

It is interesting that the main art forms selected for financial support, with the possible exception of film-making, were those involving the active participation of amateurs rather than experts. This may tie in with the earlier findings, which indicated support for the arts apparently running ahead of involvement in them. Perhaps it is only the lack of opportunities or facilities that is preventing wider participation.

VIII RELIGION

1. Respondents were asked to select from a prompt card a description of their own religion. The following picture emerged:

	(%)
Protestant/Presbyterian	64
Catholic	15
Anglican	2
Other Christian	3
Other Religion	3
Of no religious belief	12

Those aged under thirty-five were more likely to describe themselves as of no religious belief (21 per cent). The Catholic population was concentrated much more in the central belt (18 per cent) than in the north of Scotland (6 per cent).

2. Views on the influence of religion in Scottish life and attitudes were:

	(%)
Influential and beneficial	21
Influential and undesirable	13
Not particularly influential	41
Not influential enough	22
Don't know	7

Overall, then, the majority did not feel that religion has much influence in this respect and, for one in five, not as much as they would like. Both age and sex of respondents had a bearing on attitudes, with those in the younger age groups, and also men, less well disposed towards religious influence in life in Scotland:

	Sex		Age					
	Male (%)	Female (%)	18-24 (%)	25-34 (%)	35-44 (%)	45-54 (%)	55-64 (%)	65+ (%)
Influential and beneficial	23	19	15	17	19	20	23	31
Influential and undesirable	16	9	18	23	12	10	6	5
Not particularly influential	41	40	46	46	37	47	41	29
Not influential enough	17	27	15	10	27	17	34	29

3. Whatever their views on the influence of religion, however, over half of all respondents (55 per cent) believed that it was right for church leaders to speak out on social and political issues, as against 38 per cent who were opposed. Support for the voice of the Church was consistent across virtually all demographic sub-groups.

4. As far as nuclear weapons were concerned, again a narrow majority felt that there was some moral justification for these, but very much as a means of preserving peace rather than in any other situations. Given the four options from which to choose, attitudes were:

			Religion
	Total (%)	Catholic (%)	Protestant/ Other Christian (%)
(Morally justifiable)			
As a means of preserving peace	46	38	50
As a means of retaliation	7	7	8
As a pre-emptive strike/to forestall enemy attack at a time of crisis	9	7	10
Not morally justifiable at any time	40	44	36
Don't know	5	8	4

There was thus slightly stronger opposition among Catholics than Protestants and other Christians.

5. Opinions were then sought on the extent to which there should be a measure of integration between Protestants and Roman Catholics. A number of situations were read out and, for each one, respondents were asked whether or not they thought it was something that should be shared between the two:

		Total (%)	Religion Catholic (%)	Protestant (%)
Marriage	Yes	88	90	87
	No	7	9	6
Schools	Yes	87	75	89
	No	9	21	8
Communion	Yes	55	59	54
	No	31	32	32
Church buildings	Yes	68	73	67
	No	24	25	25
Church social groups	Yes	86	92	86
	No	9	5	10
Discussions on religious policy				
	Yes	86	92	85
	No	8	4	9

There was, therefore, general support for much closer links between Catholics and Protestants on all counts, irrespective of faith at present. The exception to this was schools, on which Catholics were slightly less in favour of a joint approach (albeit that a substantial majority did in fact still support this). Both parties were also less convinced about sharing Communion that any of the other situations proposed although, again, the balance of opinion remained in favour.

6. Frequency of church-going was very low, with only one in four respondents claiming to go to church once a month or more. As indicated below, however, this overall figure was accounted for largely by the poor attendance record among Protestants, with Catholics much more likely to go regularly:

	Total (%)	Religion Catholic (%)	Protestant (%)
Every week if possible	20	54	16
Once or twice a month	7	8	8
Occasionally	22	14	26
Only for special events like weddings	32	16	35
Never	18	9	14

Likelihood of attending church regularly, and even at all, was least among those aged under thirty-five, with those over sixty-five the most committed in this respect. Men were also less likely to be churchgoers than women.

7. Similar patterns were in evidence when respondents were asked how often they prayed when they were away from church although, overall, a slightly higher proportion claimed to pray than go to church on at least a weekly basis:

	Total (%)	Religion	
		Catholic (%)	Protestant (%)
Once or more a day	24	43	23
Once or more a week, but not as often as once a day	9	16	9
Occasionally	19	20	21
Only at times of crisis	7	7	8
Hardly ever	11	5	14
Never	29	9	23

There were again very distinct differences according to age and sex of respondent:

	Sex		Age					
	Male (%)	Female (%)	18-24 (%)	25-34 (%)	35-44 (%)	45-54 (%)	55-64 (%)	65+ (%)
Once or more a day	14	32	10	8	19	28	35	45
Never	41	18	48	40	25	26	18	13

8. The extent of respondents' beliefs was:

		Total (%)	Religion	
			Catholic (%)	Protestant (%)
God	Yes	78	97	85
	No	15	2	8
	Don't know	7	1	7
Christ the Son of God	Yes	75	95	82
	No	16	2	10
	Don't know	9	3	8
Life after death	Yes	50	73	51
	No	30	16	27
	Don't know	20	12	22

Conviction was thus generally stronger among Catholics than Protestants, and particularly so in respect of life after death.

As in other sections of the poll, religious belief was less evident among the young than the old, and among men than women.

NOTE:
The survey was conducted in three parts as follows:

Politics and industry: a sample of 839 adults in 36 constituencies during 7-20 January 1987.

Education, health, land use and the media: a sample of 940 adults in 40 constituencies during 22-28 January 1987.

The arts and religion: a sample of 1037 adults in 40 constituencies during 12-17 February 1987.